JUN 1 6 2009

W9-DFS-810

Robert E. Lee and the Fall of the Confederacy, 1863–1865

THE AMERICAN CRISIS SERIES
Books on the Civil War Era
Steven E. Woodworth, Professor of History, Texas Christian University
Series Editor

Robert E. Lee and the Fall of the Confederacy, 1863–1865

Ethan S. Rafuse

ROWMAN & LITTLEFIELD PUBLISHERS, INC.
Lanham • Boulder • New York • Toronto • Plymouth, UK

All maps are by Ethan S. Rafuse.

ROWMAN & LITTLEFIELD PUBLISHERS, INC.

Published in the United States of America
by Rowman & Littlefield Publishers, Inc.
A wholly owned subsidiary of The Rowman & Littlefield Publishing Group, Inc.
4501 Forbes Boulevard, Suite 200, Lanham, Maryland 20706
www.rowmanlittlefield.com

Estover Road
Plymouth PL6 7PY
United Kingdom

British Library Cataloguing in Publication Information Available

Library of Congress Cataloging-in-Publication Data:

Rafuse, Ethan Sepp, 1968–
  Robert E. Lee and the fall of the Confederacy, 1863–1865 / Ethan S. Rafuse.
    p. cm. — (American crisis series)
  Includes bibliographical references and index.
  ISBN-13: 978-0-7425-5125-1 (cloth : alk. paper)
  ISBN-10: 0-7425-5125-3 (cloth : alk. paper)
  eISBN-13: 978-0-7425-6390-2
  eISBN-10: 0-7425-6390-1
  1. Lee, Robert E. (Robert Edward), 1807–1870—Military leadership. 2. Command of
troops—Case studies. 3. United States—History—Civil War, 1861–1865—Campaigns.
4. Virginia—History—Civil War, 1861–1865—Campaigns. 5. Maryland—History—
Civil War, 1861–1865—Campaigns. 6. Pennsylvania—History—Civil War,
1861–1865—Campaigns. 7. Generals—Confederate States of America—Biography.
8. Confederate States of America. Army—Biography. I. Title.
  E467.1.L4R34 2008
  973.7'3092—dc22   2008004350

Printed in the United States of America

⊗™ The paper used in this publication meets the minimum requirements of
American National Standard for Information Sciences—Permanence of Paper
for Printed Library Materials, ANSI/NISO Z39.48-1992.

To
Charles P. Poland Jr.,
Joseph L. Harsh, and
Herman Hattaway

Contents

Preface

On the morning of May 3, 1863, Gen. Robert E. Lee rode forward from a piece of high ground in The Wilderness of Orange County, Virginia, known as Hazel Grove toward the crossroads clearing at which sat the Chancellor House. All around him, the woods were aflame, with smoke mixing with the scent and sight of hundreds of dead and wounded men to create a scene of horror almost beyond description. Moreover, the sound of continuous artillery and musket fire indicated that there remained hard work for Lee and the rest of the living to do. Nonetheless, the mood of the Confederate army around Chancellorsville was electric, for they were on the verge of pulling off one of the most incredible tactical victories in American military history.

A few days before, Maj. Gen. Joseph Hooker, commander of the Union Army of the Potomac, had seemingly placed the Army of Northern Virginia in a position where it must either make an inglorious retreat or be crushed between the two wings of a Federal army that was twice its size. But then Lee had divided his army, not once, but twice. Both moves had been bold—almost foolishly so—but they had paid off. On the evening of May 2, one corps of Lee's army had crushed the Union right. The following day, Lee's men kept up the pressure and induced Hooker to pull back from Chancellorsville. This enabled the two wings of the Confederate army to reunite for what Lee hoped would be a final push to drive the Federals into the Rappahannock River. As Lee rode among his men they greeted him with cheer after cheer.

"The scene is one that can never be effaced from the minds of those who witnessed it," one of Lee's staff officers later wrote, "as I looked upon him in the complete fruition of the success which his genius, courage, and confidence in his army had won, I thought that it must have been from such a scene that men in ancient days rose to the dignity of the gods."[1]

Less than two years later, however, Lee would find himself the third man in the Civil War signing terms for the surrender of his army to Ulysses S. Grant at Appomattox Court House.

The purpose of this book is to explain how Lee and the Confederate cause went from that moment of triumph at Chancellorsville to complete defeat in 1865. The question of how so great a general as Lee could have led his army to defeat has challenged the best minds in Civil War history for more than a century. Many have argued that the fault was not Lee's. Rather, Confederate defeat was due mainly to some other factor, such as the attrition of Confederate resources, a decline in the quality of leadership in the Army of Northern Virginia, or the poor leadership of Jefferson Davis and other politicians in Richmond. Some have placed the blame squarely on Lee himself. Lee was not, some have argued, a great general, but a severely flawed one whose strategy and tactics were in fact poor, or at least horribly unsuited to the war he was engaged in. Others have argued that Lee doggedly adhered to an operational and tactical vision that, while well-suited to the army he had in 1862 and 1863, could not succeed with the army he had to work with the last two years of the war.[2]

This book argues that strategic and operational considerations properly led Lee to a preference for offensive operations throughout the war and will trace and analyze the specific strategic, operational, and tactical problems Lee faced in such campaigns as Gettysburg, Bristoe Station, Spotsylvania, Petersburg, and Appomattox, as well as the broader strategic and operational contexts that shaped his efforts. Perhaps the most important factor behind the decline of Confederate fortunes after 1863 was the fact that Lee did not receive the generous assistance from Union military authorities he enjoyed during the first two years of the war. No explanation of Confederate defeat can ignore the fact that, as one of Lee's division commanders later put it, "the Union Army had something to do with it"—although one might be forgiven if, after following much of the literature debating the causes of Confederate defeat published in the more than 140 years since Appomattox, they were not aware of this fact.[3] Consequently, this study will not only consider matters on the Confederate side, but will also devote considerable attention to decisions and actions taken by Lee's counterparts on the Union side of the lines. Indeed, in conceiving this study I envisioned one that might more properly carry the title "Robert E. Lee and the Triumph of the Union," before being persuaded that this might confuse too many potential readers.

This book is dedicated to the three great teachers, scholars, and gentlemen under whom I had the honor and privilege to study the Civil War: Charles P. Poland Jr., Joseph L. Harsh, and Herman Hattaway. In preparing this study, I have endeavored to follow the concept laid out by Professor Hattaway in his 1997 military history of the Civil War, *Shades of Blue and Gray*.[4] For those just beginning their study of Lee and the Civil War, I hope that this study will provide them with a good understanding of the events of 1863–1865 and perhaps the inspiration—the "hook" that working with T. Harry Williams provided Professor Hattaway, and studying with Hattaway, Poland, and Harsh provided me—to further study the subject. For the members of Civil War roundtables, scholars of the war, and others already hooked and well-read on the subject, it is hoped they will find in this book an informative and enjoyable narrative and analysis of the last two years of the Civil War and why even the best efforts of one of history's greatest generals could not prevent the total defeat of his army and cause.

Notes

1. Charles Marshall, *Lee's Aide-de-Camp*, edited by Frederick Maurice (1927; Lincoln: University of Nebraska Press, 2000), 172–73.

2. Surveys of the literature on Lee and Confederate strategy can be found in Emory M. Thomas, "Rebellion and Conventional Warfare: Confederate Strategy and Military Policy," in *Writing the Civil War: The Quest to Understand*, edited by James M. McPherson and William J. Cooper Jr. (Columbia: University of South Carolina Press, 1998), and the bibliographic essay at the end of this book.

3. Carol Reardon, "Pickett's Charge: The Convergence of History and Myth in the Southern Past," in *The Third Day at Gettysburg and Beyond*, edited by Gary W. Gallagher (Chapel Hill: University of North Carolina Press, 1994), 84.

4. Herman Hattaway, *Shades of Blue and Gray: An Introductory Military History of the Civil War* (Columbia: University of Missouri Press, 1997), ix.

Acknowledgments

Without the assistance of good friends and colleagues, there is no way I could have completed this study, and it is with great pleasure that I thank them here. Steven Woodworth encouraged me to contribute a volume on Lee to Rowman & Littlefield's "American Crisis" series; read the entire manuscript with his keen, critical eye; and was a reliable source of wisdom and guidance throughout the process of writing and rewriting this study. Brooks Simpson also looked over the entire manuscript and provided much wise counsel as I put the finishing touches on it. John Hennessy and Donald Pfanz of Fredericksburg and Spotsylvania National Military Park made available to me the resources of the park's absolutely fantastic library. Chris Calkins not only did the same at Petersburg National Battlefield, but was also kind enough to read through and provide feedback on the chapters covering the Petersburg and Appomattox Campaigns. Carol Reardon read the chapters covering the Gettysburg Campaign and provided extensive and invaluable feedback on them, while Chris Stowe did the same with my treatment of operations between Williamsport and Mine Run and Mark Grimsley provided a similarly insightful and useful critique of the chapters covering the Overland Campaign. I thank all these great scholars for their assistance and guidance and, of course, accept that responsibility for whatever deficiencies exist in this work is mine alone.

I am much indebted as well to Laura Gottlieb, Niels Aaboe, Karen Ackermann, Andrew Boney, and Asa Johnson at Rowman & Littlefield for the patient support, encouragement, and many useful and needed suggestions for improving the study they provided throughout the long process of writing and preparing it for publication. I also thank the archivists and librarians at the Combined Arms Research Library, Virginia Historical Society, Platte City Branch of the Mid-Continent Public Library, Library of Virginia, and Leyburn Library at Washington and Lee University for all they did to facilitate my research efforts.

Like the Army of the Potomac, my ability to bring this project to a satisfactory conclusion depended heavily on the support I received from the home front. I could not ask for a better professional home than the U.S. Army Command and General Staff College at Fort Leavenworth, where I have received generous support from supervisors and colleagues for my efforts. I am especially thankful to department chair James Willbanks, deputy chair Rich Barbuto, and master instructor Chris Gabel for all they do to make the Department of Military History at CGSC a great place to work. I am also indebted to those colleagues at West Point and Fort Leavenworth who have collaborated with me in leading staff rides of the various campaigns covered in this study: Charles Bowery Jr., Mark Gerges, Jeffrey Gudmens, Chris Keller, Bob Kennedy, Kevin Kennedy, Curt King, Dana Mangham, Chris Stowe, and Brad Wineman. My parents provided their usual full measure of support to my efforts, as well as convenient locations from which to base expeditions to research depositories and battlefields. As always, I most appreciate the love and joy my wife, Rachel, and daughter, Corinne, bring to my life.

Finally, I thank the three great historians under whose direction I had the honor and privilege to study the Civil War: Charles P. Poland Jr., Joseph L. Harsh, and Herman Hattaway. In appreciation for the support, guidance, wisdom, and counsel they have provided throughout my career, I dedicate this book to them.

CHAPTER ONE

Chancellorsville and Its Antecedents

Despite the welcome and well-earned cheers of his men, Robert E. Lee's mind was no doubt troubled when he rode up to the Chancellor House during the morning of May 3, 1863. The cries of the wounded and the broken bodies that surrounded him provided vivid reminders of the great costs that any battle in the Civil War entailed. And what great end were these men enduring unspeakable suffering to achieve? How was their commander going to translate a tactical success he had achieved that morning into something more? Answering these questions posed a considerable challenge to any Civil War commander, for despite all the horrible bloodletting battles between the armies of the Union and Confederacy produced, the size of these armies and the tremendous fire power the weaponry of the era gave them also had the effect of making it extremely difficult to achieve truly decisive results on the battlefield itself.

This was something Lee had already learned the hard way. In his first major campaign in June 1862, Lee had, through a series of furious offensives, saved Richmond by driving Maj. Gen. George McClellan's Army of the Potomac from a position less than ten miles from the Confederate capital at Richmond to one treble that distance on the James River. Yet not only was McClellan's army able to survive the rebel onslaught intact, it also inflicted horrible casualties on Lee's army in the course of what became known as the Seven Days' Battles. Lee complained in his post-battle report that "under ordinary circumstances the Union army should have been destroyed," but could rationalize that poor intelligence, the strength of the enemy positions, and, above all, problems within his own high command had impeded achievement of this goal. These excuses were not available to explain the failure to destroy the Union army in the Second Manassas Campaign of August 1862. During that campaign, Lee and his command team managed their army with a degree of skill and smoothness that would rarely be met and never exceeded in the course of the war. Employing maneuver brilliantly, they induced a Union army commanded by Maj. Gen. John Pope to make futile attacks against a strong defensive position and, in the process, place itself in a position that was vulnerable to a crushing attack on its flank. Even though that attack was delivered and Pope's army was forced to abandon the field during the afternoon of August 30, the Federals were still able to reach the Washington defenses with their army intact and able to fight another day.[1]

That is, if the Northern people wanted them to do so. Here Lee saw his chance for ultimate victory. It was clear to Lee by at least the fall of 1862 that it was extremely unlikely he could completely destroy a Union army in battle once, much less the many times it would take to exhaust the North's ability to make war, without bleeding his own army white. (This is not to say that Lee would not look for or try to create opportunities to destroy Federal armies, just that he knew the odds were so long against achieving this goal as to make it foolish to pin his hopes on achieving it.) If he could not destroy his enemy's physical ability to make war, then hopes for Confederate independence rested on destroying the North's will to fight by raising the costs of the war in blood, treasure, and effort to an unacceptable level. The means for doing this that Lee would pursue from the time he assumed command of the Confederacy's most important army in June 1862 was to pit his army against those the United States sent into Virginia in tests of strength and skill that might raise the level of pain in the North to the point where its people would abandon the effort to restore the authority of the United States government in the Southern states—a government that before April 1861 had few servants more able or dedicated than Robert Edward Lee.

Born on January 19, 1807, at Stratford Hall, in Westmoreland County, Virginia, Lee was the offspring of two of the commonwealth's most distinguished families.[2] His mother, Ann Hill Carter Lee, was a descendant of Robert "King" Carter, whose three hundred thousand acres of land and one thousand slaves made him one of the wealthiest men in all of America during the eighteenth century and placed his family at the top of Virginia's Tidewater elite.

Figure 1.1.   General Robert E. Lee, Confederate, 1863. Library of Congress

Ann's father, Charles Carter, owned twenty-five thousand acres of land himself, including the magnificent plantation of Shirley on the James River. There, Ann married Henry Lee III, on June 18, 1793. Henry Lee's pedigree was not quite as grand as his bride's, but he had added further laurels to the Lee name during the Revolution as renowned cavalry commander "Light Horse Harry" and serving as a delegate to the Continental Congress. At the time of his marriage, Henry Lee was the governor of Virginia.

Robert Edward was the fifth of six children born to Henry and Ann Lee between 1795 and 1811. Even though those years also saw him serve in the House of Representatives (where Lee famously proclaimed his old commander, George Washington, "first in war, first in peace, and first in the hearts of his countrymen"), at the time of Robert's birth Light Horse Harry was in the process of plunging his family into deep debt. Indeed, by the time Robert was born, his father was not much of a presence in the family as a consequence of his efforts to evade creditors, who finally caught up with him in 1809 and saw to his imprisonment. By the time of his release in 1810, Ann had decided to relocate with the children to Alexandria, Virginia. There, Robert E. Lee grew up under the care of his mother and a large extended family, attending schools in central Virginia and Alexandria. In 1824, a meeting was arranged between Lee and Secretary of War John C. Calhoun to discuss the former's interest in attending the United States Military Academy at West Point. The following year he entered West Point.

After four years of academic excellence and receiving not a single demerit, Lee graduated second in the class of 1829, was commissioned into the elite Corps of Engineers, and first saw duty constructing seacoast fortifications in Georgia. Two years later he was transferred to Fort Monroe, Virginia, and further cemented his place in the Virginia elite by marrying Mary Custis, the daughter of George Washington Parke Custis, the grandson of Martha Washington from her earlier marriage. The wedding took place on June 20, 1831, at the Custis plantation on the heights overlooking the Potomac River and Washington, D.C., known as Arlington. Together, the Lees would have seven children; all three of their sons would see service in the Confederate army.

Three years after his wedding, Lee was transferred to the headquarters of the Corps of Engineers in Washington to serve as an assistant to the chief engineer. In 1837, he headed to St. Louis, Missouri, to spend four years supervising a project that would save the town by keeping the current of the Mississippi River flowing in a way that preserved its wharfs. Lee, by then a captain, followed this with a few years' work on construction projects in New York before the Mexican War broke out. Lee arrived in Mexico in August

1846 and after four relatively uneventful months in northern Mexico, joined the staff of Maj. Gen. Winfield Scott as he was making preparations for an amphibious landing against the Mexican port of Vera Cruz, the first step in a campaign from the coast to Mexico City. At Vera Cruz, Lee got his first taste of combat. He distinguished himself in the campaign against Mexico City that followed by conducting bold reconnaissances that made possible one of the most impressive military victories in all of American history. Scott afterward proclaimed Lee "the very best soldier I ever saw in the field" and developed what one man later labeled "an almost idolatrous fancy for Lee, whose military genius he estimated far above that of any other officer." At least twice during the decade and a half after the Mexican War, Scott would offer Lee high-ranking places on his staff, but these were declined by Lee on the grounds that he believed his place was in the field.[3]

Lee followed up his distinguished service in Mexico with work in Baltimore, Maryland, on what would become Fort Carroll. Then, in August 1852, he very reluctantly headed up to New York to become the tenth superintendent of the U.S. Military Academy. After a successful and pleasant, albeit at times frustrating, three-year term, he became second in command of the newly organized Second U.S. Cavalry, but not until February 1856 did he actually join his regiment in Texas. In October 1857, he left Texas upon learning of the death of his father-in-law, found out that his wife had inherited Arlington, and became by default executor of George Washington Parke Custis's estate. Although still in the army, now at the rank of lieutenant colonel, Lee remained on leave for the next few years. During this time, he managed the Custis estate and took care of his wife, whose health was failing and was all but crippled by arthritis. The former task involved, among other things, managing the five dozen or so slaves at Arlington. By the time fall came in 1859, Lee was more than ready to return to duty with his regiment in Texas. In October of that year, however, he unexpectedly found himself commanding the contingent of Federal troops tasked with suppressing John Brown's effort to stir up a slave insurrection by seizing the Federal arsenal at Harpers Ferry. After successfully carrying out this assignment, Lee finally returned to Texas in early 1860.

The product of these experiences in 1860 was a profoundly conservative man, who was dedicated to the existing social order and the institutions that supported it. The Constitution and Union were among them, as was slavery. For much of his life, Lee was a slave owner (either directly or through his family), accepted the South's "peculiar institution," relied on the labor of the slaves at Arlington, and was capable of ordering severe punishments when they proved troublesome. In line with his upbringing among the Virginia elite and experience as an army officer, Lee possessed an elitist outlook that was skeptical of human nature and believed society needed to be governed by an enlightened elite—of which Lee believed himself a member—who could govern social passions and provide reason to guide human affairs. Lee's perceptive recent biographer, Emory Thomas, has argued compellingly that the future general's attachment to order, propriety, and discipline were also rooted in shame over how his father had dissipated the family's fortune and blackened its name due to a lack of personal discipline. Other historians have alluded to the power of the Washingtonian model on Lee's behavior. In addition to their family connections, Lee and Washington both possessed volcanic tempers that they strove to keep in check and found outlets for their passions in playful flirtation with the opposite sex—and, it has been argued, in the aggressive approach to making war both men shared.[4]

When Lee returned to Texas, however, it seemed that there was little prospect of achieving much more as a military man than the high esteem of General Scott and a reputation as one of the handsomest men in the entire army. But then, the conflict between the free and slave states reached a point where it was all but inevitable that there would be a war that would dwarf all previous ones in American history and give Lee all the opportunity any man could want to gratify his military ambitions. As southern hotheads responded to Abraham Lincoln's election to the presidency in November by making good on their pledges never to accept a Republican president and began meeting to debate secession from the Union, Lee looked on with intense dismay. He had served the Union for more than thirty years and had little sympathy for secession. Yet, he qualified his devotion to the Union in a letter to a friend in January 1861 with the caveat that he believed the South could "with a clear conscience separate" if the North rejected "the just demands of the South" and "the rights guaranteed by the Constitution are denied us." "If the Union is dissolved," he added, "I shall return to Virginia and share the fortune of my people."[5]

As seven states in the Deep South declared themselves out of the Union and their leaders began creating a new nation, the Confederate States of America, Lee received a summons to report to Washington. In March, shortly after Lincoln's inauguration, Scott informed Lee that he had called him to the capital because he wanted him to participate in a project to revise the army regulations. Scott then advised Lee that he was confident the secession crisis would be resolved peacefully and showed him some documents, including correspondence between himself and members of the new administration, that led him to this conclusion. Much relieved, Lee went home to Arlington to await the organization of the revising board and, a few days later, was pleased to be officially promoted to full colonel and command of the First U.S. Cavalry.[6]

Then, on April 15, in the aftermath of the Battle of Fort Sumter, Lincoln called upon the loyal states for seventy-five thousand troops to put down what he labeled "combinations too powerful to be suppressed by the ordinary course of judicial proceedings." With his and Scott's hopes for a peaceful resolution of the crisis evaporating, on April 18 Lee was invited to a meeting with Francis P. Blair, a close adviser to Lincoln. Blair told Lee that the administration wanted him to command the field army it was raising to suppress the rebellion. The country, Blair added, looked to Lee "as the representative of the Washington family." Lee replied that although he agreed with Blair as to "the folly of Secession," he could not lead such an army. "[T]hough . . . deprecating war," he later asserted, "I could take no part in an invasion of the Southern states." Lee then met again with Scott and told him about his conversation with Blair. Scott told Lee he regretted his response to Blair's offer but that, in light of what had been said during their earlier conversation, it did not surprise him.[7]

Lee returned to Arlington after meeting with Blair and Scott and learned the following day that the Virginia convention had voted to secede from the Union. On April 20, he wrote to Scott expressing appreciation for all the general had done for him and resigning his commission from the U.S. Army. "Save in the defence of my native State," he proclaimed, "I never desire again to draw my sword." To his sister that same day, he lamented, "Now we are in a state of war which will yield to nothing. . . . I recognize no necessity for this state of things, and would have forborne and pleaded to the end for redress of grievances, real or supposed, yet . . . With all my devotion to the Union, and the feeling of loyalty and duty of an American citizen, I have not been able to make up my mind to raise my hand against my relatives, my children, my home. . . . save in defense of my native State (with the sincere hope that my poor services may never be needed) I hope I may never be called upon to draw my sword."[8]

Two days later, Lee traveled to Richmond in response to a summons from Virginia governor John Letcher and by the morning of April 23 had accepted command of all military forces in Virginia and the rank of major general. Lee spent the next few months in Richmond supervising the organization of Virginia forces and working with Letcher and Confederate president Jefferson Davis to integrate them into the larger Confederate army and navy. He followed this with an inauspicious performance in his first field command in western Virginia that fall, and then spent four months in South Carolina trying to defend too many points with too few resources and making anything but a positive impression on the locals. One good thing, aside from his promotion to full

Figure 1.2.   Jefferson Davis, future president of the Confederate States.
National Archives

general in the Army of the Confederate States of America, did come out of
Lee's experiences during this time. On dreary Sewell Mountain in western Vir-
ginia, he made the acquaintance of a fine gray stallion by the name of Jeff
Davis. While in South Carolina, Lee purchased the horse and renamed him
Traveller. Traveller quickly became Lee's favorite warhorse, and remains per-
haps the most famous in American history.[9]

Lee's efforts in western Virginia and the Deep South took place in the
context of a larger strategy that President Davis was endeavoring to implement in line with his government's mission of demonstrating its will and
ability to defend its people from Yankee invasion, one that Lee appears to
have fully endorsed. (The strategic level of war is where a nation determines

its war aims and how it will employ its resources in pursuit of those aims.) In line with this strategically defensive mission, Davis had his armies adopt an operationally defensive stance, with Confederate forces posted in such a way as to attempt to cover the entire frontier with the North. Fortunately, it was not necessary to post a soldier at every point along the border, as logistical factors made it unfeasible for the Federals to attempt to invade the South anywhere there was not access to a railroad or river. There were, however, too many potential invasion routes for the South to hope to cover every one successfully. This at first did not seem evident, as Confederate forces triumphed in just about every significant engagement along the frontier in 1861 outside of Missouri and western Virginia. But the latter region did not really have enough value to the Confederacy to make it worth the resources it would take to put up a decent fight for it, while the situation in Missouri was so confused that writing it off for a while seemed a prudent course.[10]

When major campaigns began in 1862, however, the flaws in this strategy quickly became apparent. It conceded the operational initiative to the Federals, who wisely took advantage of it to take the offensive on lines of operations that were best suited to their military strengths. (The operational level of war is where campaigns and major operations are planned and conducted within a theater. The tactical level of war is where battles and engagements are planned and executed.)[11] Although land-based lines of operations using railroads for logistical support were part of the Union war plan, Federal armies quickly demonstrated a preference for overcoming the problem of invading the South and exposing the Confederacy's pledge to protect its people and territory as a hollow fraud by traveling on water. Fortunately for the North, nature had cursed the Confederacy with a wonderful network of rivers both west and east of the Appalachian Mountains that provided superb routes of invasion.

During the late winter and spring of 1862, Union army and navy forces in the West began pushing south following the Mississippi, Cumberland, and Tennessee Rivers. Lacking anything to match the North's resources for making war on water, Confederate forces in Kentucky and Tennessee commanded by Gen. Albert S. Johnston tried to stop the Federals using land-based defenses, but these were quickly overcome by the Union army and navy with around twelve thousand Confederates trapped and taken prisoner at Fort Donelson in February. Along the Atlantic and Gulf Coasts, Union naval forces seized significant sections of the North Carolina, South Carolina, and Georgia coastlines and in April 1862 managed to capture New Orleans. Most ominously, in March the Union navy transported a massive Union army commanded by Maj. Gen. George B. McClellan from Washington to Fort

Monroe at the tip of the peninsula formed by the York and James Rivers as the first step in a campaign that the Northern public confidently expected would deliver the coup de grace to the rebellion.

On March 2, 1862, a little more than two weeks before McClellan's Army of the Potomac began arriving at Fort Monroe, Lee "very unexpectedly" received orders to leave South Carolina and return to Richmond. Eleven days later, Davis issued an order that assigned Lee responsibility for, "under the di-

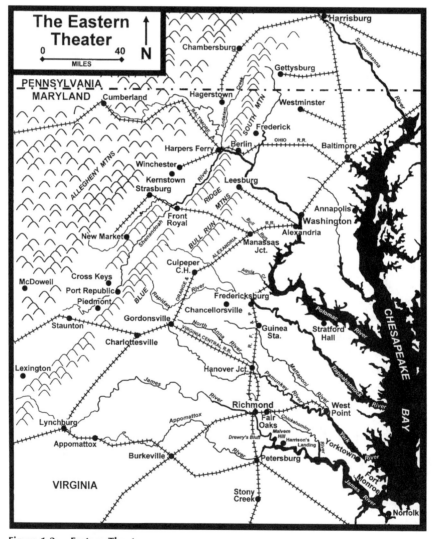

Figure 1.3.   Eastern Theater.

rection of the President, the conduct of military operations in the armies of the Confederacy." In reality, Lee immediately found himself serving chiefly as Davis's principal military adviser, rather than actually exercising command over military operations.[12]

Less than a week after Lee's appointment, McClellan's army began landing at Fort Monroe and, during the first week of April, commenced its advance up the York-James Peninsula. The first significant obstacle McClellan encountered turned out to be the weather, which was the worst this section of Virginia had seen in years. Another obstacle was thrown in McClellan's way when the Lincoln administration decided on April 3 to deny him use of the largest corps in his army. The administration did this in response to an attack on Union forces at Kernstown in the Shenandoah Valley on March 23 by a Confederate force commanded by Maj. Gen. Thomas J. "Stonewall" Jackson. Even though Jackson was soundly defeated, his attack so unnerved the Lincoln administration that it seized upon McClellan's sloppy explanation of his plan for the defense of Washington to justify denying the general the force he needed to execute his plan for a dynamic joint operation that would have quickly doomed the Confederate garrison at Yorktown. As if this were not enough, in April the U.S. War Department also decided to close its recruiting offices out of a belief that it already had enough men to deal with a rebellion that seemed to be on its knees. Unfortunately, this was not the last favor Washington would do for the Confederate cause in Virginia.[13]

Nonetheless, McClellan's offensive presented the Confederate high command with a serious problem. Although he unknowingly outnumbered the defenders at Yorktown by a substantial margin, McClellan responded to the unraveling of his plans by Washington by deciding to take Yorktown through siege operations. To the great aggravation of Lincoln, who complained the general's actions suggested "indefinite procrastination," McClellan methodically went to work implementing his plan.[14]

If Lincoln was distressed at McClellan's actions, the Confederate high command was as well. McClellan's approach was time-consuming, but it was also sure as the sunrise. To deal with it, Davis and Lee ordered Gen. Joseph E. Johnston to march his Army of Northern Virginia from its position behind the Rappahannock River to the Peninsula and combine its strength with the Yorktown garrison commanded by Brig. Gen. John B. Magruder. Johnston then went to Yorktown to assume overall command and on April 13 conducted a quick inspection to figure out what exactly he was getting into.[15]

He was appalled. Although Magruder had prepared good defensive works, it did not take long to see that it was completely beyond the power of any Confederate commander to hold on to Yorktown. McClellan's superiority in artillery, the support he received from the Union navy, and the strength and skill with which his entrenchments were being prepared were too much to resist. It was clear that, once McClellan had completed his preparations, Yorktown would be as much of a trap for Johnston's command as Fort Donelson had been for its defenders. And with that army gone, there would be little to prevent the Federals from moving swiftly up the Peninsula and taking Richmond. Perhaps if McClellan could be induced to make a poorly conceived assault with both Johnston's and Magruder's force in the Yorktown defenses, something positive might be accomplished on the Lower Peninsula, but Johnston knew his foe too well to expect that to happen. If, as he remarked after his investigation, "no one but McClellan could have hesitated to attack us" when just Magruder was in the defenses, it was futile to hope the Federal commander would change course upon learning Johnston's army was there as well. Thus, Johnston saw only one good option available: get out of Yorktown and pull back up the Peninsula before it was too late.[16]

Johnston's assessment of the situation was not well-received in Richmond. Davis and Lee could see naught but disaster for the Confederate cause in an immediate evacuation of Yorktown. After the cavalcade of calamities in the West and along the coasts, to abandon Yorktown without a serious fight might be more than the people of the South could stand without concluding that their new government and its pledge to protect them from the Yankees were hollow frauds. Then there was the problem that until the crash program to build shore defenses at Drewry's Bluff was completed, the presence of the ironclad ship CSS *Virginia* at Norfolk was the only thing preventing the Union navy from dashing up the James to the doorstep of the capital. Without possession of Yorktown, there was no way Norfolk could be held. Consequently, Davis and Lee ordered Johnston to defend Yorktown. Yet they could not and did not dispute Johnston's warning that they were courting disaster and that the prospects for a successful defense at Yorktown were as slim as the general described in a letter to Lee on April 30. "We are engaged in a species of warfare at which we can never win," Johnston bluntly observed. "McClellan . . . will depend for success upon artillery and engineering. We can compete with him in neither [and]. . . . can have no success while McClellan is allowed, as he is by our defensive, to choose his mode of war."[17] It was awful. McClellan's approach to the problem of overcoming Yorktown had put the Confederate high command in a no-win situation and rendered them militarily impotent.

Yet, as Davis and Lee were insisting that Johnston try to hold onto Yorktown, they were also moving to abandon the attempt to defend every inch of Confederate soil in favor of a new approach. The strategy of dispersing Confederate forces across the frontier, assuming the operational defensive, and ceding the initiative to the Federals had clearly failed. While the strategic aim—preservation of the Confederacy—remained unchanged, the new approach entailed taking the offensive operationally. To do this successfully, Davis and Lee recognized they would have to close the quantitative gap between the Confederate and Union armies. One way to do this was to stop dispersing their manpower along the frontier and coast and concentrate their forces in field armies, in line with Johnston's repeated calls, as the general wrote on April 22, "to assemble near Richmond as many troops as possible, those from Norfolk, North Carolina, and South Carolina to be joined by this army, then to endeavor to fight the enemy." They also recognized a different approach to raising manpower would be necessary. Consequently, during the first half of April—just as the Lincoln administration was cooperatively closing Federal recruiting offices—Davis and Lee pushed through the Confederate Congress the first conscription law in American history.[18]

It would take time, however, for these efforts to bear fruit. In the meantime, Johnston had to figure out how to defend Yorktown without losing his army. By May 3, as McClellan put the finishing touches on his plan for taking Yorktown, Johnston had concluded this was no longer possible. Thus, that day the Confederates evacuated Yorktown and began pulling back toward Richmond. Because of the danger of Union forces using their navy to slip around any position he might take up east of the Chickahominy River, Johnston could not and did not stop his retreat until he was behind that stream. There he could anchor his right flank on the James across from Drewry's Bluff, whose defenses were completed just in time to repulse a naval force that the Yankees had pushed upriver on May 15.[19]

McClellan followed Johnston cautiously and did so taking up a line of advance following the Richmond and York River Railroad. He did this in line with a promise from the Lincoln administration to restore the troops that had been taken from him at Yorktown. Over the objections of McClellan, who wanted them to join him by water, Lincoln decided these reinforcements would march south from Fredericksburg under the command of Brig. Gen. Irvin McDowell and link up with McClellan's right flank. Although a sound concept, it carried with it the mandate that McClellan make his advance on Richmond north of White Oak Swamp following the Richmond and York River Railroad, instead of shifting over to the James and basing his operations on the river—the latter prospect one that terrified Lee and the rest of the Confederate high command. Moreover, in order to link up with McDowell and be in position to attack Richmond once his forces arrived, McClellan would be compelled to divide his army between the right and left banks of the Chickahominy. If all went according to plan, though, by the end of May McClellan would have a force less than ten miles from Richmond that—in manpower, artillery, and position—could completely outmatch anything the Confederates could patch together by then.[20]

Unfortunately, all did not go according to plan. The futility of the effort to hold the Lower Peninsula impressed powerfully upon Lee the fact that if the Confederacy was to survive, its armies had to stop responding to the Federals and find some way to take the initiative. If it did not, and soon, Richmond and her defenders would surely be crushed by the combination of McClellan's and McDowell's forces. And unlike at Yorktown, abandoning the capital in hopes of finding a better place to fight elsewhere was not an option. Whatever moral and material effects the loss of Yorktown might have had would pale in comparison with the effects if the experience of Yorktown was repeated at Richmond. Moreover, even if, however unlikely it seemed, Southern morale could survive a demonstration of the Confederate government's military impotence in front of its capital, there was little hope of putting up an effective conventional resistance without the tools of war that were being produced by the Tredegar Iron Works and other Richmond industries. It was not mere sentiment that inspired Lee, in a meeting with the cabinet held in the aftermath of the fall of Yorktown, to insist, as "tears ran down his cheeks," one participant later recalled, that "Richmond must not be given up—it shall not be given up."[21]

Fortunately for Lee and his hopes of wresting the initiative from the Federals, there was the Shenandoah Valley. The results of the March engagement at Kernstown had provided a vivid demonstration of just how sensitive the Lincoln government was to affairs in that section of Virginia. It did not take much genius to wonder, if a battle in which Jackson received a pretty thorough thrashing at the hands of the Federals was enough to induce Washington to withhold an entire corps from McClellan's campaign, what would happen to those forces that were poised to march to McClellan's assistance if Jackson could be reinforced and achieve a victory or two? And if this could be done simultaneous with a counterstroke by Johnston, for whom forces were at that moment being pulled from other points in the Confederacy to reinforce his army, the combined effect could transform the war in Virginia. In reinforcing Jackson and Johnston for offensive action, Lee and Davis effectively sounded the death knell of the perimeter defense and gave birth to what the latter would label an "offensive-defensive" approach. While Confederate strategy in terms of their war aims remained defensive, the operational approach was to be offensive and made possible by concentrating Confederate forces into a few strong field armies. This approach had already paid some dividends in the West, where the momentum of Union victory had been slowed somewhat by a vicious (albeit ultimately unsuccessful) offensive at Shiloh in early April. Now it was time to put it to the test in Virginia.

Even before the fall of Yorktown, Lee had made available to Jackson two additional divisions and suggested they might be used to take the offensive in the Valley. Stonewall Jackson then proceeded to make his nom de guerre one of the more ironic in military history. From Staunton, he led his forces west to the small town of McDowell, where on May 8 he defeated a Union force attempting to push into the Valley from the west. Jackson then raced north to Front Royal where he routed a Union force commanded by Maj. Gen. Nathaniel Banks on May 23, then followed this up by crushing Banks again at Winchester two days later and chasing him north all the way to the Potomac. Predictably, the Lincoln administration overreacted to events in the Valley and decided to weaken McClellan by postponing the march of McDowell's command. Instead, Lincoln mandated that part of McDowell's command would take part in a scheme for having Union forces march into the Valley from the west and east to cut off Jackson's force. Unfortunately, Jackson responded by racing his command south with such celerity that he was not only able to elude his would-be pursuers but also administered severe beatings to them in engagements at Cross Keys on June 8 and Port Republic on June 9.[22]

While Jackson was achieving spectacular success in the Valley, the strategy of concentration and taking the offensive was achieving much less against McClellan. On May 31, Johnston launched a major offensive against two corps of McClellan's army that were south of the flooded Chickahominy. The attack initially achieved some success, wrecking one Union division and driving an entire Federal corps from its initial position. Johnston's hope of destroying the Federals south of the Chickahominy, however, would not come to fruition. McClellan responded to the Confederate attack by ordering the Union Second Corps to cross the river and go to the assistance of its comrades on the south side, which effectively stopped the Confederate offensive.[23]

The most significant of the casualties inflicted during the first day of the Battle of Fair Oaks (or Seven Pines) occurred at the very top of the Army of Northern Virginia's high command. While directing the battle during the early evening of May 31, Johnston was severely wounded. Davis learned of this turn of events as he and Lee were riding about the field in an attempt to see what was going on. After a brief meeting with the wounded Johnston and learning that his second in command could not stand the strain of army command, Davis made a fateful decision. "General Lee," he remarked as the two men directed their horses toward Richmond, "I shall assign you to the command of this army."[24] Unfortunately for Lee, by the time he assumed command of the Army of Northern Virginia, whatever opportunity there might have been to achieve a decisive victory at Fair Oaks was gone. The Confederates renewed their assaults on June 1, but made scant progress. Recognizing this, Lee ended the battle.

Richmond was still in grave danger, though. McClellan's army was strongly positioned and at some point the bad weather of that spring was going to relent and allow him to resume his inexorable advance on the Confederate capital. And it was clear that the Union commander was going to use the methods that had worked so well at Yorktown in his approach to taking Richmond. Although, unlike at Yorktown, the Confederates did not face the problem of McClellan having direct support from the Union navy, his advantage in artillery and the care and skill with which he was digging his entrenchments and preparing his offensive were just as great as they had been at Yorktown. "McClellan," Lee complained to President Davis on June 5, "will make this a battle of posts. He will take position from position, under cover of his heavy guns, & we cannot get at him without storming his works, which with our new troops is extremely hazardous. . . . It will require 100,000 men to resist the regular siege of Richmond, which perhaps would only prolong not save it." Lee then laid out to the president his plan for seizing the initiative from McClellan. "I am preparing a line that I can hold with part of our forces in front, while with the rest I will endeavor to . . . bring McClellan out."[25]

To do this, on June 10, Lee advised Davis he wished for Jackson's command, once it had finished its work in the Valley, to move to the Richmond front and "sweep down north of the Chickahominy, cut up McClellan's communications and rear." This would force McClellan's men out of their trenches and compel them to engage in a war of maneuver on Confederate terms, rather than a "battle of posts" that would favor the Federals. Lee had to act soon, though. The Federals would be vulnerable to an attempt to turn their position only as long as Lincoln's leash kept McDowell at Fredericksburg. But until McDowell arrived, the Union right would not extend far enough to prevent a Confederate force from maneuvering around it and reaching the Richmond and York River Railroad, the Army of the Potomac's supply line. Thanks to Jackson's operations in the Valley and, more importantly, Washington's response to them, the window for maneuvering around the Union right would be open long enough for Lee to take advantage.[26]

This he did beginning on June 26, opening what would become known as the Seven Days' Battles. Jackson's maneuver, although late in reaching its objectives, did have the effect of enabling him to reach the railroad, which made it impossible for McClellan to maintain his entrenched positions. Mc-Clellan, as Lee predicted, came out of his entrenchments. He did not, however, as Lee expected, fight for his supply line. Instead, he decided to take up a new one on the James River and ordered his army to march south toward that stream. This gave Lee an opportunity to strike, as McClellan's army would have to cross White Oak Swamp in order to reach the James. After taking a day to figure out what McClellan was doing, Lee developed a plan for striking a decisive blow before the Federals could reach the James.

Lee's plan, however, was too complicated, too many of his subordinates fumbled in executing it, and the Federals fought too hard for it to achieve success. McClellan managed to reach the James at Harrison's Landing and in the course of the Seven Days' Battles, his troops inflicted substantial casualties on Lee's army, especially on July 1, when they easily repulsed a poorly executed Confederate assault on their strong position in a set-piece engagement at Malvern Hill. Nonetheless, loyal Confederates breathed a heavy sigh of relief over the fact that McClellan could no longer hear the church bells of Richmond.[27]

Dealing with McClellan's operations on the Peninsula impressed upon Lee some important lessons that would shape his generalship for the rest of the war.[28] First among these was the fact that a passive defense was a loser for the Confederacy. With the Union advantage in numbers, to let a Federal commander pick the time and place where the two armies would operate would enable them to create situations that played to their advantages in numbers and firepower. Superior numbers and artillery made the Union army powerful, but slow, ponderous, and therefore ill-suited to a campaign of maneuver. In contrast, the smaller Confederate army would move quicker, be more flexible, and react faster to events than its Union counterpart. In a campaign of set-piece engagements and siege operations, these advantages were all negated, but in a fluid campaign of maneuver, they would give the Confederates a decisive advantage.

The only way to ensure the war would be one of maneuver was for Lee to seize the initiative by taking the offensive. And as the events of April–June 1862 demonstrated, the best place to do that was not east of Richmond. The lay of the land, with its confined spaces and the proximity of the rivers, was much better suited to a war of set-piece engagements and siege operations in which the advantages lay with the Federals. North of Richmond, though, the terrain was open, there was no Union navy to worry about, and the Federals were dependent on railroad-based logistics that were difficult to guard against an army that excelled at maneuver.

Unfortunately, even though the Federals were no longer at Richmond's doorstep, Lee found himself in an awful situation after the Seven Days' Battles. By reaching the James, McClellan had regained the initiative and there was little Lee could do to get it back. He could not attack McClellan in his strong position, and Federal river-based logistics were secure from attack. To be sure, McClellan gave every indication that he intended to spend some time licking his wounds before resuming operations, but that could not last forever. And when the Federals did advance they were in a place to do so effectively. Like at Yorktown, they were in direct contact with their navy and they still possessed the great strength in artillery that made the defense of that place an exercise in futility. And they had many options for exploiting their new position. McClellan could advance along the north bank of the James, with the navy enhancing his army's mobility and firepower, or cross the James and operate against the railroads that linked Richmond to the rest of the Confederacy. Regardless of where they went, under McClellan the Federals could be expected to conduct operations in the sort of methodical fashion that would offer Lee few, if any, of the sort of operational opportunities that were available when the Army of the Potomac was astride the Chickahominy.

Making matters worse for Lee was the fact that the Yankees were making a serious effort to get their act together north of Richmond. On June 26, the Lincoln administration smartly combined the forces that Jackson had so roughly handled into a single Army of Virginia and placed it under the command of Maj. Gen. John Pope. Upon taking command, Pope immediately began concentrating most of his widely scattered command around Culpeper Court House on the Orange and Alexandria Railroad. Should Pope successfully complete this task and push further south along the railroad, he could seize the railroad junction at Gordonsville and complicate Richmond's communications with the Shenandoah Valley. Then there was McDowell's force at Fredericksburg. Although technically part of Pope's army, there was the danger that they would push south along the Richmond, Fredericksburg, and Potomac Railroad toward Richmond.

Lee had to somehow pull off the trick of countering all three of these threats. If he could get away from Richmond to operate against Pope that would be terrific, for the geography of central Virginia was highly conducive to the sort of campaign of maneuver Lee needed to wage if he was to be successful against the Federals. Further enhancing the appeal of operating against Pope was the fact that that general pledged upon taking command not to conduct operations with the methodical and cautious manner that made McClellan such a threat. But as long as McClellan's army was on the James, Lee was stuck.[29]

Fortunately for Lee, the Lincoln administration once again stepped in to do him a favor. Lincoln had never liked McClellan's concept of basing the Army of the Potomac's operations on the waters of the Virginia Tidewater. The problems in the Shenandoah Valley and outcome of the Peninsula Campaign confirmed his prejudices against McClellan's ideas and fears for the safety of the Valley and Washington if the main Union army in Virginia was not between the capital and the rebels. Consequently, through newly installed general-in-chief Henry W. Halleck, on August 3 Lincoln ordered McClellan to evacuate the Peninsula and join his command with Pope's.[30]

Lincoln's decision was a godsend to Lee. He had already been compelled to send three divisions under Jackson north to counter Pope, but under strict caveats that he not do anything that might prevent their returning to Richmond immediately in the event of McClellan's resuming operations. With the evaporation of the threat from the James, Lee was free to rush his command north to deal with Pope. This he did in a magnificent campaign, in which the elements of Lee's operational approach came together in spectacular fashion. In cooperation with what had become an outstanding command team, he seized the initiative by taking the offensive and maneuvering boldly with Maj. Gen. J.E.B. Stuart's cavalry and Jackson's command during the last week of August. By doing so, he induced Pope to abandon the cautious good sense that characterized his conduct of operations during his first few weeks in command and enabled him to thwart Confederate efforts during that time to find or create opportunities to achieve decisive success. Unfortunately, by taking an aggressive approach in response to Lee's maneuvers, Pope ended up putting his army in a position on August 30 where it was open to an attack on its flank by Maj. Gen. James Longstreet's wing of Lee's army, which managed to drive the Federals from the field at the Battle of Second Manassas.[31]

Lee did not stop there. To maintain the initiative and force the Yankees into another campaign of maneuver before they could recover from their whipping at Manassas, Lee pushed his command across the Potomac into Maryland. There were more than operational considerations behind this decision, though, as it was a clear extension of Lee's views on how to achieve the South's strategic objective of securing Northern recognition of its independence. Just as the string of defeats ceding the operational initiative to the Federals had produced earlier in the year dragged down Confederate morale, Lee hoped that the string of victories that would flow from dictating the time and place of operations through aggressive, offensive operations would have a depressing effect on the enemy. This was, as he saw it, the only possible means for securing Confederate independence. The Confederacy could never destroy the ability of the North to make war, so its only chance for victory was to erode the will of the North to make war. The way to do this was to encourage the idea in the North that, however desirable, the task of restoring the Union was not acceptable from a cost-benefit standpoint. The way to do this was by winning victories on the battlefield that would frustrate the North and raise the costs of the war in blood, treasure, and patience to the point that to the Northern public, crushing the Confederacy, even if feasible, was not worth it.[32]

This could not be done by any of the other courses of action available to Lee after his victory at Manassas. Lee did not and never would have the means to successfully attack or besiege Washington, he did not have the logistical support to remain in northern Virginia, and falling back to the Rappahannock River or Shenandoah Valley would cede the initiative to the Federals—with all the danger that had been demonstrated to carry. Moreover, in July the Lincoln administration had reopened its recruiting offices, calling upon the states to provide three hundred thousand more troops. Once these troops had received the training, equipment, and seasoning to make good the losses of the first half of 1862, whatever advantage the Confederates might have gained through their more effective mobilization policies in 1861 and early 1862 would be gone and the balance of manpower would tip in favor of the Union for good. Moving into Maryland would, Lee correctly surmised, force the Lincoln administration to put these new troops in the field before they were ready. "Two grand armies of the United States that have been operating in Virginia, though now united, are much weakened and demoralized," Lee proclaimed to Davis on September 3. "We cannot afford to be idle and though weaker than our opponents in men and military equipments, must endeavor to harass, if we cannot destroy them. . . . As long as the army of the enemy is employed on this frontier I have no fears for the safety of Richmond."[33]

Unfortunately for Lee, Pope's defeat forced Lincoln to once again turn to McClellan, who brought to command the qualities necessary to foil Lee's plan. McClellan's organizational ability enabled him to move out of Washington much faster than Lee expected. Consequently, McClellan was able to catch the Confederates when their army was awkwardly divided due to Lee's decision to detach part of his command for an operation against Federal garrisons at Martinsburg and Harpers Ferry. McClellan also conducted his operations in his usual methodical, low-risk fashion, which enabled him to seize positions that robbed Lee of the operational initiative and give the Confederate leader no opportunity to get it back. He then drove Lee's army from South Mountain, countered every subsequent attempt by Lee to resume a campaign of maneuver, and came within a razor's edge of completely destroying the Army of Northern Virginia at the Battle of Antietam (or Sharpsburg). Despite the capture of more than ten thousand Federal troops at Harpers Ferry, Lee returned to Virginia on September 19–20, 1862, in defeat.

After Antietam, Lee and McClellan licked their wounds for several weeks, during which Lee formally organized his army into two wings (they would be officially designated "corps" once the Confederate Congress legally authorized such organizations in November). Lee responded by directing Longstreet's wing of the army to march to Culpeper to keep McClellan from reaching the Orange and Alexandria Railroad far south enough to menace Gordonsville. Meanwhile, he kept Jackson's wing in the Shenandoah Valley, where by threatening McClellan's line of supply east of the Blue Ridge, he compelled the Federal commander to take measures that ensured Longstreet would achieve his objective. Nonetheless, McClellan was able to reach Warrenton and set up a new line of supply on the Orange and Alexandria during the first week of November. Lincoln, however, had had enough of McClellan and on November 7, Maj. Gen. Ambrose Burnside replaced him as commander of the Army of the Potomac.[34]

Burnside, recognizing his appointment was in effect a demand for action, did not disappoint. Within days after taking command, he proposed abandoning the Orange and Alexandria to make a rapid march to Fredericksburg, cross the Rappahannock, and advance south from there following the Richmond, Fredericksburg, and Potomac Railroad. Lincoln was unenthusiastic about the plan. From a position on the Orange and Alexandria, Burnside would stand directly between the Confederates in Washington. Moving south and east carried the risk of giving the rebels an opportunity to operate beyond his right flank and menace the Union capital. Burnside, however, thinking much like Lee, believed that by taking the initiative and moving quickly he would force the Confederates to react to him, which would preclude their making any move toward Washington. Lincoln finally agreed to Burnside's plan, but had Halleck warn: "He thinks it will succeed if you move rapidly; otherwise not."[35]

Any concern that Lee might take advantage of Burnside's move by taking the offensive proved groundless. Lee had little inclination to undertake a major offensive campaign so late in the season and, as Burnside expected, a rapid Union march from Warrenton to Fredericksburg compelled Lee to react to the Federal move and follow Burnside to Fredericksburg. Unfortunately for Burnside, his plan to quickly get his 120,000-man army across the Rappahannock came to naught, as Halleck's lack of diligence prevented pontoon bridges from reaching the Army of the Potomac when they were expected. This gave Lee time to reach Fredericksburg and post his 78,000 men in a strong defensive position on the heights just outside town. After his efforts to find a better alternative failed, Burnside decided to directly assault Lee's position. It did not require boldness or the initiative for Lee to prevail in the defensive battle he fought at Fredericksburg on December 13, 1862. Although a Federal division managed to penetrate Jackson's portion of the line near Prospect Hill and, had the man responsible for that wing of Burnside's army acted with more energy, could have caused serious trouble, when the day was over Lee had won a clear tactical victory, inflicting about 12,600 casualties while suffering fewer than 5,400 of his own. Watching the enemy make futile assault after futile assault on Longstreet's impregnable position, Lee remarked, "It is well that war is so terrible, or we should grow too fond of it."[36]

Yet Fredericksburg was not an entirely positive experience for Lee, for as Jackson accurately predicted before the battle, "*we will whip the enemy, but gain no fruits of victory.*" Due to the power of the Union army, especially its artillery, at no time during the battle did an opportunity arise where Lee could seize the initiative and exploit his success. Indeed, a few months later Lee would confide to a junior officer that after Fredericksburg, "I was much depressed. We had really accomplished nothing." Moreover, even the relative disparity in casualties contained cause for concern. In Washington, Lincoln soberly noted that even though Burnside had lost: "more men than did the enemy . . . if the same battle were to be fought over again, every day, through a week of days, with the same relative results, the army under Lee would be wiped out to its last man, the Army of the Potomac would still be a mighty host, the war would be over, the Confederacy gone."[37]

Few generals, if any, were as cognizant as Lee was of this "awful arithmetic." The only way the Confederacy could hope to achieve some kind of attritional equality was if the armies were engaged in operations in a manner that might make it possible to deal the Yankees heavy blows without wasting Confederate strength disproportionately. If the armies were in camp, the inevitable losses to sickness, accidents, and the other hazards that would take place would wear the Confederates down disproportionately—even without taking into account the South's inferior ability to feed, supply, and provide medical care to its men. This was one of the reasons Lee would always be anxious to take the offensive. At Fredericksburg, that had not been necessary to achieve a tactical victory. But it was foolish to always expect the Yankees to be so accommodating as to make gross tactical errors—that is unless they were thrown off balance, which could best be achieved by taking away their ability to dictate the time and place of engagements. The only way to do this was to seize the initiative through offensive action.

The worst possible scenario from Lee's perspective, and one he feared would be adopted if he remained operationally passive, was that the Yankees would attempt to replay the Peninsula Campaign instead of letting the war be fought in northern and central Virginia where geography favored a war of maneuver. Indeed, during the late fall of 1862, Lee expressed grave concern that McClellan might be able to act on his desire to return to the James after he finished revitalizing his army after Antietam.[38] Although Lee could not have known it, Lincoln rendered his concerns on this score moot. By the time Burnside's tenure as commander of the Army of the Potomac ended in late January 1863, even though a number of officers in the Army of the Potomac made it clear they wanted to return to the Peninsula, Lincoln had done Lee the great favor of eliminating returning to the Peninsula as an option. At Lincoln's decree, Union military might in Virginia would be employed on a line of operations that played to Confederate military strengths in maneuver.

As previously noted, Lincoln's experiences with McClellan had reinforced his strong dislike for the idea of basing the main Federal effort in the East on the rivers of the Virginia Tidewater. Lincoln and Halleck, the president's principal military advisor, believed with almost religious fervor in concentration of force on a single line of operations. To let the Army of the Potomac travel to the Peninsula again, while leaving enough forces in northern Virginia to ensure the security of Washington and the Shenandoah Valley, would violate this principle. Moreover, Lincoln concluded that the best that could be achieved from operations based on the James was a siege of Richmond. The notion of his Army of Northern Virginia being trapped inside earthworks in front of its capital, of course, terrified Lee. However, Lincoln hated the idea of his own army being stuck in earthworks in front of Richmond. From behind their fortifications, the Confederates, Lincoln and Halleck postulated, could hold off many times their number so long that it would exhaust Northern patience as much, if not more than, an occasional defeat in battle. Strong fortifications would also allow the Confederates, while holding off a much larger force, to detach forces for operations elsewhere, either in the West where Lincoln and Halleck were pinning their hopes for victory or against Washington. Just as important, to let the Army of the Potomac return to the James would be a de facto acknowledgment that McClellan had been right and the president wrong in their debate over lines of operations. Such an admission over such an important military matter would be devastating to Lincoln. It would vindicate a commander whose methods still enjoyed great popularity within the army, yet were mocked as wrong-headed and perhaps treasonous by a large and vocal segment of the Republican Party whose support Lincoln could not afford to lose. Consequently, Lincoln and Halleck decided the Army of the Potomac would simply have to do the best it could north of Richmond. If that meant condemning the Army of the Potomac to a line of operations that favored the Confederates, bloody battles, and operational stalemate, Lincoln accepted that and hoped for success in the West.

Yet the Union "headquarters doctrine," as historians Herman Hattaway and Archer Jones have labeled it, was not without its merit. First, even if it kept the Army of the Potomac away from the James River line where it was most potent, as long as that army's commanders conducted operations with caution and good sense, they could deny Lee any opportunity for the sort of truly decisive victories his strategy needed to succeed. And there was the "awful arithmetic" that dictated that even operational stalemate and tactical setbacks contained within them, in the form of attrition, benefits for the Union cause. More important, though, Lincoln correctly sensed Lee and his subordinates preferred to conduct operations as far away from the Confederate capital as possible. Lincoln also correctly perceived that Lee's offensive-minded operational vision meant that there was a good chance Confederate forces would again move far enough north that an opportunity would be created, as in the Maryland Campaign, for the Army of the Potomac to catch them outside the protection of fortifications and far from their base at Richmond and deliver a truly crushing and decisive blow. Thus, although the headquarters doctrine offered immense relief to Lee by ensuring there would be no return to the Peninsula for the Army of the Potomac in 1863, it did provide a framework for Union operations that, if not optimum, still carried considerable hazard for the Confederacy.[39]

As if this were not enough, even as Lincoln was relieving Lee of his anxieties regarding the Union army going to the James, strategically his government was taking actions that further illustrated the powerful odds the Confederacy had to contend with—and provided powerful testimony to the fact that the North's determination to preserve the Union remained strong. The Thirty-seventh Congress that began in December 1861 ended in March 1863 having passed a strong conscription law that made all able-bodied men between twenty and forty-five subject to being drafted, a national banking act to ensure that the North's immense financial resources would be more efficiently and effectively applied in the contest with the South, and established the first federal income tax in United States history.[40]

Yet for the Confederacy's leading general there was a silver lining in all of this. To be sure, these revolutionary measures provided a vivid reminder of the North's ability to make war and a demonstration of the determination of its leaders in Washington to do so. However, they were greeted with great unease, and in some places outright defiance, in much of the North. In combination with the Emancipation Proclamation, they fueled a growing discontent with the Lincoln administration and the war (although not necessarily with the restoration of the Union, an important distinction that has been lost on many observers). Consequently, Lee was still able to retain hope for "a revolution among their people" against the war. At the same time, he did not think he and his army could passively await events, but had to be an active agent in shaping them. "Nothing can produce a revolution," he believed, "except systematic success on our part."[41]

Yet, as he was writing these words, the means Lee had at his disposal for achieving systematic military success were significantly diminished. In mid-February 1863, he found himself compelled to detach Longstreet and two divisions from the Army of Northern Virginia to southeast Virginia. The Federals had sent reinforcements to the region and in addition to countering this it was hoped that Longstreet would be able to gather supplies there as well. Longstreet's expedition would produce few positive results at a cost of reducing Lee's army to the point where it was outnumbered two to one by the Federal army on the other side of the Rappahannock. Further adding to Lee's woes were major health problems that began in March. What at first seemed to be merely a heavy cold had the general battling intense pain in his chest, back, and arms for most of April and May. Biographers Douglas Southall Freeman and Emory Thomas have concluded Lee's ailment was probably angina pectoris, a serious heart condition for which there was no remedy, only means for alleviating the symptoms. Although his condition improved once the weather did, Lee would not be the same man physically in 1863 that he was the year before. Several months after the worst of his symptoms had passed, he confided to a family member, "I have felt very differently since my attack of last spring, from which I have never recovered."[42]

Burnside's relief from command brought a new man to the head of the Army of the Potomac, one closer to Pope than McClellan in temperament—a fact that "Fighting Joe" Hooker made clear by assuring anyone who listened in Washington that he was no "McClellanite." Indeed, Hooker had made his reputation as an aggressive fighting general who did not make war with the spade and shovel, but with bold maneuvers and hard fighting. And Hooker proved an able commander. He revitalized the Army of the Potomac after its post-Fredericksburg "Valley Forge" and developed a superb operational plan that very nearly vindicated all the faith he had encouraged the North to invest in him.

During the last week of April 1863, Hooker began putting his plan into motion. He ordered two corps of his 130,000-man army to recross the Rappahannock at Fredericksburg and menace the Confederates there, while the rest of his army moved north and west toward crossings of the Rappahannock and Rapidan rivers located well above Fredericksburg in an attempt to turn Lee's left flank. When it was clear that Hooker's main effort was the turning movement, Lee left part of his 60,000-man army at Fredericksburg under the direction of Maj. Gen. Jubal Early and marched the bulk of his command west toward Chancellorsville. Lee's move induced Hooker to halt his advance just west of Zoan Church and withdraw to a defensive position in the thick Wilderness around Chancellorsville. Seeing no prospect for a successful direct assault against Hooker's position, Lee boldly ordered Jackson's corps to make a long march on May 2 to a point from which it could fall upon the Federals west of Chancellorsville.[43]

Fortunately for Lee, when Jackson began his attack, he found that the officer responsible for the Federal position around and to the west of Wilderness Church, Maj. Gen. Oliver O. Howard, had disregarded warnings from Hooker to be prepared. Jackson surprised the Federals with his late-afternoon attack and drove Howard's routed command back along the Orange Turnpike toward Chancellorsville. Early in the morning of May 3, as he tried to figure out how to unite the two divisions immediately under his direction with Jackson's forces and keep up the pressure on the Federals so they could not rally and turn what was a fluid situation into a more set-piece one, Lee learned that Jackson had been seriously wounded. Lee responded by placing Jackson's forces under Stuart and twice sent orders to that officer stating the necessity that "the glorious victory thus far achieved be prosecuted with the utmost vigor, and the enemy given no time to rally. As soon . . . as it is possible, they must be pressed, so that we can unite two wings of the army . . . work by the right wing, turning the positions of the enemy, so as to drive him from Chancellorsville, which will again unite us. Everything will be done on this side to accomplish the same object."[44]

By mid-morning on May 3, Stuart and Lee had managed to close the gap between them, enabling Lee to ride forward to claim possession of the crossroads around Chancellorsville. It was the pinnacle of his success as a tactical commander. Yet despite the brilliant success of the past two days it was far from certain on May 3 that Lee could achieve a decisive victory at Chan-

Figure 1.4.   Major General Joseph Hooker, Union, c. 1860–1865. Library of Congress

cellorsville. Hooker still enjoyed a superiority in manpower of two to one over the Confederates, and much of the force the Federal commander had under his immediate command had not even been engaged yet. If the Yankees were allowed just a little breathing space to allow them to regroup in a strong position, they would present Lee with a considerable—and perhaps insurmountable—tactical problem. Consequently, after uniting the two wings of his army, Lee's first ambition was to maintain the pressure on the Federals in hopes that he could catch them in a confused state between Chancellorsville and the Rappahannock. Unfortunately, at this point a message reached Lee informing him that the Federal forces at Fredericks- burg commanded by Maj. Gen. John Sedgwick had broken through the Confederate defenses there and were advancing on his rear. Lee had no choice but to reluctantly give up his hopes of continuing to push Hooker and dispatch four brigades under the command of Maj. Gen. Lafayette McLaws east. They arrived at Salem Church shortly after the situation had been stabilized by a tough battle that brought the Federal advance to a halt. The next morning, Lee sent more forces to Salem Church, which, thanks in part to the commanding general's personal intervention, helped drive Sedg- wick's forces back against the Rappahannock at Scott's Ford, which the Fed- erals crossed the night of May 4–5.[45]

With that problem solved, Lee returned to Chancellorsville to deal with Hooker, who had prepared a strong defensive position covering the Rappa- hannock crossing at U.S. Ford. Upon reaching Chancellorsville, Lee decided to attack on May 6, hoping to deliver the coup de grace to Hooker's com- mand. Fortunately for Lee, by the time dawn arrived on May 6, the Federals were gone and his army was spared what would surely have been a suicidal assault. As if the two-to-one Union advantage in numbers were not enough, Hooker had had nearly three full days to prepare his position for the sort of set-piece defensive fight the Army of the Potomac excelled in. Not surpris- ingly, Hooker's subordinates were confident and eager to continue the battle. However, Hooker's faculties had been badly impaired by a serious head injury he suffered earlier in the battle, which dulled his usual good judgment and enthusiasm for a fight. Nonetheless, Lee was unhappy when he learned of Hooker's retreat and subjected division commander Dorsey Pender, who had what proved to be the dubious honor of reporting Hooker's departure, to a display of his volcanic temper. "Why General Pender!" Lee exclaimed after receiving his subordinate's report, "That is what you young men always do. You allow those people to get away. I tell you what to do, but you don't do it." Waving his hand in exasperation, Lee then told Pender: "Go after them and damage them all you can."[46]

Lee's frustration on the morning of May 6 was rooted in part in the fact that Chancellorsville had provided a vivid demonstration of the danger of surrendering the initiative to the Federals. By remaining on the defensive, a consequence of the reduction of his numbers for use elsewhere, Lee had al- lowed the Federals to catch him at a disadvantage and largely choose the time and place of the fighting. It was only through incredibly risky tactics and luck beyond belief that the Army of Northern Virginia did not suffer a catastrophic defeat. If not for Howard's negligence, Jackson would not have achieved as much as he did on May 2; if not impaired by his injury, the usually able Hooker would have undoubtedly handled his army with greater skill and determination in the days that followed.

Moreover, despite these gifts from Dame Fortune and the tactical brilliance he and his army had displayed at Chancellorsville, Lee, as evidenced by his tirade on the morning of May 6, was not completely satisfied with the outcome of the campaign. To be sure, he had won a magnificent victory, preserving his position south of the Rappahannock and forcing the Yankees to make a humiliating retreat back to their camps. But he had been unable to achieve anything that really altered the operational or strategic situation in a way that tipped the military balance in favor of the Confederacy. Indeed, there was much to suggest just the opposite. The costs in time and lives at Chancellorsville had been extremely high—almost to the point of negating all the positive effects of the battle. The Army of Northern Virginia's losses totaled 13,100 killed, wounded, and missing. True, Hooker's total losses were greater (about 16,800), but these could be replaced; thus, the relative attrition rates were decidedly pro-Union, with the only thing really accomplished being the return of the Union army to the camps north of the river from which they had started the campaign.

This, of course, was an impressive achievement, given the odds Lee had faced. Yet, as far as the moral effect of the victory was concerned, this too was disappointing. Indeed, if Lincoln could find a silver lining in Fredericksburg, there was no reason to expect Chancellorsville to produce any great change in his determination to press on with the war. To be sure, upon receiving word of Hooker's defeat, Lincoln's first response was: "My God! My God! What will the country say!" Yet, as more information about the battle came in, the Union president regained his equilibrium and, after a quick visit to Hooker and his army, came away with his confidence in ultimate victory fully intact.[47]

Notes

1. Lee to Cooper, March 6, 1863, in *The Wartime Papers of Robert E. Lee*, edited by Clifford Dowdey and Louis H. Manarin (Boston: Little, Brown, and Co., 1961), 221.

2. For information on Lee's background and pre-Civil War life, I have mainly relied on Emory M. Thomas's superlative *Robert E. Lee: A Biography* (New York: W.W. Norton, 1995), 24–190.

3. Ibid., 140; Lee to Thomas, June 16, 1859, Robert E. Lee Papers, Special Collections, Leyburn Library, Washington and Lee University, Lexington, Virginia. (Hereafter cited as Lee Papers, WL)

4. Thomas, *Robert E. Lee*, 17. The Washington connection is most fully addressed in Richard B. McCaslin, *Lee in the Shadow of Washington* (Baton Rouge: Louisiana State University Press, 2001).

5. Lee to Carter, January 16, 1861, Lee Papers, WL.

6. William Allan, "Memoranda of Conversations with General Robert E. Lee," in *Lee the Soldier*, edited by Gary W. Gallagher (Lincoln: University of Nebraska Press, 1996), 9–10, 12.

7. Abraham Lincoln, "Proclamation Calling Militia and Convening Congress," April 15, 1861, in *The Collected Works of Abraham Lincoln*, edited by Roy P. Basler, 7 vols. (New Brunswick, NJ: Rutgers University Press, 1953), vol. 4: 332; Lee to Reverdy Johnson, February 25, 1868, quoted in *Wartime Papers of R.E. Lee*, eds. Dowdey and Manarin, 4; Allan, "Memoranda," 10, 12.

8. Lee to Scott, April 20, 1861, in *Wartime Papers*, eds. Dowdey and Manarin, 9; Lee to Anne Marshall, April 20, 1861, ibid., 9–10.

9. Douglas Southall Freeman, *R.E. Lee: A Biography*, 4 vols. (New York: Charles Scribner's Sons, 1934), vol. 1: 644–46.

10. Department of Defense, *Joint Publication 1-02: Department of Defense Dictionary of Military and Associated Terms as Amended through 17 October 2007* (Washington, DC: U.S. Department of Defense, 2001–07), 516. The discussion in this chapter of the Confederate high command's perimeter strategy and the decision in mid-1862 to eschew it in favor of a more aggressive strategy has been heavily influenced by the unmatched analysis of these matters contained in Joseph L. Harsh, *Confederate Tide Rising: Robert E. Lee and the Making of Southern Strategy, 1861-1862* (Kent, OH: Kent State University Press, 1998), 31–39, 53–73.

11. DoD, *Joint Publication 1-02*, 394, 532.

12. Lee to Carter Lee, March 14, 1862, Lee Papers, WL; General Orders No. 14, March 13, 1862, U.S. War Department, *The War of the Rebellion: A Compilation of the Official Records of the Union and Confederate Armies*, 70 vols. in 128 parts (Washington, DC: Government Printing Office, 1880–1901), ser. 1, vol. 5: 1099. (Hereafter cited as *OR*; all references are to series 1 unless otherwise noted.)

13. Ethan S. Rafuse, *McClellan's War: The Failure of Moderation in the Struggle for the Union* (Bloomington: Indiana University Press, 2005), 201–6, 221.

14. Lincoln to McClellan, May 1, 1862, in *Works of Lincoln*, ed. Basler, vol. 5: 203.

15. Special Orders No. 6, April 12, 1862, *OR*, vol. 11, pt. 3: 438; Taylor to Huger, April 13, 1862, ibid., 438–39.

16. Joseph E. Johnston, *Narrative of Military Operations* (New York: D. Appleton, 1874), 111–13; Johnston to Lee, April 22, 1862, *OR*, vol. 11, pt. 3: 456; Johnston to Cooper, May 19, 1862, ibid., pt. 1: 275.

17. Johnston to Lee, April 30, 1862, ibid., pt. 3: 477.

18. Johnston to Lee, April 22, 1862, ibid., 456.

19. Johnston to Cooper, May 19, 1862, ibid., pt. 1: 275–76.

20. McClellan to Stanton, August 4, 1863, ibid., pt. 1: 24–31; Johnston to Lee, April 29, 1862, ibid., pt. 3: 473; Lee to Johnston, May 17, 1862, in *Wartime Papers*, eds. Dowdey and Manarin, 175.

21. Harsh, *Confederate Tide Rising*, 64–65; John H. Reagan, *Memoirs, with Special Reference to Secession and the Civil War* (New York: Neale Publishing, 1906), 139.

22. Lee to Jackson, May 1, 1862, in *Wartime Papers*, eds. Dowdey and Manarin, 163; Lincoln to McDowell, May 24, 1862, in *Works of Lincoln*, ed. Basler, vol. 5: 232; Jackson to Chilton, March 7, April 10, 14, 1863, OR, vol. 12, pt. 1: 470–72, 701–08, 711–16.

23. Johnston to Cooper, June 24, 1862, ibid., vol. 11, pt. 1: 933–35; McClellan to Stanton, June 1, 1862, ibid., 751–52.

24. Freeman, *R.E. Lee*, vol. 2: 74.

25. Lee to Davis, June 5, 1862, in *Wartime Papers*, eds. Dowdey and Manarin, 184.

26. Lee to Davis, June 10, 1862, ibid., 188.

27. The course and outcome of the Seven Days' Battles are examined in Sears, *To the Gates of Richmond*, Brian K. Burton's *Extraordinary Circumstances: The Seven Days Battles* (Bloomington: Indiana University Press, 2001), and Carol Reardon's wonderfully insightful "From 'King of Spades' to 'First Captain of the Confederacy': R.E. Lee's First Six Weeks with the Army of Northern Virginia," in *Lee the Soldier*, ed. Gallagher, 309–30.

28. This discussion of Lee's strategic and operational vision has been heavily influenced by the unmatched analysis of these matters in Harsh, *Confederate Tide Rising*, 53–73.

29. Order Constituting the Army of Virginia, June 26, 1862, in *Collected Works of Abraham Lincoln*, ed. Basler, vol. 5: 287; in his analysis of this situation, Joseph Harsh aptly describes Lee as "spread-eagled." Harsh, *Confederate Tide Rising*, 98–100, 105–115.

30. Halleck to Burnside or Stevens, August 1, 1862, OR, vol. 12, pt. 3: 524; Halleck to McClellan, July 30, August 3, 1862, ibid., vol. 11, pt. 1: 76–77, 80–81.

31. Harsh, *Confederate Tide Rising*, 108–18. The authoritative work on Second Manassas is John J. Hennessy, *Return to Bull Run: The Campaign and Battle of Second Manassas* (New York: Simon & Schuster, 1993).

32. The best study by far of Lee's failed venture into Maryland in September 1862 is Joseph L. Harsh, *Taken at the Flood: Robert E. Lee and Confederate Strategy in the Maryland Campaign of 1862* (Kent, OH: Kent State University Press, 1999), although useful accounts will also be found in Stephen W. Sears, *Landscape Turned Red: The Battle of Antietam* (New York: Ticknor & Fields, 1983) and D. Scott Hartwig, "Robert E. Lee and the Maryland Campaign," in *Lee the Soldier*, ed. Gallagher, 331–55.

33. Lee to Davis, September 3, 1862, in *Wartime Papers*, eds. Dowdey and Manarin, 292–93.

34. Special Orders No. 234, Hdqrs. Army of Northern Virginia, November 6, 1862, OR, vol. 19, pt. 2: 698–99; McClellan to Stanton, August 4, 1863, ibid., pt. 1:

86–89; Lee to Cooper, August 19, 1863, in *Wartime Papers*, eds. Dowdey and Manarin, 323–24.

35. Halleck to Burnside, November 14, 1862, OR, vol. 21: 84.

36. For a superb study of the Fredericksburg Campaign in all of its aspects, see George S. Rable, *Fredericksburg! Fredericksburg!* (Chapel Hill: University of North Carolina Press, 2002). Frank O' Reilly's *The Fredericksburg Campaign* (Baton Rouge: Louisiana State University Press, 2003) is more focused on the military aspects of the battle. An excellent shorter account is in Daniel E. Sutherland, *Fredericksburg and Chancellorsville: The Dare Mark Campaign* (Lincoln: University of Nebraska Press, 1998), 28–68.

37. Hill to Dabney, July 1, 1864, D.H. Hill Papers, Library of Virginia, Richmond, Virginia (italics in the original; repository hereafter cited as LV); Heth to Jones, June 1877, *Southern Historical Society Papers*, edited by R. A. Brock, 52 vols. (1876–1959; Millwood, NY: Kraus Reprint Co., 1977), vol. 4: 153 (hereafter cited as *SHSP*); William O. Stoddard, *Inside the White House in War Times: Memoirs and Reports of Lincoln's Secretary*, edited by Michael Burlingame (Lincoln: University of Nebraska Press, 2000), 101.

38. James Longstreet, "The Battle of Fredericksburg," in *Battles and Leaders of the Civil War*, edited by Robert U. Johnson and Clarence C. Buel, 4 vols. (New York: Century, 1885), vol. 3: 70.

39. Herman Hattaway and Archer Jones, *How the North Won: A Military History of the Civil War* (Urbana: University of Illinois Press, 1983), 264–66, 328–37, 347–50, 466–70.

40. James M. McPherson, *Ordeal by Fire: The Civil War and Reconstruction* (New York: McGraw Hill, 2001), 225–26, 384–85.

41. Lee to G.W.C. Lee, February 28, 1863, in *Wartime Papers*, eds. Dowdey and Manarin, 411.

42. Freeman, *R.E. Lee*, vol. 4: 525; Thomas, *Robert E. Lee*, 278–79; Lee to his wife, October 28, 1863, in *Wartime Papers*, eds. Dowdey and Manarin, 616.

43. Lee to Cooper, September 23, 1863, ibid., 460–62. Excellent accounts of the Chancellorsville campaign are provided in Sutherland, *Fredericksburg and Chancellorsville*, 128–81, and Stephen W. Sears, *Chancellorsville* (New York: Houghton Mifflin, 2002), while an excellent examination of Lee's performance is provided in Robert K. Krick, "Lee at Chancellorsville," in *Lee the Soldier*, ed. Gallagher, 357–80.

44. Lee to Davis, May 3, 1863, in *Wartime Papers*, eds. Dowdey and Manarin, 452; Lee to Stuart, May 3, 1863, ibid., 451–52.

45. Lee to Cooper, September 23, 1863, ibid., 465–68; Sedgwick to Williams, May 15, 1863, OR, vol. 25, pt. 1: 559–61.

46. Lee to Davis, May 7, 1863, in *Wartime Papers*, eds. Dowdey and Manarin, 457; Clement A. Evans, ed. *Confederate Military History: A Library of Confederate States History*, 12 vols. (New York: Thomas Yoseloff, 1962; 1899), vol. 3: 392.

47. David Herbert Donald, *Lincoln* (New York: Simon & Schuster, 1995), 435–38.

CHAPTER TWO

From the Rappahannock to the Susquehanna

The second week of May 1863 found the Federals still far from Richmond, while the Confederacy, in Lee and his army, had a force that seemed capable of anything. The Chancellorsville Campaign had ended with Hooker's army back on the north side of the Rappahannock and Confederates everywhere taking pride in yet another magnificent tactical performance by the Army of Northern Virginia. But how was the South to win the war? That Chancellorsville did not seem to bring the Confederate cause much closer to victory in the war was clear to Lee as he digested news of Hooker's retreat. And it was clear the cost at Chancellorsville had been very high. As bad as the butcher's bill was when night fell on May 6, in the week that followed the battle's costs seemed to increase exponentially on account of the loss of Stonewall Jackson.[1]

Late on May 2, Jackson had been riding through the Wilderness west of Chancellorsville in an attempt to gather information and see if more could be accomplished that night. After reaching a point just west of his outer skirmish line, Jackson suddenly decided to turn around. Shortly thereafter, some North Carolina troops, hearing Jackson and the officers accompanying him riding toward them and compatriots to the south exchanging fire with some Pennsylvanians in their front, opened fire. Two bullets struck Jackson's left arm and a third slammed into his right hand. After receiving first aid, Jackson was carried through the Confederate lines on a journey that eventually ended in a small house at Guinea Station. His left arm was amputated early on May 3, and when one of those tending to Jackson encountered Lee four days later, he was told, "Give [Jackson] my affectionate regards, and tell him to make haste and get well, and come back to me as soon as he can. He has lost his left arm but I have lost my right." Lee's words and prayers (he confided to a chaplain on the ninth that he had "wrestled in prayer for him last night, as I never prayed, I believe, for myself") were not enough. On May 10, he notified Richmond it was his "melancholy duty to announce to you the death of General Jackson. He expired at 3:15 p.m. today. His body will be conveyed to Richmond on the train tomorrow."[2]

As Jackson's body made its way to its final resting place in Lexington, Virginia, Lee traveled to Richmond on May 14 for a meeting with President Davis. The chain of events that led to what would be one of the most important councils of war in the history of the Confederacy began on the ninth. That day Lee received a message from Richmond in which Secretary of War James Seddon proposed taking troops from the Army of Northern Virginia and sending them west to support Confederate operations there. Lee replied that he would comply with an order to do this, but argued: "The adoption of your proposal is hazardous, and it becomes a question between Virginia and the Mississippi. The distance and the uncertainty of the employment of the troops are unfavorable." Lee's response did not surprise Davis, who remarked in his endorsement on the message, "The answer of General Lee was such as I should have anticipated, and in which I concur."[3]

Nonetheless, Lee deemed it necessary to elaborate on his objections in another message to Seddon. Any troops sent from Virginia, he argued, would not reach Mississippi until it was past the time they could do any good. Lee also diplomatically expressed skepticism as to whether the troops would be effectively used by western commanders, whose record so far in the war, it need not be said, did not exactly inspire confidence. In the meantime, he stated, the absence of those troops from Virginia would "be sensibly felt." Given the fact that it was "greatly outnumbered by the enemy," Lee argued the Army of Northern Virginia in fact needed reinforcement, without which it "may be obliged to withdraw into the defenses around Richmond." The following day Lee reiterated these points in a report to Richmond about Federal movements that led him to the conclusion that "Virginia is to be the theater of action, and this army, if possible, ought to be strengthened." Lee also suggested that if Richmond was concerned about the pressure the Federals were exerting along the southern coasts (and by extension elsewhere), a reinforced Army of Northern Virginia might be able to do something to alleviate it if "it could get in a position to advance beyond the Rappahannock."[4]

Finally, on May 14, Lee traveled to Richmond to confer with Davis and Seddon on the matter. Three days later Lee left the capital having gotten what he wanted. The best course of action, Lee persuaded Davis and Seddon, would not be to send troops from the Army of Northern Virginia west, but to let the Confederacy's best commander once again lead its best army north. His arguments had no doubt been sharpened prior to his trip from testing them out in discussions with Lt. Gen. James Longstreet, who, upon Jackson's death, was by far first among Lee's subordinates. That Lee managed to win Longstreet over to his way of thinking was no mean feat. Longstreet saw merit in proposals for reinforcing the western armies with troops from the Army of Northern Virginia, in part because it might provide an opportunity to gratify his own ambitions for a higher command, something that was not going to come his way in Virginia. Nonetheless, after he had discussed the matter with Lee, Longstreet, as Davis, Seddon, and all but one member of Davis's cabinet would, came around to his commander's point of view.[5]

He was correct to do so. One could be forgiven, now and then, for questioning what events proved to be a perilously risky venture, for on the surface it appeared the cause of Southern independence was holding up rather well in May 1863. Union operations along the Mississippi against Vicksburg had been floundering for months, with Maj. Gen. Ulysses S. Grant having tried a number of schemes designed to capture or at least neutralize the great Confederate bastion on the Mississippi. The failure of each and every one of them raised such concern in Washington that the Lincoln administration decided to send an official from the War Department to Mississippi to see whether Grant was up to the task before him. For its part, since taking a serious beating at the beginning of the year at the Battle of Murfreesboro, Maj. Gen. William S. Rosecrans's Army of the Cumberland had not shown much inclination to venture forth from its camps near Nashville in pursuit of its objective of rescuing the Unionist population of East Tennessee. And, of course, there were the victories at Fredericksburg and Chancellorsville to inspire hope in the Confederate faithful.

Yet, even though things appeared to be going well on all three of the war's major fronts, the cause of Southern independence was in fact in deep trouble. The men recruited under Lincoln's call for troops the previous summer were fully trained and in the field, decisively tipping the balance sheet in terms of military manpower. In addition, by the late spring of 1863 Union financial and material resources were finally being managed with an efficiency and effectiveness that, if not all they could be, nonetheless put Confederate efforts in this regard to shame. These developments did not get the sort of headlines that events on the battlefield did, but were important ones in the war of exhaustion in which the North and South were engaged. Moreover, during the spring of 1863 signs appeared that at least some members of the Union high command had turned a corner in terms of fully getting their act together. The most important developments appeared in Mississippi. The first was Grant's seemingly sudden emergence as a master of the operational art; another was Lincoln's acting on his belief that opening the Mississippi River was the Union war effort's number one priority in 1863. The effect of these developments was a brilliant campaign in Mississippi that by the third week of May would trap a major Confederate army in Vicksburg and render impotent a force commanded by Gen. Joseph Johnston that had been organized to rescue the town and its defenders—with more Union troops headed Grant's way to make his victory certain. The most significant of these, symbolizing the shift in Union strategic priorities, was the Union Ninth Corps, which eight months earlier had been battling Lee's army at Antietam.[6]

Meanwhile, the prospect of achieving decisive success in Tennessee was shrinking daily. In Gen. Braxton Bragg, the Confederacy had a commander in central Tennessee of some ability, but one who was plagued by overweening subordinates who constantly second-guessed his decisions. Moreover, in Rosecrans, the North had an able commander who was not going to give Bragg an opening by rushing precipitously into the logistically problematic task of conducting offensive operations in middle and eastern Tennessee. Although his meticulous preparations severely tried the patience of Washington, they also made it unlikely he would do anything that might provide encouragement to Confederates' hopes in that theater.[7]

As a consequence of these developments, the Confederacy possessed an unpromising menu of strategic choices in mid-May 1863. To not a few observers, the contrast between Confederate troubles in the West and its impressive record in Virginia led them to an understandable conclusion: that there was a need to spread the South's military resources and talent a bit more widely, which could be accomplished by sending a large contingent from Lee's army west to Mississippi or Tennessee. That Lee's success in persuading the Davis administration to agree to his proposal to keep his army together and lead it north into Pennsylvania led to a bloody defeat that surpassed even Chancellorsville in the toll it took on the Army of Northern Virginia—and could well have been an even greater disaster for the Confederacy—makes it tempting to argue for the road not taken and that Lee should have remained on the operational and tactical defensive in Virginia.

The fact is, though, that Lee was correct both to resist the diminution of his army and in his argument for taking the offensive. There was and is little reason to believe Lee was wrong to think that troops detached from his army would not arrive in Mississippi at a time or place where they could do enough good to compensate for the cost such an effort would entail, both financially and in terms of the greater disadvantage Lee would have had to operate under while his troops were diverted to Mississippi. Even if reinforcements from the Army of Northern Virginia could have reached Mississippi in a timely manner (something Lee very properly doubted, given the exceedingly poor condition of Confederate infrastructure), Grant's ability as a commander and the fact that the North was itself sending significant reinforcements to the area—and could easily have increased its effort had it been necessary— makes it rather unlikely that even the best of commanders (which the South definitely did not have in the area) could have saved Vicksburg.

The case for Lee's taking the offensive, on the other hand, was as compelling as it had ever been. Lee correctly believed after Chancellorsville that he and his political masters, as always, faced a situation where they "must decide between the positive loss of inactivity and the risk of action" and that there was "nothing to be gained by this army remaining quietly on the defensive." He faced an enemy army that was superior in numbers, sure to take another stab at the offensive in the future, and led by a commander smart enough to avoid another affair as one-sided as Fredericksburg had been. And Lee could not afford many more battles like Chancellorsville, which he later claimed left him "more depressed than after Fredericksburg." Although a victory, Lee had to have understood that Chancellorsville had been a very close call and that the Army of Northern Virginia had prevailed at a cost that nearly canceled out whatever tactical and operational benefits had been gained. Even more worrisome to Lee was the possibility that, if left to determine how and when the next major campaign in Virginia was to be made without distraction, the North might come to its senses and have the Army of the Potomac take up a more favorable line of operations, such as the York-James Peninsula. Indeed, in late May an evidently alarmed Lee expressed concern that the Federals were planning a move designed to either hold the Army of Northern Virginia in place while Union forces on the Peninsula attacked Richmond or pave the way for transferring Hooker's command to the James. Of course, there was no way Lincoln and Halleck were ever going to let a commander of the Army of the Potomac do this. Not being privy to the internal workings of the Union high command, though, there was no way Lee could know this.[8]

Regardless of what the Federals were contemplating after Chancellorsville, Lee properly believed he would be better off with the initiative in his own hands so he would have greater control over the operational and tactical situation. To do this, he could not wait for the Federals to make the next move, but had to take the offensive. A direct attack on the Federal army at Falmouth was not an option, though. Even with the return of Longstreet's command from Suffolk, Hooker still enjoyed a great advantage in numbers. The Federals also possessed secure lines of communication that Lee could not maneuver against effectively, as he had in the Second Manassas Campaign. Thus, any attempt to cross the Rappahannock anywhere in the vicinity of Fredericksburg, in itself a difficult proposition given the obstacles to a successful forced river crossing, could only result in a set-piece engagement that would play to Federal advantages in numbers, engineering, and firepower. If Lee could achieve any sort of victory in such a battle, it was easy to see it would not produce benefits commensurate with the cost. Crossing the Rappahannock a bit further upstream from Fredericksburg, but still east of the Blue Ridge was also problematic. It would put the Army of Northern Virginia in a potential vice between Hooker's army and the Washington defenses, with both Federal forces logistically secure, while making it difficult for Lee to sustain his own army. A supply line back to Richmond would be almost impossible to defend, and there was no way to make up for this by foraging in war-ravaged northern Virginia.

Thus, Lee chose what was the best plan available. Staying south of the Rappahannock, the Army of Northern Virginia would march north and west to the gaps in the Blue Ridge and then move through them into the Shenandoah Valley. Upon entering the Valley, Lee's legions would turn north to drive off Union forces that had been occupying the northern end of the Valley. Once this had been accomplished, Lee would base his next move on circumstances. He believed—correctly—that his army's presence in the Valley would force the Army of the Potomac to leave its secure position at Falmouth and move north, but that there would be nothing to preclude the Army of Northern Virginia's pushing across the Potomac into Maryland (where the Shenandoah Valley becomes the Cumberland Valley) and then into Pennsylvania.

At the least, these moves would provide Virginia a respite from operations, enabling it to recuperate some from the strain that two major armies placed on the state's resources, and enable Lee to feed his army in a rich and heretofore untouched agricultural region. The importance of such logistical considerations in Lee's thinking, as one recent historian has pointed out, cannot be overestimated.[9] At the same time, logistics were not the only considerations shaping Lee's vision of the campaign. Lee also based his actions on his understanding of how political considerations would shape the Union response to his moves. There was no way the Lincoln administration could tolerate the presence of the Confederacy's premier army in Pennsylvania at any time, and, with gubernatorial elections scheduled in the commonwealth for November, the summer of 1863 was not the best of times. The armies that fought for the Union were raised by the states, and there were few governors who had been more critical to the Union war effort than Andrew Curtin of Pennsylvania, under whose direction the state had raised well over one hundred regiments. These units were critical to—indeed the "keystone" of—the entire Union effort in the East and were the backbone of the Army of the Potomac. The overthrow of the Curtin government at Harrisburg by voters angry at the violation of Pennsylvania's territorial integrity, and its replacement with a Democratic one that was less zealous in its support for the Lincoln administration and the war, would have a serious impact on the Federal war effort.

Thus, Lee surmised, the Union government would demand that Hooker give chase to the Army of Northern Virginia and fight it wherever it decided to go. This was not the only option available to the commander of the Army of the Potomac, however. Indeed, there was much to recommend instead taking advantage of Lee's move to the Valley to make a thrust against Richmond, or to just move west and north a bit to a position from which the Army of the Potomac could both interpose itself between Lee's army and Washington and cut Lee off from Richmond. Both moves carried relatively little risk, and if they led to a battle, the Army of the Potomac would be able to fight with their logistics secure and under conditions that favored the Federals operationally and tactically. Lee, however, assumed the Lincoln administration would not permit an Army of the Potomac commander to pursue either course, but would instead compel him to rush northward across the Potomac in search of the Army of Northern Virginia in a way that would keep the initiative in Lee's hands in a region that was superbly suited to the sort of maneuver warfare at which his army excelled.

The geography of the region where Lee expected the outcome of his foray north of the Potomac would be determined was distinguished by a series of ridgelines and valleys that separated the Chesapeake Bay from the Cumberland Valley. Bordering the Cumberland Valley to the east was South Mountain, which was known as the Blue Ridge south of the Potomac. South Mountain separated the Cumberland Valley from the Monocacy River and the various streams that formed its watershed. An eastern spur of South Mountain, known as Catoctin Mountain, split off from the main ridge south of the Maryland-Pennsylvania border, with the Middletown Valley separating the two ridgelines. South of the Potomac this ridgeline was known as the Catoctin and Bull Run Mountains, with the Loudoun Valley between it and the Blue Ridge. Separating the Monocacy River watershed, whose principal settlements included Frederick and Taneytown south of the Mason-Dixon

Line and Gettysburg north of it, from Washington and Baltimore in the tidewater region north of the Potomac was Parr's Ridge.

In order to reach the Cumberland Valley and fulfill the Lincoln administration's mandate to hunt down and bring the Army of Northern Virginia to battle as soon as possible, Lee could hope Hooker would be compelled to spread out his army and maneuver it in such a way that it would be difficult to concentrate it in one place quickly. Indeed, Lee planned to maneuver his own army in such a way as to compel the enemy to do this and create opportunities for the smaller and quicker Army of Northern Virginia, whose possession of the initiative and superior cavalry could be expected to give it

Figure 2.1.   The Gettysburg Campaign.

greater situational awareness than its foe, to strike hard blows at the Federals when their forces were divided and unprepared. If the Army of the Potomac could be decisively defeated, it would most likely have to be through a series of engagements in which segments of the Federal army would be crushed in detail, rather than a single grand engagement in which both armies were concentrated and fighting in a set-piece manner. Such victories would have the benefits of, at a minimum, forcing a badly battered Army of the Potomac to draw back to lick its wounds, which would give the Army of Northern Virginia more time to spare Virginia logistically while depressing morale in the North—hopefully to the point where it might produce the political revolution in the North Lee had long sought that could end the war.

What kind of battle did Lee expect to fight when his army was once again in contact with the Army of the Potomac? Longstreet claimed after the war that Lee committed himself, in their pre-campaign conversations, to fighting on the tactical defensive in any engagement with the Federals.[10] There is little reason to believe this was the case, and not just because Longstreet's memory on matters related to Gettysburg was not always reliable. The fact is that Lee, like any good commander, would not formulate in his mind a narrow vision of how any particular campaign would develop, but would approach the campaign flexibly so as not to limit his ability to respond to events on their own terms. Of course, experience and his own intuition had led him to a sound understanding of what operational and tactical conditions would be most favorable to his army. He could reasonably expect that his movements in Pennsylvania would compel the two armies to maneuver in the open and create a situation in which the one that was faster and better able to react quickly to circumstances would have the advantage. This would hopefully make it possible for the Army of Northern Virginia to avoid fighting a set-piece engagement with the Army of the Potomac in which the Federals' logistics were secure, their forces were concentrated, and their superior firepower could be brought to bear. It was a solidly conceived campaign plan and probably the only one that held out any prospect of achieving a victory of sufficient scale to turn around the steady crumbling of the Confederacy under the weight of Federal power in May 1863, even though in retrospect, it is clear that Lee's hopes that he could achieve such victories and that they could produce so profound an effect on the North politically were based on assumptions that pushed perilously close to the edge, if not beyond the limits of the possible.

Before he could begin his campaign, though, Lee first had to reorganize his army. Jackson's death had left a major void in the chain of command. Lee remarked in a letter to one of his division commanders on May 21 that he hoped Stonewall's spirit would "raise up many Jacksons in our ranks" but expressed grave concern about whether it had worked its magic yet. The army was magnificent, he proclaimed: "There were never such men in an army before. They will go anywhere and do anything if properly led. But there is the difficulty—proper commanders. Where can they be obtained? . . . our army would be invincible if it could be properly organized and officered."[11]

The day before, Lee had written to Davis discussing these very issues and told the president he welcomed the opportunity to reorganize the army. "I have for the past year felt that the corps of this army were too large for one commander," he confided, "Each corps contains when in fighting condition about 30,000 men. These are more than one man can properly handle & keep under his eye in battle." Lee told Davis he would have addressed the problem by now had the task of identifying men besides Jackson and Longstreet who were capable of handling corps proven easier. With Jackson's death, however, the time to find them had clearly run out. Thus, Lee informed Davis he thought Maj. Gen. Richard S. Ewell and Maj. Gen. Ambrose P. Hill could be recommended for elevation. Although he had not had much contact with him, Lee felt able to proclaim Ewell "an honest, brave soldier, who has always done his duty well." Hill, he stated, was "upon the whole . . . the best soldier of his grade with me." Ewell would take Jackson's place as commander of a three-division Second Corps, while, to create the Third Corps for Hill to command, Lee proposed reducing Longstreet's First Corps to three divisions and combining Richard H. Anderson's, Hill's, and a newly organized division into a new corps. In line with their new responsibilities, he asked that Ewell and Hill be promoted to lieutenant general. Lee's recommendations were quickly approved, which enabled him to issue orders on May 30 announcing the Army of Northern Virginia's new organization.[12]

Less than a week later, the great campaign began. On June 3, two of Longstreet's divisions began moving toward Culpeper Court House, and were followed to that place over the next two days by Ewell's command. While Hill's command remained at Fredericksburg to watch the Federals and comply with Lee's order to make "such disposition as will be best calculated to deceive the enemy, and keep him in ignorance of any change in the disposition of the army," Longstreet, Ewell, and Stuart's cavalry finished concentrating their forces at Culpeper Court House by June 8. Lee himself arrived the next morning and after a review of Stuart's cavalry (which Lee advised his wife "was a splendid sight . . . Stuart was in all his glory"), Lee expected his command would push west the next day to lead and screen the advance of the rest of the army to the Blue Ridge. Neither Lee nor Stuart anticipated events on June 9 would take a very different course and in a way that suggested that concerns Lee had recently expressed over the strength of his cavalry relative to the enemy's were well founded.[13]

As Lee began moving west, evidence that something was going on reached Hooker's headquarters. He initially suspected the Confederates were planning on crossing the Rappahannock "with a view to the execution of a movement . . . to cross the Upper Potomac, or to throw his army between mine and Washington." If this was the case, Hooker proposed on June 5 to "pitch into his rear," and asked Lincoln if to do so would violate his mandate to remember "always the importance of covering Washington and Harper's Ferry." Lincoln immediately threw cold water on Hooker's proposed course of action, objecting that the Confederates south of the Rappahannock could hold him off from behind entrenchments, while Lee attacked his forces north of the river or moved against Washington. Divided by the Rappahannock, the Army of the Potomac would be left, wrote Lincoln, "like an ox jumped half over a fence and liable to be torn by dogs front and rear, without a fair chance to gore one way or kick the other."[14]

Yet by crossing the Rappahannock in large force to attack Lee's rear as he proposed, Hooker would in fact have seized the initiative and forced Lee to react to him, without losing the ability to position his army in such a way that Lee would have had a difficult time achieving the sort of decisive, successful engagement the Confederacy needed. Clearly, the possibility that the Federals might do something along the lines of what Hooker proposed weighed heavily on the minds of Lee and Davis as they debated whether to move the Army of Northern Virginia to the Shenandoah Valley and whether forces that could be sent to that army should be held back in order to protect Richmond. What effect Hooker's plan might have had is suggested by Lee's decision to halt the movement of his forces toward Culpeper upon learning Hooker had pushed a force across the Rappahannock downstream from Fredericksburg near Deep Run. This offers grounds for questioning whether Lincoln was correct in his fears of what Lee might do in response to implementation of Hooker's plan. And even if Lee had acted as Lincoln and Halleck feared, there is reason to believe that they were overly pessimistic as to the consequences. In order to interpose a strong force between Hooker and Washington, Lee would have had to divide his own army and either attack Hooker's superior army in its defenses around Falmouth or move into a position where it could be trapped between the anvil of the Washington defenses and the hammer of Hooker's army. In sum, Hooker's plan and the thinking behind it were hardly, as one historian has proclaimed, "completely wrong."[15]

Hooker, of course, understood his proposal had been effectively vetoed and turned to the problem of dealing with the situation he faced in that context. The day after his exchange with Lincoln, Hooker reported he had decided to break up what reports were indicating to be the assembly of a large Confederate cavalry force around Culpeper bent on "mean mischief," by "send[ing] all my cavalry against them, stiffened by about 3,000 infantry." On the morning of June 9, this Union force of nearly eleven thousand cavalry and infantry, operating under the command of Maj. Gen. Alfred Pleasonton, crossed the Rappahannock with orders from Hooker to "disperse and destroy" the rebel force at Culpeper. Pleasonton then launched a two-prong attack against Stuart's encampments around Brandy Station. In a hard fought day-long battle, Stuart managed to rally his surprised command of 9,500 and force the Federals to fall back across the Rappahannock. Lee arrived on the field during the battle but did nothing to interfere with Stuart as he conducted it. And despite the vigor with which the Federals had fought at Brandy Station, it did little to cause him to rethink his general operational intentions. On June 10, Lee instructed Ewell's corps to resume its march toward the Blue Ridge and sent orders to commanders in the Valley notifying them that Ewell would soon be arriving and directing them to report to him and provide him with all the intelligence they could find.[16]

As Ewell's command was making its way to the Valley on June 10, Lee decided for some reason to address political matters in a letter to Davis. He expressed concern that the belligerence of journalists and other public figures in the South was having a negative effect on the prospects for encouraging and exploiting demonstrations of support for peace in the North. He warned Davis that given the enemy's superiority "in numbers, resources, and all the means and appliances for carrying on the war, we have no right to look for exemptions from the military consequences of a vigorous use of these advantages." Although he urged that the South continue to make the most of the means at their disposal to fight and hope for blessings from God on their efforts, Lee also argued "it is nevertheless the part of wisdom to carefully measure and husband our strength, and not to expect from it more than in the ordinary course of affairs it is capable of accomplishing." Southern resources, he noted, were "constantly diminishing" and the gap between them and those available to the North could be expected to grow—but only "if they continue united in their efforts to subjugate us." Thus, Lee told Davis he believed the Confederacy must make every effort to divide and weaken the North and give all possible encouragement, "consistently with truth, to the rising peace party of the North." He then suggested that to that end an effort should be made to disingenuously suggest to the North that perhaps a settlement could be reached short of Confederate independence. Once enough people in the North scented peace, he suggested they might become so intoxicated with the thought of ending the war that they would not resume it even if they ultimately found the South's determination to remain independent could not be swayed. He closed by asking Davis to indicate whether he approved these views, but added that even if the president deemed them "inexpedient or inadvisable, I think you will nonetheless agree with me that we should at least abstain from measures or expressions that tend to discourage any party whose purpose is peace."[17]

Two days after Lee sent this message to Davis, Ewell's lead division entered the Shenandoah Valley via Chester Gaps and the Second Corps subsequently pushed north in two powerful columns. On June 14, Ewell skillfully maneuvered his command and routed a Union force at Winchester, the hub of Union operations in the lower Valley. Although their commander, Maj. Gen. Robert Milroy, managed to flee to safety at Harpers Ferry, by the time night fell on June 15 more than 4,400 Union soldiers were prisoners, and Ewell had acquired a veritable mountain of captured supplies and equipment. As this was occurring, one of Ewell's divisions marched to Martinsburg on the Potomac and forced the Federals to abandon the town. With the exception of the remnants of Milroy's command and the garrison at Harpers Ferry under whose protection Milroy had taken refuge, the entire lower Valley now belonged to Ewell, and the roads to and across the Potomac were clear. The fighting around Winchester also offered a demonstration of Ewell's skill as a commander. "Ewell," one officer later exulted, "was quick, skillful and effective—in fact, Jacksonian."[18]

As Ewell was marching to Winchester, Lee continued to monitor the movements of Hooker's army. By June 13, he had evidence that Hooker was extending his forces along the northern bank of the Rappahannock, but was unsure as to the Federal commander's intentions. Neither, for that matter, was Hooker. If, in the words of one Confederate, the fight at Brandy Station had "made the Union cavalry," Hooker could be forgiven for missing that development in the days that followed, for Pleasonton was unable to provide him with a good sense of what the Confederates were doing. This did not, however, prevent Hooker from proposing, if it turned out the Confederates were moving westward, to "march to Richmond at once. . . . I do not hesitate to say that I should adopt this course as being the most speedy and certain mode for giving the rebellion a mortal blow." The merits of such a move were no less compelling than those of the plan Hooker had proposed on June 5. Indeed, if nothing else, Hooker correctly perceived that the bridgehead he had established at Deep Run was frustrating whatever plans Lee had by "caus[ing] the enemy to hesitate in moving forward."[19]

Figure 2.2.   Richard S. Ewell, Confederate, c. 1860–1870. Library of Congress

Of course, Hooker knew he would not be free to operate purely on his own judgment and could not have been surprised when Lincoln and Halleck vetoed his plan. Both men clearly believed that the logistical network around Richmond and the fortifications the Confederates had constructed around the city presented a formidable obstacle to an attacking army that could not be overcome in an acceptable amount of time. From this flowed their conviction that, as Lincoln advised Hooker, even if the general were to reach Richmond that very day, he could not take the city in time to prevent his "communications, and with them your army" from being "ruined." Hooker, however, reasoned that it would not be too difficult, if the advance was coordinated with movements by forces already on the Peninsula under the command of Maj. Gen. John Dix, to send enough troops south to operate against Richmond from a new and secure line of communications based on the rivers of the Tidewater, while leaving plenty available to be sent north of the Potomac. Unsaid, though suggested by his observation that Lee's movements to the west had been checked by the danger of his driving south to Richmond, was Hooker's sense that there would not be much danger of the rebels moving north in significant numbers when their capital was threatened anyway. In this, he was probably correct. As previously noted, Lee believed the Confederacy could not survive the loss of its capital, something he thought inevitable if a significant Union force reached a point from where it could conduct river-based siege or quasi-siege operations against Richmond. Thus, it is difficult to see how Lee could not have reacted to a thrust southward by the Union army by falling back toward Richmond as fast as he could in an attempt to stop Hooker before he got too close to the capital.

This is not to say, though, that the course of action Lincoln imposed on Hooker had little merit. "I think Lee's army, and not Richmond is your sure objective point," Lincoln argued, before laying out what he saw as the two possible Confederate courses of action. If Lee remained behind the Rappahannock, Lincoln advised Hooker to "fret him and fret him." However, Lincoln was more excited, and justifiably so, at the prospect of Lee's heading north. This, he believed would break what since the previous November had been an operational stalemate along the Rappahannock in which the Union army could "fret" Lee, but needed a great deal of luck to achieve anything truly decisive. If the Confederates left the area and headed north, though, it would completely transform the situation in a way that Lincoln accurately perceived could create an opportunity for a decisive Union victory. "If he comes toward the Upper Potomac," he advised Hooker, "follow on his flank and on his inside track, shortening your lines while he lengthens his." If the situation were to develop so favorably, Lincoln urged Hooker to not just fret Lee, but "Fight him . . . when opportunity offers."[20]

On June 11, the day after receiving this message from Lincoln, Hooker had orders issued to his corps commanders directing them to get ready to move. Early on the twelfth he directed two corps to push west to Bealeton and Catlett's Stations and Pleasonton's cavalry to move to Warrenton Junction on the Orange and Alexandria Railroad. On June 13, having finally gotten information indicating that Ewell's and Longstreet's corps were marching toward the Valley, Hooker advised Halleck that "instructions of the President, approved by yourself . . . compel me, in view of this movement of the enemy, to transfer the operations of this army from the line of the Aquia to the Orange and Alexandria." One wing of the army composed of four corps, he reported, would move north to Manassas Junction, while another composed of three corps would march to Dumfries.[21]

Undoubtedly, June 14 brought Lee both great relief and satisfaction. Not only was Ewell grandly smashing Milroy's command at Winchester, but reports from Hill that Hooker had abandoned his bridgehead at Deep Run and was pulling back entirely from the river made it possible for Lee to order Longstreet's and Hill's corps to head west toward the Blue Ridge. On June 15, Lee directed Longstreet to have Maj. Gen. John Bell Hood's division cross the Rappahannock and enter the Loudoun Valley, with Maj. Gen. Lafayette McLaws's and Maj. Gen. George Pickett's divisions (the latter able, now that the threat of a Federal thrust against Richmond was gone, to march north from Hanover Junction and Richmond to join the rest of the corps) moving forward to follow Hood along the eastern edge of the Blue Ridge or move into the Valley. The next day, orders were sent to Hill to leave Fredericksburg, move west, and "follow Longstreet as closely as you can" until his corps reached Chester Gap. There, the Third Corps would move into the Valley. Meanwhile, the First Corps would move north along the western edge of Loudoun Valley until it reached Manassas Gap or Ashby's Gap.[22]

The task of covering the army's eastern flank and keeping track of the enemy was entrusted to Stuart's cavalry, and on the seventeenth they found themselves hotly engaged with Federal cavalry pushing west into the Loudoun Valley. The day before Lee issued orders for Longstreet's movement, Hooker was at Dumfries and learning the fate of Milroy's forces in the Shenandoah Valley was weighing heavily on the minds of Lincoln and Halleck. He notified Washington the following day that four corps and the cavalry were in position around Manassas Junction and Centreville, then moved his headquarters to Fairfax Station that afternoon. That same afternoon, a message reached Hooker from Halleck reporting the loss of Winchester and Martinsburg, advising him he was "entirely free to operate as you desire against Lee's army, so long as you keep his main army from Washington," and suggesting that he next direct his army toward Leesburg. Hooker replied by advising Lincoln and Halleck of the departure of Hill's command from Fredericksburg with the evident objective of joining the rest of Lee's army on the Upper Potomac, and that if the enemy intended to cross the river, "it is not in my power to prevent it."[23]

In line with Halleck's suggestion, on June 16 Hooker began pushing with "vigor and power" in the direction of Leesburg. There he could take up a position from which he could counter any enemy move and possibly relieve the garrison at Harpers Ferry, which had abandoned the town to take refuge in the fortifications on Maryland Heights. At the same time, Hooker was increasingly frustrated at his inability to get clear and satisfactory information about Lee's movements and intentions. Consequently, on June 17, Hooker directed Pleasonton to take the main body of the army's cavalry to the hamlet of Aldie, located at a gap in the Bull Run Mountains, and push from there into the Loudoun Valley along the roads to Winchester, Berryville, and Harpers Ferry. "You have a sufficient cavalry force to do this," Pleasonton was instructed, "Drive in pickets . . . and get us information."[24]

By that day, Lee had moved his headquarters from Culpeper, following Longstreet's command to the town of Markham east of Manassas Gap. There on the seventeenth he directed Ewell to push a division across the Potomac to Hagerstown, while deceiving the Federals into thinking that he intended to operate against Harpers Ferry. He also sent a message to Longstreet, whose movements through the western edge of Loudoun Valley had not had the effect Lee hoped of "deceiv[ing] the enemy as to our ultimate destination" (because Hooker in fact was completely unaware of them), approving his decision to move into the Valley. He then directed Longstreet to push north as fast as he could in order to reach Ewell and enable the Second Corps to push into Maryland "at least as far as Hagerstown." In the meantime, he would await Hill's corps as it pushed into the Valley through Chester Gap and moved north toward the Potomac.[25]

As Lee made these dispositions for his infantry corps on June 17, a contingent from Pleasonton's cavalry suddenly appeared at the western end of Aldie and Thoroughfare Gaps intending to fulfill their commander's wish, in the words of one historian, "to pick a fight with the first Rebel cavalry he found in the Loudoun Valley." At Aldie and Middleburg, the Federal and Confederate cavalry clashed in sharp engagements that ended with neither side able to claim a truly decisive victory. The following day, Pleasonton continued to try to gather information as to what the Confederates were doing, but his efforts came to naught as Stuart's men thwarted his efforts. On the nineteenth, Pleasonton made another attempt to break through Stuart's screen, but only suffered another thrashing at Middleburg. Two days later, Pleasonton tried again, this time assisted by an infantry brigade from the Fifth Corps. These enabled Pleasonton to drive the Confederate cavalry off after a tough fight at Upperville and push forward toward Ashby's Gap. At this point, however, Confederate resistance stiffened, leading Pleasonton to determine that he had accomplished all he could and pull back to Aldie. Pleasonton had gotten the fight he wanted, but his efforts uncovered little new information for his commanding general and few insights as to what Lee's intentions were.[26]

The fighting in Loudoun Valley naturally had an effect on Lee's movements. When evidence of the fighting at Aldie and Middleburg arrived on June 18, with the possibility that Pleasonton's force might in fact be the vanguard of the entire Army of the Potomac, Lee felt compelled to respond. By nightfall on June 18, two of Ewell's divisions were in Maryland, with one of Longstreet's divisions under orders to march to Shepherdstown to allow the last of Ewell's divisions to cross the Potomac. However, Pleasonton's actions forced Lee to order that division of Longstreet's command not to move to Shepherdstown but to take up a position at Snicker's Gap so it would be available if Stuart got in trouble or if Hooker was making a major push into Loudoun Valley. With the repulse of Pleasonton's men at Aldie and Middleburg, Lee had a dispatch sent to Longstreet directing him to hold his command "in readiness to move in the direction of the Potomac." But when Pleasonton renewed his efforts on June 20, these orders were countermanded so Longstreet could secure Ashby's and Snicker's Gaps and be in a position from which he could aid Stuart. When it became clear on June 22 that Pleasonton had had enough and his appearance was not the prelude to a push by Hooker's army into Loudoun Valley, Lee wrote to Ewell, "If you are ready to move, you can do so. I think your best course will be towards the Susquehanna. . . . If Harrisburg comes within your means capture it." The following day Lee directed Longstreet to move his corps to Berryville, Martinsburg, and Williamsport, and then cross the Potomac into Maryland. Now, though, it would be following behind Hill's corps, which during the night had passed behind Longstreet's command while it watched the Blue Ridge gaps.[27]

If how the three infantry corps were to proceed was clear during the last week of June, Lee faced a question regarding what to do with Stuart and his cavalry. At some point during his three days battling Pleasonton, Stuart told Lee that he believed he could make another ride around the Federal army. Maj. John Mosby, commander of a unit of partisan rangers operating in northern Virginia, had advised Stuart that the position of Hooker's army would make such a move a fairly low-risk proposition and Stuart, perhaps eager to pull off a stunt that would silence critics who had found his performance at Brandy Station wanting, embraced the idea. More important, if Stuart and a considerable body of cavalry could operate between Hooker and Washington, they might interdict Union communications, demoralize the Yankee populace, and exacerbate Lincoln's impatience, all of which could leave the Army of the Potomac more out of sorts than it was expected to be as it marched in pursuit of Lee's army. Lee agreed to the plan, provided it did not prevent Stuart from quickly reaching Ewell to cover his right flank as he moved through the Cumberland Valley or alleviating headquarters' concerns that Hooker might "steal a march on us and get across the Potomac before we are aware."[28]

Lee's orders reached Stuart via Longstreet, who forwarded them on June 22 with a note stating that Lee was amenable to Stuart's moving with three brigades "via Hopewell Gap and passing by the rear of the enemy," but that if the route was not clearly practicable, "You had better not leave us." The following day, Lee wrote directly to Stuart authorizing him to "judge whether you can pass around their army without hindrance . . . and cross the river east of the mountains." Regardless of what route he took, Lee insisted that after crossing the Potomac Stuart must quickly "move on & feel the right of Ewell's troops, collecting information, provisions, & c." Stuart, of course, exercised the discretion Lee provided to do what he wanted: attempt another ride around the Army of the Potomac. Given Stuart's track record of success in riding around the Union army, Lee can be forgiven for authorizing him to attempt to do so again. Yet, given the consequences of this decision, it is clear this was a terrible mistake.[29]

If Lee's actions and decisions during those fateful days were in any way rooted in a belief that he faced a demoralized enemy commander who was not up to the job before him, he was acting on a decidedly faulty assumption. After Chancellorsville, Lincoln had resisted calls for Hooker's removal on the grounds that one did not throw away a gun just because it misfired once, and events were proving the wisdom of this decision. In mid-June 1863, the Federal commander was smartly responding to Lee's movements. From his headquarters at Fairfax Station and then Fairfax Court House, Hooker spent the third week of June digesting news of the fighting in the Loudoun Valley and hoping the Confederates were in fact intending to cross the Potomac. If

Figure 2.3.   Brigadier General James E. B. Stuart, Confederate, c. 1863. National Archives

they did, Hooker, like Lincoln, saw a magnificent opportunity. He could then maneuver his army and the forces at Harpers Ferry in such a way as to cut off Lee from the Potomac, which would allow Hooker to bring him to battle at a time and place of his own choosing. And while Stuart and Pleasonton battled in the Loudoun Valley, Hooker maneuvered the rest of his army in such a way as to put him in a good position to do this. By June 21, Hooker had the Army of the Potomac well in hand east of the Catoctin–Bull Run Mountains, with his most advanced corps holding positions near Leesburg, near Aldie Gap, and at Thoroughfare Gap. From these positions, Hooker's command could easily move north across the Potomac into the Monocacy Valley toward Pennsylvania or west toward Harpers Ferry and the Shenandoah Valley, depending on circumstances, and do so in a way that would not compromise the security of Washington in the slightest.[30]

Blissfully unaware of all of this and the potential danger they posed to his army, Lee pushed Hill and Longstreet's commands toward the Potomac. On June 23 he advised Davis that Ewell's corps was advancing toward the Susquehanna, while Hill's was expected to be at Shepherdstown by the end of the day and Longstreet to "follow tomorrow." The next day, as Hill's corps crossed the Potomac at Shepherdstown, Ewell marched up the Cumberland Valley with his lead division passing through Chambersburg, and Longstreet marched to the Potomac crossing at Williamsport. "Every indication promises a more successful campaign even than the last," one Confederate soldier advised his family on June 23. "Ewell has already opened it finely, the omens are most auspicious and we are confident of a brilliant expedition. . . . victory will inevitably attend our arms in any collision with the enemy."[31]

On June 25, Lee reached Williamsport and crossed the river there with one of Longstreet's divisions. Just before reaching the river, though, Lee, wrote a letter to Davis in which he again advised the president that he believed greater efforts should be made to identify and adopt courses of action that might "repress the war feeling in the Federal states." He also reported that he was compelled to abandon his communications southward due to having insufficient troops to protect them, but made sure to reassure Davis as to the wisdom of the move across the Potomac that compelled him to take this step. By pushing north, he told Davis, he believed he could force "Hooker's army across the Potomac and draw troops from the south, embarrassing their plan of campaign in a measure, if I can do nothing more and have to return."[32]

After crossing the river, Lee, with the gravity of the situation perhaps further impressed upon him by the physical act of crossing the Potomac, decided to write to Davis. He again advised the president that it was his opinion that "we cannot afford to keep our troops awaiting possible movements of the enemy, but that our true policy is, as far as we can, so to employ our own forces as to give occupation to his at points of our selection." Lee also, as he had been for a few days, advocated the organization of a body of troops from the forces around Richmond and in the Carolinas at Culpeper Court House under the command of Gen. Pierre G. T. Beauregard.[33]

Lee selected Beauregard in part because of the prestige that officer enjoyed as a result of his victories in the 1861 battles of Fort Sumter and Manassas. Beauregard's reputation, Lee had predicted on June 23 "would give magnitude to even a small demonstration" in the minds of the Lincoln administration, whose "well known anxiety . . . for the safety of its capital would induce it to retain a large force for its defence." (Lee's request for Beauregard was also probably motivated by his earlier trouble securing cooperation from Maj. Gen. Daniel H. Hill, commander of troops in North Carolina, in the effort to reinforce the Army of Northern Virginia after Chancellorsville—and an anticipation that Beauregard's presence might take the quarrelsome Hill down a notch.) Beauregard's force would not only, Lee argued, "sensibly relieve opposition to our advance." He also thought Beauregard might compel the Federals to draw troops away from the coast and "we might even hope to compel the recall of some of the enemy's troops from the west." "It should never be forgotten," Lee concluded, "that our concentration at any point compels that of the enemy, and . . . tends to relieve all other threatened localities." However, it turned out that with Dix's forces on the Peninsula then carrying out orders to threaten an advance against Richmond from the east, there was no way Davis would or could send any more forces north. There would be no Beauregard diversion.[34]

Nonetheless, as it pushed north through the Cumberland Valley, there appeared to be naught but smooth sailing for the Army of Northern Virginia. On June 26 and 27, Ewell's corps resumed its march toward the Susquehanna. Two of his three divisions continued to move up the valley toward Harrisburg, occupying Carlisle on the twenty-seventh, while the other, commanded by Maj. Gen. Jubal Early, crossed South Mountain and advanced toward York via Gettysburg. While at Carlisle, Ewell ordered an engineer and some cavalry to Harrisburg to reconnoiter the city's defenses as a preliminary to an advance against the Pennsylvania state capital. Meanwhile, by the evening of June 27, Early's division had reached the outskirts of York and found nothing to prevent its commander from carrying out his plan to continue on to Wrightsville on the Susquehanna the following day. For their part, Longstreet's and Hill's commands enjoyed equally easy advances as they marched from the Potomac to Hagerstown and then pushed across the Mason-Dixon line to Chambersburg and Fayetteville on June 27.[35]

        That same day, however, Lee felt compelled to address the matter of how his men were treating the civilians they encountered in Pennsylvania. Six days earlier, in the spirit of his remarks to Davis that every effort must be made to avoid provoking Northerners in order to diminish their "war feeling," Lee issued General Orders No. 72. These were designed to guide his army's behavior "while in the enemy's country" and forbid "any person belonging to or connected with the army" from damaging or taking any civilian property, with the exception of designated officers in the army's various supply departments. These officers were to secure supplies through requisitions upon local authorities, with receipts issued to provide compensation for dispossessed civilians.[36]

These regulations, however, proved almost unenforceable, and the Army of Northern Virginia laid a heavy hand on the towns and civilians in its path. The urge to plunder a rich, well-cultivated region was too much for Lee's hungry legions to resist, while many easily found agreement with a Richmond newspaper that urged them to "take deep and signal revenge for the injuries that have been inflicted upon us. . . . [and] make the whole Pennsylvania Valley astonishment to future generations. . . to reimburse ourselves for the incalculable injury which has been inflicted on us." The ugliest aspect of the entire episode was the deliberate targeting of African-Americans for abduction so they could be sent south to be enslaved. How much Lee personally knew about this behavior is unclear, but upon reaching Chambersburg, he had learned enough to consider it necessary on June 27 to issue General Orders No. 73. In this document he wrote that he had "observed with marked satisfaction the conduct of the troops on the march" but expressed regret that there had "been instances of forgetfulness on the part of some . . . that we make war only on armed men, and that we cannot take vengeance for the wrongs our people have suffered without lowering ourselves." He closed by once again instructing his men to "abstain with most scrupulous care from unnecessary or wanton injury to private property" and directed all officers to "arrest and bring to summary punishment" anyone who violated his orders on this matter.[37]

The general might as well have saved his breath. The men of Lee's army were determined to reap all the benefits they could from being part of an invading army (after all, a desire to make the North, rather than Virginia, feed his army was one of the factors that led Lee to cross the Potomac in the first place), and their officers were disinclined to stop them in any case. Indeed, on June 30 a single officer managed to send back to Martinsburg, "750 Sheep, 140 Cattle, 40 Horses, 3 Wagons loaded with a dry goods store and hardware store and 19 negroes." While it is too much to dismiss his actions as insincere propaganda gestures, Lee could not have been blind to the fact that, as one officer informed his family, "Our people are devastating Pennsylvania." Moreover, if he thought he could weaken the North's war spirit through gentle treatment of their land, the fact that New York's and Pennsylvania's government and citizenry assembled a decent, although by no means awe-inspiring body of troops to defend the Susquehanna, certainly offered grounds for questioning that assumption.[38]

Although undoubtedly displeased at having to take his men to task for their behavior, Lee was quite confident on June 27 regarding the operational situation. According to Brig. Gen. Isaac Trimble, who was accompanying the army even though he had no formal command, that afternoon Lee called him to his tent, asked him for his opinion as an engineer regarding the region around Gettysburg, and "said hereabout we shall probably meet the enemy and fight a great battle." It is tempting to dismiss Trimble's postwar description of Lee foreseeing a great battle at Gettysburg four days before it began as too good to be true; however, Lee had advised Ewell the previous day that he believed they would end up fighting the Federals near Frederick or Gettysburg. Moreover, Trimble's recollection of what else Lee said during their conversation no doubt accurately reflected the Army of Northern Virginia commander's sense of the situation and hopes for what the future would bring. "Our army is in good spirits," Trimble recalled Lee saying, "not over fatigued, and can be concentrated on any point in twenty-four hours or less." Although he had not heard anything from Stuart as to whether the Federals had yet crossed the Potomac, Lee was confident he would meet Hooker's army in a highly favorable operational situation. "They will come up," he predicted, "probably through Frederick; broken down with hunger and hard marching, strung out on a long line and much demoralized, when they come into Pennsylvania. I shall throw an overwhelming force on their advance, crush it, follow up the success, drive one corps back and another, and by successive repulses and surprises before they can concentrate; create a panic and virtually destroy the army."[39]

Lee was not alone in his confidence regarding the outcome of any engagement with the Federals in Pennsylvania. "It has been said," one division commander later wrote, "that the *morale* of an army is to numbers as three to one. If this be correct the Army of Northern Virginia was never stronger than on entering Pennsylvania . . . there was not an officer or soldier in the Army of Northern Virginia, from General Lee to the drummer boy, who did not believe, when we invaded Pennsylvania in 1863, that it was able to drive the Federal army into the Atlantic Ocean." When a delegation of ministers asked Ewell upon his arrival in Carlisle if there would be any objections to their praying for President Lincoln during their upcoming Sunday services, the general jauntily replied, "Not at all. I know of no man who is more in need of your prayers."[40]

But if Lee and his army were full of confidence in late June 1863, their compatriots elsewhere were not faring so well. Three days before Lee laid out for Trimble his vision for how he would defeat the Army of the Potomac, Rosecrans's army had finally begun moving in Tennessee. Within a week, Rosecrans had executed a series of skillfully conceived maneuvers that demonstrated Rosecrans, like Grant, possessed a superb grasp of the operational art. Despite terrible weather, by July 1 Bragg's army had been compelled to abandon its position around Tullahoma and make a retreat that would not end until it was behind the Tennessee River at Chattanooga. As if this were not enough, on June 20 whatever hope Lt. Gen. John C. Pemberton, the commander of the Confederate army trapped in Vicksburg, might have had that the army being assembled in Mississippi under Gen. Joseph Johnston's command would come to his rescue received a fatal blow. That day a message arrived from Johnston advising Pemberton that despite his best efforts to build up his force, it was "too weak to save Vicksburg." As if this were not enough, six days earlier, the Union Ninth Corps had arrived on the scene to make the capture of Vicksburg a certain thing, and there was no chance the Lincoln administration was going to fulfill Lee's hope that it would respond to the Army of Northern Virginia's presence north of the Potomac by recalling troops from the west. Thus, by the last week of June 1863 hopes that a tide that had long been running against the Confederacy, and was evidently gaining strength, might be reversed rested primarily on Lee somehow pulling off something spectacular in Pennsylvania.[41]

Whether this was possible, though, would be as much up to Lee's opponent as himself. And in late June Hooker had no intention of playing by the script Lee wanted him to follow and was in fact following one that offered the possibility of putting the Army of Northern Virginia in serious danger. Although great alarm and fear was expressed in the North over the Confederate invasion, Lincoln could not contain his jubilation over the development. "I believe you are aware," Lincoln advised Hooker on June 16, "that since you took command of the army I have not believed that you had any chance to effect anything until now. As it looks to me, Lee's now returning toward Harper's Ferry gives you back the chance [to destroy Lee's army] that I thought McClellan lost last fall." In response to a message from the governor of New Jersey reporting that his people were "apprehensive that the invasion of the enemy may extend to her soil" and wanted McClellan restored to command, Lincoln coolly informed the governor that his view of the situation was completely wrong. Not only, Lincoln proclaimed, were fears that the Confederates might reach New Jersey groundless, but Lee's movement into Pennsylvania in fact presented the Union army with "the best opportunity we have had since the war began." "We cannot help beating them," Lincoln advised a member of his cabinet on June 26, "if we have the man. How much depends in military matters on one master mind!"[42]

Hooker, of course, did not need Lincoln to point out to him that Lee's movements presented him with a fantastic opportunity, and had no doubt that he was "the man" to take advantage of it. On June 25, Hooker ordered

three corps under the overall command of Maj. Gen. John Reynolds to cross
the Potomac at Edwards Ferry and move to Middletown, with the mission of
watching the passes in South Mountain that connected the Middletown Valley with the Cumberland Valley. The rest of the army would follow
Reynolds's wing across the Potomac, with one corps then pushing west toward Harpers Ferry, while three corps, under Hooker's personal direction,
moved up the Monocacy Valley toward Frederick. By the evening of June 27,
the various units of the Army of the Potomac had nearly reached their re-
spective destinations. Once it reached Harpers Ferry, the corps Hooker had
dispatched to that place would link up with the garrison and menace Lee's
line of retreat down the Cumberland Valley. Meanwhile, the forces around
Frederick would cover Washington and Baltimore in case Lee decided to
cross South Mountain and move into the Monocacy Valley, with Parr's Ridge
offering a number of points where a good defensive position could be established.[43]

Of course, there was some risk in dividing the Army of the Potomac this
way. Indeed, Lee had entered Pennsylvania and was maneuvering his army in
an attempt to induce Hooker to incautiously divide the Army of the Potomac and enable the Army of Northern Virginia to bring it to battle before
it could be reconcentrated in a good fighting position. However, from its position in the Middletown Valley, Reynolds's wing of the army was admirably
situated to quickly cover the modest distances that separated them from their
comrades in the Cumberland and Monocacy Valleys. Indeed, contrary to
what Lee predicted in his conversation with Trimble, by June 27 Hooker's
movements had shaped the situation so that if anyone was going to be approaching the coming battle "broken down with hunger and hard marching"
there was a very good chance it would be the Army of Northern Virginia.
However much consternation Lee's presence north of the Potomac might
have caused in the North, the good sense with which Hooker was managing
his army certainly gave Lincoln reason to hope that the "best opportunity"
the Union had had in months would not be wasted.

Yet, however skillfully he was managing the situation in front of him during the last week of June 1863, Hooker could not overcome a severe problem
that had been brewing behind him—and it was not Stuart's cavalry. At the
heart of it was the fact that, as Hooker advised Lincoln more than a week before moving his army across the Potomac, "I have not enjoyed the confidence
of the major-general commanding the army." Lincoln, as Hooker pointed
out, had "long been aware" of the fact that deep animosity existed between
Hooker and Halleck. In the months after Hooker assumed command of the
army, Lincoln had attempted to work around this by communicating directly

with the Army of the Potomac commander. This arrangement could not stand the strain the events of June 1863 placed upon it, which led Hooker to advise the president that as long as he did not have the confidence of the general-in-chief, "we may look in vain for success." Lincoln responded by making it clear that if Hooker was saying the good of the country demanded that a choice be made between himself and Halleck, he had to understand that this was not a contest in which he could prevail. Halleck's ability to provide advice that largely confirmed the president's own sense of things and willingness to serve as a lightning rod for critics inside and outside the army had made the general-in-chief too important to Lincoln both politically and personally. Thus, late on June 16, Lincoln bluntly told Hooker, "To remove all misunderstanding, I now place you in the strict military relation to General Halleck of a commander of one of the armies to the general-in-chief of all the armies. . . . I shall direct him to give you orders and you to obey them."[44]

Hooker got the message and determined to work with the hand he had been dealt. Nonetheless, a test of strength with Halleck was inevitable. It came over Hooker's desire to have some say over the garrison at Harpers Ferry, which was technically outside his command authority, in line with his desire to have a strong force operating against Lee's rear in the Cumberland Valley. On the evening of June 26 Hooker advised Halleck that he was planning to visit Harpers Ferry the next day and asked if there was "any reason why Maryland Heights should not be abandoned" to make the forces there available for use in the field. Halleck replied the following morning that he deemed Maryland Heights too important a point to be abandoned. Hooker immediately wrote back that he had found ten thousand men at Harpers Ferry who could be of service in the field but would be "of no earthly account" if they remained where they were and begged Halleck to bring the matter to the attention of the president and secretary of war.[45]

Before Halleck could act on this request, though, an incident occurred that convinced Hooker that he had no choice but to throw down the gauntlet. Shortly after sending the aforementioned message, Hooker was at the headquarters of Maj. Gen. William French, commander of the Harpers Ferry garrison, when he learned Halleck had flatly directed French, "Pay no attention to General Hooker's orders." At 3:00 p.m., a bare five minutes after Hooker's earlier report arrived, another message from the general reached Halleck. "My original instructions require me to cover Harper's Ferry and Washington," Hooker proclaimed in this message, "I beg to be understood that I am unable to comply with this condition with the means at my disposal, and earnestly request that I may be relieved from the position

I occupy." To the general's surprise, early on the morning of June 28, he found himself greeting two unexpected visitors at his headquarters. One of them was Col. James Hardie, who had just made an all-night trip from Washington carrying orders from the War Department that informed Hooker his request to be relieved from command of the Army of the Potomac had been received and acted on. The other visitor was Maj. Gen. George Gordon Meade, the man Washington had ordered to take his place.[46]

How and whether this development would alter the course of events, of course, remained to be seen. Nonetheless, it was clearly something Lee would have to take into account as he pondered how he was to win a victory north of the Potomac decisive enough to save the badly faltering cause of Southern independence. Already, unbeknownst to Lee, the Federal army had moved into positions from which it could not only dash any hopes for such a victory, but inflict a crushing defeat that would dramatically hasten the fall of the Confederacy. Yet when Lee arose on the morning of June 28, 1863, he was blissfully ignorant of this, and there seemed to be no reason to rethink the vision of how the campaign would develop that he had laid out for Trimble the day before. The change in Union commanders, however, was an important development, and once news of it reached Lee, it would invariably compel him to reconsider some of the assumptions upon which he was basing his operations. It would not be the last event to force the general to do some serious rethinking that fateful June 28, 1863.

Notes

1. Readers interested in the events between Chancellorsville and the end of Hooker's tenure as commander of the Army of the Potomac will find excellent full accounts in Edwin B. Coddington, *The Gettysburg Campaign: A Study in Command* (1968; New York: Simon & Schuster, 1997), 3–179; Stephen W. Sears, *Gettysburg* (New York: Houghton Mifflin, 2003), 1–124; and, Steven E. Woodworth, *Beneath a Northern Sky: A Short History of the Gettysburg Campaign* (Wilmington, DE: Scholarly Resources, 2003), 1–36. Lee's generalship and conduct during this phase of the war are the particular focus of Scott Bowden and Bill Ward, *Last Chance for Victory: Robert E. Lee and the Gettysburg Campaign* (Conshohocken, PA: Savas Publishing, 2001), 1–144.

2. Robert K. Krick, "The Smoothbore Volley that Doomed the Confederacy," in *The Chancellorsville Campaign: The Battle and Its Aftermath*, edited by Gary W. Gallagher (Chapel Hill: University of North Carolina Press, 1996), 107–42; James I. Robertson, *Stonewall Jackson: The Man, the Soldier, the Legend* (New York: Macmil-

lan, 1997), 725–53; Freeman, *R.E. Lee*, vol. 2: 560, 562; Lee to Seddon, May 10, 1863, in *Wartime Papers*, eds. Dowdey and Manarin, 283.

3. Lee to Seddon, May 10, 1863 (with Davis endorsement), OR, vol. 25, pt. 2: 790.

4. Lee to Seddon, May 10, 1863, ibid., 790; Lee to Davis, May 11, 1863, in *Wartime Papers*, eds. Dowdey and Manarin, 483–84.

5. James Longstreet, "Lee in Pennsylvania," in *The Annals of the Civil War*, edited by Gary W. Gallagher (1878; New York: Da Capo Press, 1994), 416; Reagan, *Memoirs*, 121–22.

6. The Vicksburg Campaign has been superbly examined in two recent works: William L. Shea and Terrence J. Winschel, *Vicksburg Is the Key: The Struggle for the Mississippi River* (Lincoln: University of Nebraska Press, 2003), and Michael Ballard, *Vicksburg: The Campaign that Opened the Mississippi* (Chapel Hill: University of North Carolina Press, 2004).

7. Bragg's troubles are chronicled in Steven E. Woodworth, *Jefferson Davis and His Generals: The Failure of Confederate Command in the West* (Lawrence: University Press of Kansas, 1990); Rosecrans's problems are effectively described in Larry J. Daniel, *Days of Glory: The Army of the Cumberland, 1861–1865* (Baton Rouge: Louisiana State University Press, 2004), 225–28, 233, 237–39, 248–49, 257–64.

8. Heth to Jones, June 1877, SHSP, vol. 4: 154; Lee to Seddon, May 30, June 8, 1863, in *Wartime Papers*, eds. Dowdey and Manarin, 498, 504–5; Lee to Elzey, May 27, 1863, ibid., 494; Lee to Davis, May, 30, 1863, ibid., 496.

9. Reagan, *Memoirs*, 120, 150; Kent Masterson Brown, *Retreat from Gettysburg: Lee, Logistics, and the Pennsylvania Campaign* (Chapel Hill: University of North Carolina Press, 2005), 12–16.

10. Longstreet, "Lee in Pennsylvania," 417.

11. Lee to Hood, May 21, 1863, in *Wartime Papers*, eds. Dowdey and Manarin, 490.

12. Lee to Davis, May 20, 1863, ibid., 488–89; Hdqrs. Army of Northern Virginia, Special Orders No. 146, May 30, 1863, OR, vol. 25, pt. 2: 840.

13. Lee to Davis, June 7, 1863, in *Wartime Papers*, eds. Dowdey and Manarin, 502–03; Lee to his wife, June 19, 1863, ibid., 507; Lee to Hill, June 5, 1863, OR, vol. 27, pt. 3: 859; Lee to Cooper, July 31, 1863, ibid., vol. 27, pt. 2: 305.

14. Hooker to Lincoln, June 5, 1863, ibid., pt. 1: 30; Lincoln to Hooker, June 5, 1863, ibid., 31.

15. T. Harry Williams, *Lincoln and His Generals* (New York: Alfred A. Knopf, 1952), 252.

16. Hooker to Halleck, June 6, 1863, OR, vol. 27, pt. 1: 33; Butterfield to Pleasonton, June 7, 1863, ibid., pt. 3: 27–28; Lee to Jenkins, June 10, 1863, in *Wartime Papers*, eds. Dowdey and Manarin, 510; Lee to Imboden, June 10, 1863, ibid.

17. Lee to Davis, June 10, 1863, ibid., 507–09.

18. Ewell to Chilton, —— 1863, OR, vol. 27, pt. 2: 439–42; Donald C. Pfanz, *Richard S. Ewell: A Soldier's Life* (Chapel Hill: University of North Carolina Press, 1998), 290.

19. Lee to G.W.C. Lee, June 13, 1863, in *Wartime Papers*, eds. Dowdey and Manarin, 414; H.B. McClellan, *I Rode with Jeb Stuart: The Life and Campaigns of Major General J.E.B. Stuart* (Bloomington: Indiana University Press, 1958), 294; Hooker to Lincoln, June 10, 1863, OR, vol. 27, pt. 1: 34–35.

20. Lincoln to Hooker, June 10, 1863, ibid., 35.

21. Circular, Headquarters Army of the Potomac, June 11, 1863, ibid., pt. 3: 67; Hooker to Howard, June 12, 1863, ibid., 69; Itinerary of the Army of the Potomac and cooperating forces, June 5–July 31, 1863, ibid., pt. 1: 141; Hooker to Halleck, June 13, 1863, ibid., 38.

22. Lee to Davis, June 15, 1863, in *Wartime Papers*, eds. Dowdey and Manarin, 515; Lee to Longstreet, June 15, 1863, ibid., 516; Lee to Hill, June 16, 1863, ibid., 517.

23. Lincoln to Hooker, June 14, 15, 1863, OR, vol. 27, pt. 1: 40, 43; Hooker to Halleck, June 15, 1863, ibid., 40; Halleck to Hooker, June 15, 1863, ibid., 42; Hooker to Lincoln, June 15, 1863, ibid., 43, 43–44.

24. Hooker to Lincoln, June 16, 1863, ibid., 47; Hooker to Halleck, June 16, 1863, ibid., 40–41, 46; Halleck to Hooker, June 16, 17, 1863, ibid., 46, 49; Williams to Pleasonton, June 17, 1863, ibid., pt. 3: 172.

25. Lee to Ewell, June 16, 1863, in *Wartime Papers*, eds. Dowdey and Manarin, 518; Lee to Hill, June 16, 1863, ibid., 517; Lee to Longstreet, June 17, 1863, ibid., 518.

26. Sears, *Gettysburg*, 97–101.

27. Lee to Ewell, June 19, 22, 1863, in *Wartime Papers*, eds. Dowdey and Manarin, 521, 524; Ewell to Chilton, ———, 1863, OR, vol. 27, pt. 2: 439; Longstreet to Chilton, July 27, 1863, ibid., 357–58.

28. Lee to Stuart, June 22, 1863, in *Wartime Papers*, eds. Dowdey and Manarin, 521.

29. Longstreet to Stuart, June 22, 1863, OR, vol. 27, pt. 3: 915; Lee to Stuart, June 23, 1863, in *Wartime Papers*, eds. Dowdey and Manarin, 526.

30. Donald, *Lincoln*, 440; Hooker testimony, 1865, in U.S. Congress, *Report of the Joint Committee on the Conduct of the War*, 3 vols. (Washington, DC: Government Printing Office, 1863), vol. 1: 177; Itinerary of the Army of the Potomac and cooperating forces, June 5–July 31, 1863, OR, vol. 27, pt. 1: 142.

31. Lee to Davis, June 23, 1863, in *Wartime Papers*, eds. Dowdey and Manarin, 530; Anderson to Palmer, August 7, 1863, OR, vol. 27, pt. 2: 613; Ewell to Chilton, ———, 1863, ibid., 443; Rodes to Pendleton, ———, 1863, ibid., 551; Edwards to Lanny, June 23, 1863, Leroy S. Edwards Letters, bound vol. 334, Fredericksburg and Spotsylvania National Military Park Library, Fredericksburg, VA (repository hereafter cited as FSNMP).

32. Longstreet to Chilton, July 27, 1863, OR, vol. 27, pt. 2: 358; Lee to Davis, June 25, 1863 in *Wartime Papers*, eds. Dowdey and Manarin, 530–31; Entry for June 25, 1863, Franklin Gardner Walter Diary, bound vol. 138, FSNMP.

33. Lee to Davis, June 25, 23, 1863, *Wartime Papers*, eds. Dowdey and Manarin, 527–28.

34. Lee to Davis, June 23, 25, 1863, ibid., 527–28, 532–33; Cooper to Lee, June 29, 1863, OR, vol. 27, pt. 1: 75–76; Davis to Lee, June 28, 1863, ibid., 76–77.

35. Ewell to Chilton, ———, 1863, ibid., pt. 2: 443; Early to Pendleton, August 22, 1863, ibid., 465–66; Longstreet to Chilton, July 27, 1863, ibid., 358; Anderson to Palmer, August 7, 1863, ibid., 613.

36. Hdqrs. Army of Northern Virginia, General Orders No. 72, June 21, 1863, ibid., pt. 3: 912–13.

37. Richmond Daily Dispatch, June 22, 26, 1863; General Orders No. 73, June 27, 1863, in Wartime Papers, eds. Dowdey and Manarin, 533–34.

38. Johnson to his wife, June 30, 1862, Bradley T. Johnson Papers, Special Collections, William R. Perkins Library, Duke University, Durham, NC, copy in bound vol. 380, FSNMP.

39. Isaac R. Trimble, "The Battle and Campaign of Gettysburg," SHSP, vol. 26: 121; Jedediah Hotchkiss, Make Me a Map of the Valley: The Civil War Journal of Stonewall Jackson's Topographer, edited by Archie P. McDonald (Dallas: Southern Methodist University Press, 1973), 155.

40. Heth to Jones, June 1877, in SHSP, vol. 4: 151–52; (Staunton, VA) Vindicator, October 2, 1863.

41. Steven E. Woodworth, Six Armies in Tennessee: The Chickamauga and Chattanooga Campaigns (Lincoln: University of Nebraska Press, 1998), 19–46; Shea and Winschel, Vicksburg Is the Key, 168–72; Ulysses S. Grant, Personal Memoirs of U.S. Grant (New York: Charles L. Webster, 1885), 321.

42. Lincoln to Hooker, June 16, 1863, Works of Lincoln, vol. 6: 281; Parker to Lincoln, June 29, 1863, OR, vol. 27, pt. 3: 409; Lincoln to Parker, June 30, 1863, Works of Lincoln, vol. 6: 311; Williams, Lincoln and his Generals, 258.

43. Coddington, Gettysburg Campaign, 122–26; Itinerary of the Army of the Potomac and co-operating forces, June 5–July 31, 1863, OR, vol. 27, pt. 1: 143.

44. Hooker to Lincoln, June 16, 1863, ibid., 45; Lincoln to Hooker, June 16, 1863, ibid., 47.

45. Hooker to Halleck, June 26, 27, 1863, ibid., 58, 60; Halleck to Hooker, June 27, 1863, ibid., 60.

46. Walter H. Hebert, Fighting Joe Hooker (Indianapolis: Bobbs-Merrill, 1944), 245; Hooker to Halleck, June 27, 1863, OR, vol. 27, pt. 1: 58, 60; Charles F. Benjamin, "Hooker's Appointment and Removal," in Battles and Leaders of the Civil War, edited by Robert U. Johnson and Clarence C. Buel, 4 vols. (New York: Century, 1885), vol. 3: 241–43.

CHAPTER THREE

Gettysburg

As news of the change in command traveled out to the various corps in the Army of the Potomac and Meade struggled to get a handle on his new job during the morning of June 28, 1863, Robert E. Lee was beginning to get concerned about the lack of news from Stuart. Several days had passed since Lee gave his cavalry commander authority to try to ride around the Army of the Potomac, and it was clear Stuart had yet to fulfill his mission of finding and covering the right of Ewell's corps, which was well advanced from the rest of the army's concentration around Chambersburg.[1]

There is little evidence, though, that Lee's confidence regarding his situation, a confidence rooted in ignorance of just how much danger Federal movements over the past few days had put his army in, had diminished much since his conversation with Trimble the previous day. While waiting for news from Stuart, Lee decided the most pressing matter on his plate was the situation with the Second Corps, and he sent a message to Ewell ordering him to advance from Carlisle to Harrisburg and expect Longstreet to be there soon to support him in an attack on the Pennsylvania state capital. When he received this message Ewell was already making preparations for such a move, while to the south the lead elements of Early's division were already at Wrightsville on the banks of the Susquehanna.[2] At army headquarters, this appeared to be the only event of any real significance on June 28, and when darkness fell, it seemed that the latest in a string of surprisingly trouble-free days was coming to an appropriately uneventful end.

Then, shortly after 10:00 p.m., a messenger reached Lee with alarming news. A spy by the name of Henry Harrison, whose services Longstreet had secured in Virginia, was reporting that the Army of the Potomac had crossed into Maryland. Although usually skeptical of information gathered by scouts, this news, if true, was far too important to be ignored. Lee asked for Harrison to personally report to army headquarters and tell him exactly what he had learned. Harrison informed Lee that he had personally encountered two Union corps at Frederick and learned that another two were near South Mountain. The Federals, Lee immediately realized, were in the process of stealing the initiative from him—if they had not done so already. This was not all, Harrison advised the general. "Fighting Joe" Hooker no longer commanded the Army of the Potomac; George Meade did.[3]

Although undoubtedly troubled that news of these developments had not come from the source they should have, Lee knew he had no time to waste in adjusting his plans. Orders were quickly dispatched to Ewell to abandon whatever plans he had for forcing the Susquehanna and to pull back down the Cumberland Valley to rejoin the rest of the army. By the next morning, Lee had decided the army would concentrate at Cashtown, near the gap where the road linking Chambersburg with Gettysburg crossed South Mountain, and ordered Hill's corps to move toward Cashtown, with Longstreet to follow the next day. Early that morning, Lee also sent orders to Ewell directing him to have his two divisions in the Cumberland Valley cross South Mountain south of Carlisle and "move in the direction of Gettysburg, via Heidlersburg." At Heidlersburg, Ewell was to "join your other divisions to Early's. . . . [I]t is preferable for you to keep on the east side of the mountains. When you come to Heidlersburg you can either move directly on Gettysburg or turn down to Cashtown."[4]

Once the approximately seventy-five thousand men in the Army of Northern Virginia were again concentrated near Cashtown, Lee would reassess the situation before determining his next move. His ability to formulate and execute an effective plan would, of course, depend in no small part on what the Army of the Potomac was doing. Lee took some comfort in the thought that the sudden change in command might produce an awkward transitional period in the Federal army that could create a window of opportunity for the Army of Northern Virginia. At the same time, though, he re-

alized it would be no easy task to find, create, or take advantage of any opportunity that might arise. "General Meade will commit no blunder in my
front," he warily advised one of his subordinates shortly after the Federal
change in command, "and if I commit one he will make haste to take advantage of it."[5]

Unfortunately for Lee, he was correct in his assessment of his new foe and
wrong to hope that the change in command might have a detrimental effect
on the Army of the Potomac. Many in the Army of the Potomac high command had not held Hooker in high regard personally when he ascended to
command of the Army of the Potomac, and their disdain for him had been reinforced by how the Chancellorsville Campaign played out. Their displeas-
ure at Lincoln's decision not to heed their appeals for a change in command
after Chancellorsville was obvious to anyone who had contact with the
Army of the Potomac, and their distrust of their commander was further exacerbated during the march from the Rappahannock to Maryland by
Hooker's unwillingness to take them into his confidence regarding his intentions. Meade, however, was respected and trusted by nearly all of his corps
commanders and could count on their full cooperation and obedience—in
part because he was a conservative and methodical commander in the Mc-
Clellan mold who was unlikely, as Lee recognized, to commit a significant
blunder. This was bad news for Lee, as one of the assumptions that guided
him as he decided on and conducted the campaign into Pennsylvania was
that he could induce the commander of the Army of the Potomac to make
rash decisions and handle his army in an overly aggressive manner that
would create opportunities for the Army of Northern Virginia to achieve a
decisive victory. True to his nature, upon assuming command Meade approached the operational problem he faced in a cautious and methodical
manner. His mission, as laid out by Halleck, was to "keep in view the important fact that the Army of the Potomac is the covering army of Washington
as well as the army of operation against the invading forces of the rebels. You
will, therefore, maneuver and fight in such a manner as to cover the capital
and also Baltimore." Even though he still had yet to gain a decent sense of
exactly where the enemy was and what his intentions were, by seven in the
morning of June 28, Meade had concluded he "must move toward the
Susquehanna, keeping Washington and Baltimore well covered."[6]

Meade inherited an enviable operational situation from Hooker. As dawn
broke on June 28, the Army of the Potomac was divided into three wings occupying positions in the Cumberland, Middletown, and Monocacy Valleys with
the ability to quickly shift back and forth, and with their logistics secure. What
the fate of Lee's army might have been had this course of action continued to

be pursued is open to conjecture, but it is easy to see how it might have been far worse than it eventually would be. Nonetheless, not liking the small risk that having his forces separated in this way carried and believing he could not both advance toward the Susquehanna and maintain a strong presence in the Cumberland and Middletown Valleys, Meade abandoned Hooker's approach. He decided to concentrate his entire command, except for a small force to be left at Harpers Ferry, east of South Mountain at and around Frederick. The Federal army would then move northward between Parr's Ridge and South Mountain in such a way that would cover Washington and Baltimore and alleviate the fears of the authorities in Harrisburg by compelling Lee to pull back from the Susequehanna. Once this had been accomplished, Meade would look for a good position to concentrate his army where it would cover Washington and Baltimore, have secure logistics, and pose a threat to Lee's communications with Richmond. This would force the Confederates to either retreat down the Cumberland Valley with their eastern flank potentially vulnerable to attack, or to attack Meade in his chosen position. Although different from Hooker's, Meade's plan was also a very good one. It carried with it the potential of fulfilling Lincoln's hope that the opportunity for a decisive victory created by the Confederate invasion of Pennsylvania would not be missed.

The first step in Meade's plan, the concentration of his army around Frederick, was completed by the time Harrison's report reached Lee on June 28. The following day, Meade directed Maj. Gen. John Reynolds to take the three corps he had marched over from the Middletown Valley north toward Emmitsburg and Gettysburg, with a cavalry division commanded by Brig. Gen. John Buford screening their advance. Meade hoped this would induce Lee to pull back the forces he had advanced to the Susquehanna from Harrisburg, thus eliminating the menace to the Pennsylvania state capital. With the exception of Reynolds's wing, Meade intended for the rest of the army to "incline to the right," but not too far lest it undermine his ability to "hold my force well together." Two corps would move from Frederick to the pike linking Gettysburg with Westminster, the terminus for the Western Maryland Railroad. Once it reached the pike, these corps would serve as the Army of the Potomac's center, with a cavalry division screening its advance. Meade's largest corps would move toward Manchester, which was on the road connecting Gettysburg with Baltimore via Hanover, and once there would serve as the Union right wing, also with a cavalry division screening its front and flank. The last of the Army of the Potomac's corps would take up a position near Taneytown and serve as a reserve, while, taking advantage of the authority Halleck had denied Hooker but granted him over the garrison, Meade intended for French's troops at Harpers Ferry to move to Frederick to secure the Union rear.[7]

As Meade moved out from Frederick on June 29, Lee was issuing orders for the reconcentration of his army at Cashtown and anxiously awaiting their execution. The orders to Ewell evidently did not reach that officer until most of the day had passed. Consequently, it was not until the next morning that a division from each of the Second Corps's two columns was on the march toward their rendezvous at Heidlersburg, with Ewell's third division accompanying the corps's wagons and reserve artillery as they moved down the Cumberland Valley toward Chambersburg. Meanwhile, Hill advanced his three divisions from Chambersburg across South Mountain toward Cashtown, with his lead division reaching the town by the end of the day. Two of Longstreet's divisions followed Hill's march from Chambersburg (the third remained behind to guard the army's rear) and spent the night of June 29–30 west of Cashtown Pass at Greenwood. Thus, by the time night fell on June 29, Lee's effort to reconcentrate his army was proceeding well. Whether this move or the particular way it was being executed were appropriate in relation to the movements of the enemy was an open question, though, for Stuart was still absent and out of touch (with a staff officer reporting that he was still south of the Potomac only two days earlier), and Lee could not determine where he, or more importantly the enemy, exactly was.[8]

While Lee monitored the concentration of his army from Greenwood on June 30, a brigade from Hill's lead division pushed forward that morning from Cashtown to Gettysburg with orders from its commander to "search the town for army supplies (shoes especially), and return the same day." As they approached Gettysburg, though, Hill's men unexpectedly spotted enemy troops in the town whose numbers and origin they could not determine. They responded by calling off the supply-gathering mission and pulling back to Cashtown to report their findings, which reached Hill that evening. While Hill mulled over this information, the division Ewell had marched across South Mountain from Carlisle reached Heidlersburg, while Early's division was close enough that its commander could meet with Ewell that night. Ewell told Early that he had just received orders from Lee to continue moving toward Hill, but whether he did so via Cashtown or Gettysburg was left to his discretion. Ewell also advised Early that a dispatch from Hill had arrived reporting the arrival of his command at Cashtown and that he intended to march the two divisions from the Second Corps he had on hand to Cashtown in the morning.[9]

The assumption that Hill would be at Cashtown when the Second Corps could be expected to arrive on July 1 would prove incorrect as a consequence of a chain of events the Third Corps commander set in motion the night of June 30. In response to a request from a subordinate, Hill authorized another expedition to Gettysburg to gather supplies and, he later wrote, "discover what was in my front." If any concerns or objections regarding such a course of action crossed Lee's mind when Hill advised him of his intentions, he did not communicate them to Hill. Indeed, the commander of the division that was to advance to Gettysburg later recalled being told by Hill on the evening of June 30 that he had discussed the situation with Lee and been assured that "the enemy are still at Middleburg, and have not yet struck their tents."[10]

What Hill's men had seen in Gettysburg on June 30 were elements from the cavalry division covering Reynolds's wing of the Army of the Potomac. By then, evidence had reached Meade that the Confederates were moving two corps toward Gettysburg and that his movements had relieved Harrisburg from the threat posed by Ewell's command. The latter development eliminated the original rationale for pushing Reynolds's wing so far ahead of the rest of the army and led Meade to begin developing a new course of action. On June 30, he directed two officers to reconnoiter and prepare a defensive position behind Pipe Creek. Once this had been accomplished, Meade could pull back Reynolds's wing to link up with the rest of the Army of the Potomac in a well-prepared defensive position between Middleburg and Manchester behind Pipe Creek. There Meade would effectively cover Washington and Baltimore, possess secure logistics, pose a threat to Lee's line of retreat back to Virginia through the Cumberland Valley, and perhaps compel the Army of Northern Virginia to take the offensive in a set-piece battle in which the Union would have every advantage. On the morning of July 1, Meade put the finishing touches on his plan and issued what became known as the Pipe Creek Circular, which ordered the withdrawal of Reynolds's wing from its advanced position to join the rest of the Army of the Potomac behind Pipe Creek.[11]

By the time Meade issued the Pipe Creek Circular, however, events were already driving history toward a different channel. Instead of pulling his army back to fight the rebels from a good defensive position at Pipe Creek on July 1, Meade would be forced to fight a battle that day that was very different from the one he wanted. Although caught by surprise by the particular course events took, to the great fortune of the Army of Northern Virginia, events on July 1 played out in a manner that was very close to how their commander wanted and needed an engagement with the Federals to develop north of the Potomac.

The fighting began north and west of Gettysburg, when Hill's men retraced their steps from Cashtown and encountered first an extremely well-led division of Union cavalry and then an entire Union corps. As the fight developed that morning, Lee was riding with Longstreet, whose corps was moving through Cashtown in South Mountain. When the sound of battle reached Lee he immediately rode forward to Cashtown to find out what was going on. Upon arriving at Cashtown, Lee tried to gain some information from General Hill. All the corps commander could tell him, one of Lee's staff officers later recalled, was that "the advance of [Maj. Gen. Henry] Heth's division had encountered the cavalry of the enemy near Gettysburg. Instructions had been sent to General Heth to ascertain what force was at Gettysburg, and, if he found infantry opposed to him, to report the fact immediately, without forcing an engagement."

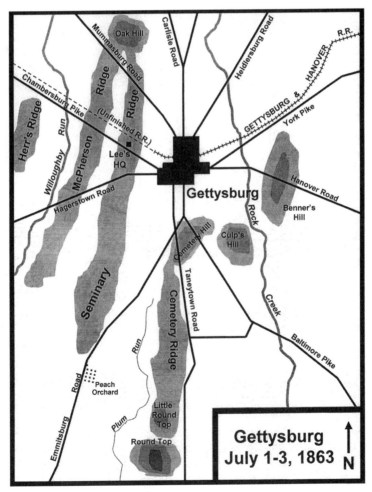

Figure 3.1.   Battle of Gettysburg.

Hill then left Cashtown for the front, while a visibly agitated Lee remarked to one of his division commanders, "I cannot think what has become of Stuart. I ought to have heard from him long before now. . . . In the absence of reports from him, I am in ignorance as to what we have in front of us here. It may be the whole Federal army, it may only be a detachment."[12]

In fact, it was only a detachment of the Army of the Potomac that Hill had stumbled into a fight with. Nonetheless, ignorant of Meade's plan to pull back to Pipe Creek, its commander, Reynolds, decided he was not going to give up any ground without a fight and on his own initiative ordered more Union troops to Gettysburg. Reynolds's decision was to Lee's good fortune. It meant that the Yankees would, as Lee hoped, be making the fight with a segment of their army that was well in advance of its comrades, who would have to make hard, tiring marches to reach a battlefield where they would be vulnerable to attacks against one or both of their flanks. It was almost exactly the scenario Lee had sketched out for Trimble four days earlier. All that was needed was for the Army of Northern Virginia to react properly to the situation and, without information from Stuart to base their moves on, enjoy a little luck. They got it. On the morning of July 1 Ewell once again proved that he possessed more than a little of the good fortune that had so often marched with Jackson. Upon learning that morning of Hill's advance on Gettysburg, Ewell deduced this meant the army's point of concentration would be at that town, and countermanded his orders to march from Heidlersburg to Cashtown. Instead, the two divisions Ewell had with him would move toward Gettysburg from the north. As it turned out, this meant that they would arrive at a perfect position from which they and their comrades in the Third Corps could make Lee's vision of how he wanted a fight to develop when he crossed the Potomac a reality and produce a nightmare for the Federals, in which they found themselves in the exact situation their commander wanted to avoid.[13]

That this was the case was anything but apparent, though, when one of Ewell's staff officers, Campbell Brown, reported to Lee at Cashtown to advise him of Ewell's decision. Brown found Lee consumed by a "peculiar searching, almost querulous impatience" due to the lack of information he had about the situation in front of him, and desperate to find out where the man responsible for providing it was. When Brown responded to Lee's queries by reporting that Second Corps headquarters had heard nothing from Stuart either, Lee could not contain his exasperation. After all, when he had issued the orders authorizing Stuart's detachment from the army, they were crystal clear that he must do nothing to preclude his being in contact with the Second Corps by at least this point in time. Even worse, it seemed the enemy did have a vague sense of Stuart's movements, which was more than anyone in the Army of Northern Virginia could claim. He had told Stuart, a clearly exasperated Lee explained to Brown, "to cross one of the upper fords along the Eastern base of the [Blue] Ridge, & [be in] constant communication with me—& rather than abandon communications to fall back into the Gaps of the mountain,—but he has gone off clear around Gen'l Meade's army & I see by a paper that he is near Washington. A scout reports Meade's whole army marching this way, but that is all I know about his position." Understandably more concerned about the danger that was clear and present, as opposed to the opportunity that might be developing, Lee then sent Brown back to Ewell with the message that he was to "send out to his left & try to open communications with Gen'l Stuart," with the understanding that, given the circumstances, concentrating the Army of Northern Virginia rather than fighting the Federals was the first priority. Consequently, when Brown returned to Second Corps headquarters he advised Ewell that Lee "did not want a general engagement brought on till the rest of the army came up."[14]

Finally, shortly after noon, Lee decided he could no longer hang back at Cashtown and spurred Traveller forward along the road to Gettysburg. As he reached a point less than five miles from Gettysburg, it became clear that, regardless of his wishes, the actions of the Third Corps had sparked a significant fight. At the same time, it did not seem that Hill's command, although a bit roughed up, was positioned in such a way that it was in serious danger or that the task of completing the concentration of the Army of Northern Virginia was in any sort of jeopardy. Then, however, at around three in the afternoon, the Second Corps began arriving on the scene from the north in such a way that it seemed to their commanders that "It was too late to avoid an engagement," as Ewell later wrote. Due to poor leadership, though, the first of Ewell's divisions to reach the field suffered a severe mauling at the hands of the Federals. As Ewell's men were engaging the enemy, one of Hill's division commanders asked Lee for permission to renew the attack from the west to support the Second Corps's efforts. Lee refused to provide it. "I am not prepared to bring on a general engagement today," he explained. "Longstreet is not up."[15]

Shortly thereafter, though, Ewell's second division arrived and crushed the right flank of the Union corps that had gone into position north of the town. This completely transformed the situation. Lee was nothing if not quick to recognize when fortune had provided the sort of opportunity he had been looking for. Longstreet or no Longstreet, Stuart or no Stuart, a decisive victory now seemed within reach for the Army of Northern Virginia. Thus, Lee relinquished his earlier caution and issued orders to Hill to resume and Ewell to press his attacks. Within an hour, the Union positions north and west of Gettysburg were shattered, and the Federals were retreating through the town's streets in hopes of finding sanctuary on the high ground to the south.

The scale of the Confederate victory on July 1 and whether it would be a truly complete one, Lee quickly recognized as he discussed the situation with Hill late that afternoon, would depend on whether Federal commanders could maintain possession of a high hill south of Gettysburg on which a cemetery was located. From their command post on Seminary Ridge west of the town, Lee and Hill could see the Federals already had a "strong force of infantry and artillery" on Cemetery Hill and had no intention of giving up this position voluntarily. In the course of the day, however, two divisions from the Third Corps had taken a severe beating at the hands of the Federals, whom Hill confided to one man, seemed to be fighting "with a determination unusual to them." Consequently, Hill believed these two divisions were too exhausted to resume the attack. Hill's third division was at that moment approaching the field, but Lee, who was with its ill corps commander at the time, evidently decided it would not be committed to a fight for the high ground south of Gettysburg that evening. From prisoners taken in the course of the fighting that day, it was revealed that the Army of Northern Virginia had fought only two corps from the Army of the Potomac and, Lee later wrote, "that the remainder of that army . . . was approaching Gettysburg."16

With Stuart gone, Lee had very few means available for determining whether this was the case and if so, how soon Union reinforcements would arrive. Consequently, he decided that it was necessary to keep Hill's fresh division in reserve. If Cemetery Hill were to be taken on July 1, it would have to be done by Ewell; thus, Lee sent an aide to the Second Corps commander with directions "to carry the hill occupied by the enemy if he found it practicable, but to avoid a general engagement until the arrival of the other divisions of the army." Even though his command had not taken as bad a beating as Hill's, Ewell ultimately determined that taking Cemetery Hill was not "practicable" that evening. Given the many problems organizing such an attack posed, the strength of the Federal forces on the hill, and the energy and effectiveness with which they were rallying—not to mention the fact that reports reached Ewell of Federal forces west of his position who might fall upon the flank and rear of his command if it did make the attack—he was wise do so. Nonetheless, the fact that the Federals were still holding the high ground south of town when the fighting ended on July 1 meant that Lee found himself faced with a situation that had developed and would continue to develop in a way that would favor his opponent and inexorably increase the odds the Army of Northern Virginia faced at Gettysburg.17

Lee began contemplating the problem he might face if the Federals could not be driven from the high ground south of Gettysburg even before his orders to consider whether and how the Second Corps might attack Cemetery Hill reached Ewell. Not long after Lee sent these, Longstreet found him at his headquarters where the road connecting Cashtown and Gettysburg crossed Seminary Ridge. After Lee described the situation, Longstreet quickly looked over the terrain and suggested the next step should be to move south around the Union left and secure a position between Meade "and Washington, threatening his left and rear." This, he believed, would force the Federals "to attack us in such position as we might select," in which case the Confederates were sure to beat them. "Impressed," Longstreet later recalled, "with the idea that, by attacking the Federals he could whip them in detail," Lee rejected his lieutenant's advice. If the enemy continued to hold their position south of Gettysburg the next morning, Lee bluntly told Longstreet, "we must attack him." Longstreet was not pleased. If the enemy was still holding their positions, he replied, "it will be because he is anxious that we should attack him—a good reason, in my judgment, for not doing so."[18]

As Lee and Longstreet talked, a member of Ewell's staff told them the Second Corps commander was willing to attempt to take Cemetery Hill, but believed a supporting attack was needed. Longstreet advised Lee that his lead division was at that moment at least an hour's march away. When it became apparent shortly thereafter that Ewell was not going to attempt to take Cemetery Hill, Lee decided he needed to talk to him. Upon reaching Ewell's headquarters, Lee asked him and the two Second Corps division commanders present if they could attempt an attack the next day. When they expressed skepticism as to the possible success of such a move, Lee proposed pulling their commands back through Gettysburg to shorten and strengthen the army's position. This course of action did not appeal to Ewell and his lieutenants either, which led Lee to raise the possibility of having Longstreet's command attack the Union left on July 2. This prompted a suggestion from the Second Corps high command. They believed that if Longstreet did make such an attack and it achieved some measure of success, their units could then join the battle with a good prospect of decisive success. Lee returned to Seminary Ridge and thought through his options in light of what Longstreet and the Second Corps's leadership had told him.[19]

Unfortunately, there was much that remained unknown. Where was the rest of the Army of the Potomac, what were Meade's intentions, and what were those elements going to do in line with them? This lack of information did much to diminish the appeal of Longstreet's idea of trying to move around

Figure 3.2. James Longstreet. Francis Trevelyan Miller, *The Photographic History of the Civil War*, vol. 10 (New York: The Review of Reviews Co., 1911), 245

the Union right. Moreover, what Lee did know argued for aggressive action to be taken as quickly as it could be done. Consolidating his hard-won position or pulling back to the South Mountain passes and hoping to entice the Federals to attack him was not a particularly good option. By July 1 the Army of Northern Virginia had been living off the land for several days, exhausting the region in which it had been operating, and without a secure and reliable source of supply, the Federals, who were moving up from good bases of operations at Washington and Baltimore with a good road and rail network behind them, could simply starve him out. Lee could try to reestablish a new supply line through the Cumberland Valley; however, this would entail detaching a considerable force from the Army of Northern Virginia to deal with the Federals he had left at Harpers Ferry. And Lee vividly recalled how such a move the previous September had nearly resulted in the destruction of his army.

Moreover, if the Federals were determined to fight at Gettysburg, Lee could see an opportunity. He had crossed the Potomac hoping, indeed needing, to put his army in a situation where it was attacking a part of the Army of the Potomac. Every piece of evidence Lee had before him as July 1 came to a close indicated he might have an opportunity at Gettysburg to do this and win the sort of decisive victory he had crossed the Potomac to achieve, but that the window for doing so was rapidly closing. Meade would no doubt make a strong effort to concentrate his army as quickly as he could on the heights south of the town, and once this had been accomplished Lee would find himself facing a numerically superior army on terrain that their firepower and numbers could make all but invulnerable to attack. Consequently, every hour, every minute that passed tilted the balance further toward the Federals—and made it less likely that Lee would be able to achieve anything more than he had on July 1. If, on the other hand, Meade decided not to continue the fight at Gettysburg, that meant the two Union corps that had been bruised but not destroyed on July 1 would soon rejoin their comrades on ground selected by their commander. If this were accomplished, it would almost be certain that the next time Lee faced the Federals he would be at an even greater disadvantage than he might face at Gettysburg on July 2.

And so Lee had little choice but to attack, and he spent the morning of July 2 developing a plan for doing so. Early that morning, a member of Lee's staff was ordered to conduct a reconnaissance to determine how far south the Federal position on Cemetery Hill ran. When the officer returned he reported the Federal line extended south from Cemetery Hill along Cemetery Ridge, but ended short of two prominent hills, Little Round Top and Big Round Top. This information and a series of conversations with his subordinates confirmed in Lee's mind that the best course of action would be the one he had formulated the night before. Even though the First Corps commander made it abundantly clear that he did not like the idea of attacking at Gettysburg, Lee decided that the two divisions from Longstreet's command that were then arriving on the field would move south behind Hill's corps and maneuver until they reached a position from which they could attack the Union left flank. To facilitate Longstreet's efforts, the two divisions from Hill's corps that had been engaged on July 1 would "threaten the enemy's center" on Cemetery Hill, while to their right the third division from the Third Corps would "cooperate . . . in Longstreet's attack." Meanwhile, Ewell's command would "make a simultaneous demonstration upon the enemy's right, to be converted into a real attack should opportunity offer."[20]

Such an attack would be incredibly difficult, as Lee understood from experience, to coordinate or supervise very closely. This was largely a consequence of the very limited means Civil War generals possessed for exercising command and control over any force of significant size. Consequently, in all but the most ideal circumstances, the only practically feasible way to manage an army in the field was for a commander to give his subordinates general instructions as to what was expected of them in his overall operational or tactical plan and then provide them with plenty of leeway to handle the details and exercise individual initiative. In recognition of this, Lee had come to believe well before July 1863 that providing close supervision over a battle did, as he advised a Prussian officer who was accompanying the army in Pennsylvania, "more harm than good" and that all he could do was "think and work with all my powers to bring my troops to the right place at the right time; then I have done my duty." Once he had done this and issued the orders for execution of the general plan, in Lee's mind he had no choice but to accept that responsibility for events had passed from his hands to those of "God and . . . subordinate officers."[21] (At the same time, it should be noted that Lee was too good a commander to follow a generally sound principle dogmatically and there would be a number of occasions during the war when, facing circumstances where it was both practicable and necessary to do so, he in fact exercised close supervision over his subordinates.)

Further complicating Lee's ability to manage the battle at Gettysburg was the fact that, as a consequence of the events of July 1, the Federals south of Gettysburg possessed a much shorter and more compact line than the Confederates. Moreover, Meade had the advantage of operating on interior lines, which made the task of exercising command and control easier for the Federal commander and gave him the ability to respond to events much quicker than Lee could. Operating on a much longer exterior line, Lee found himself facing an extremely difficult task in coordinating the movements of widely separated elements of his army and exercising effective command and control over them. As Lee could not have been unaware, this was an almost exact reversal of the situation he had faced the previous September at Antietam. There his army had fought on interior lines, and Lee was able to communicate with subordinates and manage his forces much more effectively than had his Federal counterpart, which played no small role in Lee's ability to avoid a truly catastrophic defeat at the hands of a far superior foe. Now, though, it was Lee who found his already outnumbered army on the offensive and too widely spread out for him to hope to exercise close control over all of its elements to ensure their attacks were closely coordinated.

Of course, whether Lee's decisions would be vindicated by events on July 2 would depend greatly on his opponent's actions. When news arrived from

Reynolds of the fighting at Gettysburg on the morning of July 1, Meade had developed his plan to withdraw to Pipe Creek and await events there. However, he did not overrule his subordinate's decision to fight for the town. In doing so, Meade recognized he was allowing a segment of his army to do battle at a point far from its base with an enemy that was already quickly concentrating on that point—the very situation he wanted to avoid. The only explanation for Meade's actions is the high regard he had for Reynolds's judgment, which undoubtedly led him to assume that Reynolds would not be making a fight at Gettysburg if the situation were at all unfavorable. Then news reached Meade that Reynolds had been killed, placing management of the battle in the hands of less trusted officers. Still committed to the Pipe Creek plan but willing to adapt to circumstances, Meade remained at the headquarters he had established to oversee the plan's implementation and dispatched one of his trusted subordinates, Maj. Gen. Winfield Scott Hancock, to Gettysburg to take charge of the situation. Hancock was also to advise Meade as to whether the situation at Gettysburg warranted discarding the Pipe Creek plan and ordering the Army of the Potomac to concentrate at Gettysburg.

Upon receiving Hancock's assessment that "the character of the position [was] favorable," Meade "determined to give battle at this point; and, early in the evening of the 1st, issued orders to all the corps to concentrate at Gettysburg." By the time Meade himself reached Gettysburg shortly after midnight, two corps had already arrived to join the two that had been badly bloodied, but by no means destroyed, on July 1. Three more were on the way, and when they arrived, Meade would be in an extremely strong position with about ninety-three thousand men concentrated on good terrain that enabled them to apply their superior firepower in a set-piece battle—the very sort of situation Lee had crossed the Potomac and shaped his operations to avoid. Yet on the morning of July 2, the situation still retained a great deal of the fluidity the Confederates needed if they were to achieve a decisive tactical success and perhaps translate it into something more. Both commanders recognized the Army of Northern Virginia was capable of committing a great deal of mischief and that a decisive Confederate victory at Gettysburg, although its prospects were declining with every moment that passed, was by no means outside the realm of possibility on July 2. However, what chance there was for the sort of victory the Confederacy needed at Gettysburg depended greatly on whether Meade would discredit Lee's earlier prediction by committing a serious blunder. Meade had let events on July 1 get out of his control and develop the way they had, and paid the price by suffering a crushing defeat. He was determined not to let this happen again. In case it did, though, Meade prudently kept the idea of falling back to the Pipe Creek position under consideration.[22]

At around eleven in the morning, Lee finished making his plans, and Longstreet's two divisions began their march to get into position to strike the Union left. It took them until after 4:00 p.m. to do this and begin their attack. Once it began, Longstreet's attack initially went very well, driving the Federals from their initial positions and inflicting serious losses on the Army of the Potomac. Meanwhile, from his headquarters on Seminary Ridge, Lee, in line with his recognition of the limitations the deployment of his army imposed on his ability to actively direct the battle, did little to try to manage the battle. Indeed, one observer noted the general spent much of his time after the fighting began sitting alone on a tree stump, using his field glass to monitor the situation and occasionally conversing with Hill and a member of his staff. With Longstreet and Ewell making their attacks so far from each other and their commander not really able to exercise tight supervision over both their efforts, it is not surprising that the commitment of force to the battles on either end of the line was not as well-coordinated or timed as might have been optimal. Consequently, Meade was able to take advantage of his interior lines and the greater degree of command and control he enjoyed over his forces to blunt Longstreet's attack and maintain control of key terrain on Cemetery Ridge and Little Round Top. The story was the same on the Union right, where the Federals were able to repulse assaults by Ewell's command against Culp's Hill and Cemetery Hill.[23]

Although the performance of the Federal high command on July 2 was anything but flawless, the sort of victory Lee was pursuing when he crossed the Potomac and had achieved on a small scale on July 1 did not come on the second day of battle. To make matters worse for Lee, that afternoon the last of Meade's corps reached the battlefield, and by the time the fighting ended that day it was clear that if there was to be any more fighting at Gettysburg, Lee would face the Federals in exactly the situation they wanted to be in: concentrated and in well-established positions from which they could fight a set-piece battle. In short, barring some miracle, the dramatic events of July 2 almost completely eliminated whatever slim prospect Lee had for winning a decisive victory at Gettysburg.

This, of course, is much clearer in retrospect than it was when Lee was contemplating his options during the night of July 2–3. The first thing to consider was the possibility that Meade might decide that he had had enough and try to retreat from Gettysburg. However, Meade had spent two days concentrating his forces in a strong position that his army had fought bitterly to hold on to, and now had before him the prospect of fighting the sort of defensive set-piece battle in which the Federal army excelled. It was unlikely that he would give up such an advantageous and hard-won position now. At the same time, for the Army of Northern Virginia, leaving Gettysburg, whether to return to Virginia or just in search of a better position to fight from, also remained out of the question. For the Confederates to leave the field at this point would be to concede defeat, something Lee was loath to do and seemed rather unnecessary on the night of July 2–3, given the fact that his army had delivered some hard blows to the enemy over the past two days. Moreover, a Confederate retreat from Gettysburg could hardly be expected to have a negative effect on Northern morale, much less deliver the crushing blow to the North's will to continue the war the Confederacy needed if it was to survive.

Longstreet continued to urge adoption of his plan to maneuver around the Union left in order to find a good position that would compel the Federals to attack, but Lee correctly recognized that Meade was too prudent an officer to not take steps to counter such a move. In addition, Lee had yet to exhaust every option available to him at Gettysburg. One would be to go on the defensive, either by adjusting and strengthening his position at Gettysburg or by pulling back to South Mountain, and hope the Federals could be induced to attack; however, Lee was keenly aware that the logistical concerns that limited his ability to remain in one place for any extended period of time were no less compelling on July 3 than they had been on July 2. It also no doubt seemed unreasonable to expect Meade, who had done nothing so far to contradict Lee's earlier assessment of him as a properly cautious and prudent general, to follow a script prepared by his opponent and go on the offensive in a way that would give the Confederates an opportunity for the sort of victory it needed north of the Potomac.

Further shaping Lee's thinking on July 3 was the fact that his only feasible escape route from Gettysburg was through the South Mountain passes at Fairfield and Cashtown and then south through the Cumberland Valley, and there was the danger that while the Army of Northern Virginia waited for Meade to attack, a Federal force might interdict its line of retreat. Lee had knowingly accepted the risks associated with operating with a potentially vulnerable line of retreat about a week earlier when he decided not to do anything about French's command at Harpers Ferry. By July 3, however, Lee had to also be concerned about the force the Federals had assembled under the command of Maj. Gen. Darius Couch for the defense of Harrisburg and the Susquehanna. (In fact, early on July 3 Meade sent messages to French, whose force was then at Frederick, and Couch letting them know he expected them to help the Army of the Potomac take advantage of a Confederate withdrawal from Gettysburg.)[24]

That Lee was concerned about the situation in his rear on the third was evident in his order that morning for a force of cavalry "to be sent at once to the vicinity of Fairfield" to secure the right and rear of the army. This proved a wise precaution, for a brigade from Buford's cavalry division was in fact on the prowl beyond the southern flank of both armies on July 3, and one of its regiments would make a stab at a Confederate wagon train near Fairfield during the afternoon. Fortunately for Lee, his order was promptly acted on by Brig. Gen. William E. "Grumble" Jones, whose three regiments managed to rout the Federals in a fierce engagement near Fairfield and force them to abandon their effort to seize the town.[25]

Consequently, if Lee were to achieve his strategic and operational goals at Gettysburg, the onus was on him to make something happen. Based on the reports he received from his subordinates, it appeared that the attacks on the Union right and left had come within a whisker of success, with the timely arrival of reinforcements on the Union side seeming to have been the difference on the southern end of the field. Moreover, even though July 2 had ended with the entire Federal army finally concentrated at Gettysburg, Lee could take some solace in the fact that he himself would have relatively fresh forces to employ on July 3. In addition to having the third division from Longstreet's corps available for action on July 3, Stuart's long-missing cavalry had finally returned.

Stuart had arrived at Lee's headquarters on Seminary Ridge on July 2 while Longstreet's men were moving into position for their attack. Stuart had ridden around the Federal army, but it had taken considerably longer than anticipated. The route through the Bull Run Mountains Stuart expected to take turned out not to be clear, as Mosby had reported, but occupied by the Yankees. Instead of doing the prudent thing and return to the Army of Northern Virginia upon learning of this development on June 25, Stuart exercised the discretion Lee had granted him to attempt another ride around the Army of the Potomac. He pushed his cavalry further south until he found an unobstructed route through the mountains and crossed the Occoquan River further downstream than he had anticipated in order to ensure that he was behind the Federal army, and then pushed north through Fairfax County to the Potomac. After crossing the Potomac early on June 28, the same day Longstreet's spy brought Lee news that the Army of the Potomac was in Maryland, Stuart attacked a Federal wagon train at Rockville, Maryland and seized 125 wagons and their teams. Accompanied by these new acquisitions, Stuart pushed north expecting to find Ewell near the Susquehanna and fulfill his mission of making contact with and covering the Second Corps's flank. On June 30, however, Stuart's efforts to reach Ewell were further delayed when he found himself engaged in a sharp fight with Union cavalry at Hanover. By the time the fighting at Hanover ended, Ewell's men were pulling back from the Susquehanna. The following day, Stuart reached Carlisle and found Ewell's men long gone. Shortly thereafter, he received a message from Lee stating that the army was heavily engaged at Gettysburg, and he and his cavalry were to proceed to that place without delay.[26]

The ferocity of Lee's anger toward Stuart was evident to all who witnessed their uncomfortable reunion on July 2. Stuart immediately attempted to explain and justify his disappearance, but only provoked Lee into, one man later recalled, "cut[ing] him short with a voice that smoldered: 'I have not heard a word from you for days, and you the eyes and ears of my army!'" After taking his young cavalry commander to task for his recent actions, Lee turned to the problem at hand and instructed Stuart to take his cavalry to the extreme left of the army and position them where they could facilitate Ewell's operations by covering his left flank.[27]

Although frustration over Stuart's absence and the effect it had on the army's fortunes over the past few days were unquestionably the principal reasons Lee was unable to restrain his temper in dealing with Stuart on July 2, it may also have been a manifestation of physical illness. After the war, one of Stuart's aides recalled being dispatched to Lee's headquarters with a report during the evening of the second but being told on his arrival that he could not see the general. Thinking this odd, as Lee usually received reports from Stuart personally, the aide then began discussing matters with the general's staff before seeing the commander of the Army of Northern Virginia "come out of his tent hurriedly and go to the rear several times while I was there." Seeing Lee walking "as if he was weak and in pain" Stuart's aide asked some of the members of the general's staff what the problem was and was told, "General Lee was suffering a good deal from an attack of diarrhea."[28]

Whatever his physical condition might have been during the evening of July 2, Lee still hoped he could resume the offensive early the next day. With Stuart's men in place to support Ewell and Longstreet's third division, Maj. Gen. George Pickett's, expected to finally be on the field by morning, Lee intended to initiate the battle on the third in the same fashion as he had on the second—with attacks on the Union right and left. "The general plan," he later wrote, "was unchanged. Longstreet, reinforced by Pickett's three brigades . . . was ordered to attack the next morning, and General Ewell was directed to assail the enemy's right at the same time." During the night of

July 2–3, Ewell received orders from Lee "to renew my attack at daylight Friday morning" and promptly began taking steps to comply.[29]

Lee's belief that the course of action he had planned for July 3 had a chance of success rested on achieving a "proper concert of action" that had been lacking the previous day. Ewell did his part. Although he faced an extremely strong Federal position in his front, Ewell made a determined attempt to carry it early on July 3. Longstreet, however, on his own initiative, had taken measures to prepare for the move he had long been advocating, "renewing the attack by my right, with a view to pass around the hill occupied by the enemy on his left, and to gain it by a flank and reverse attack." Moreover, due in part to his preoccupation with this endeavor, Longstreet did not make the necessary arrangements to ensure Pickett's division would arrive on the field before daylight so it could carry out its part in Lee's plan for July 3. By the time Lee learned of these developments and that they would preclude Longstreet's making an attack simultaneous with Ewell's command, it was too late. The Second Corps was already engaged in a fierce battle for Culp's Hill that would end around 11:00 a.m. with the well-positioned Federals having bloodily repulsed Ewell's assault.[30]

In light of these developments, Lee altered his plan. Just as Longstreet was preparing to make his attempt to maneuver around the Union left, Lee arrived at his command post and told him that he now wished to make an attack against the Union center on Cemetery Ridge with Pickett's division, supported by the rest of the First Corps. Longstreet objected, but Lee would not be deterred. There was, as he saw it, no other viable option. Retreat from the battlefield remained unacceptable, while going over to the defensive would place too much control over the situation in the hands of the enemy and offered little prospect of bringing about the decisive success Lee needed in any case. Ewell's efforts that morning had proven the Union right was too strongly held for success to be hoped for there, while Longstreet's plan for moving around the Union left could not be undertaken without stretching the Army of Northern Virginia even more perilously thin and, given the disposition of the Union army at that time, was completely impractical in any case—although Longstreet did not see it this way.

Besides, it was not unreasonable to think that in order to blunt the furious attacks Longstreet and Ewell had made against his right and left over the past twenty-four hours, Meade might have weakened his center to the point that a successful assault might be possible. When it was clear that Lee's intention to attack was not to be put off, Longstreet objected that the two divisions from his corps that had been engaged on July 2 were exhausted and that if they were to attempt an attack along the lines Lee was proposing, their flank and rear would be exposed to fire from the Federals on Little Round Top. Lee then decided that those two divisions would not participate in the attack and Pickett would instead be assisted by a division and two brigades from Hill's corps that had been unengaged on July 2. Longstreet accepted this arrangement, but still thought, he wrote a few weeks later, "The distance to be passed over under the fire of the enemy's batteries, and in plain view, seemed too great to insure great results, particularly as two-thirds of the troops to be engaged in the assault had been in a severe battle two days previous." Despite his lieutenant's coolness to the whole scheme, Lee evidently had no reservations about placing responsibility for the preparation and execution of the assault in Longstreet's hands.[31]

Shortly after 1:00 p.m., Confederate gunners commenced the preliminary bombardment of the Union position. About two hours later, Longstreet reluctantly ordered the infantry forward and, as the First Corps commander had predicted, the charge proved to be an exercise in futility. A few hundred or so men managed to penetrate the Federal line, but they were too few to hold the position, and by 4:30, the survivors of the charge were falling back to Seminary Ridge. Lee rode out among them as they returned, comforting his men as he endeavored to rally them in case the Federals attempted a counterattack. "Form your ranks again," he called out to them, "when you get back to cover. We want all good men to hold together now. . . . It was all my fault this time." When a grief-stricken Pickett responded to Lee's efforts by stating, "I have no division now," the commanding general replied, "Come General Pickett, this has been my fight and upon my shoulders rests the blame." To one distraught brigade commander, Lee remarked, "Never mind, General, *all this has been* MY *fault*—it is *I* that have lost this fight, and you must help me out of it in the best way you can."[32]

Lee's fears that the Federals might attempt a major counterattack that evening proved unfounded. Elements from the Union Fifth and Sixth Corps advanced from their positions on the southern end of the field to drive off the units from Longstreet's command positioned there and reclaim ground that had been lost on July 2, but the day proved too far advanced and Meade was too prudent a commander to try to put together a major effort hastily. Nonetheless, it was clear on the night of July 3 that there was nothing more that the Army of Northern Virginia could hope to achieve at Gettysburg and, although the army had been so exhausted during the three days' fighting that a retreat back toward Virginia carried with it a great deal of danger, it simply could not stay north at Gettysburg. There was no choice but to retreat.

As if the events at Gettysburg were not bad enough, July 3 was also a day of gloom for the cause of Southern independence due to events in Mississippi and Tennessee that led one official in Richmond to proclaim in his diary on July 12, "This week just ended has been one of unexampled disaster since the war began." As Lee was learning that Longstreet's activities would preclude a simultaneous attack with Ewell's command during the morning of July 3, Bragg's command was retreating from Tullahoma and, most significantly, white flags were appearing over the Confederate works at Vicksburg. Shortly thereafter, as Lee was coming to his decision to instead attack the Union center, two of Pemberton's subordinates were riding forward from the Confederate lines carrying a message proposing an armistice to the two sides to negotiate the surrender of Vicksburg. After a contentious interview with Pemberton, Grant drafted terms for Vicksburg's surrender, and shortly after midnight he and Pemberton agreed that the latter would officially surrender the city and his army at ten that morning, ensuring that Independence Day 1863 would be a day of celebration for the North. When Lincoln learned of what had happened at Vicksburg, he exulted, "Now, if General Meade can complete his work, so gloriously prosecuted thus far, by the literal or substantial destruction of Lee's army, the rebellion will be over."[33]

Of course, all Lee could see before him on the night of July 3–4 was the peril his own army faced at Gettysburg. Consequently, after conferring with his subordinates at Hill's headquarters on the Cashtown Road he began preparations that evening for a retreat to the Potomac. The first step was to strengthen the army's line by shortening it. Consequently, orders went out to Ewell to pull back from his position in front of Cemetery Hill and Culp's Hill and link up with the left of the Third Corps on the ridges west of Gettysburg, while Longstreet was directed to pull his divisions back from their advanced positions south of town and link up with Hill's right. Lee also ordered the army's supply trains and wounded to be moved west to Cashtown, where on July 4 they were to meet up with cavalry units commanded by Brig. Gen. John Imboden that were to escort them to Williamsport. At Williamsport, they and the rest of the Army of Northern Virginia would cross the Potomac and then proceed to their final destination at Winchester. The plan for the entire movement to Williamsport was spelled out in orders Lee issued on July 4. Hill's corps would lead the march west from Gettysburg, proceeding on the evening of the fourth to the pass in South Mountain at Fairfield. Longstreet's corps, and then Ewell's, would follow and, after passing through Hill's position at the pass, go into bivouac west of the mountain. Ewell and Hill would "alternately take the front and rear" as the army moved from Cashtown and Fairfield down the Cumberland Valley to Hagerstown and Williamsport, with Stuart's cavalry screening the army's movements.[34]

As preparations for the retreat were underway, Lee also decided to prepare a quick report for President Davis of recent events. Despite his concession that "our own loss has not been light," Lee was decidedly circumspect in his report and hardly provided a fully accurate sense of the extent of the setback the army had suffered at Gettysburg or the extremely dangerous situation it was in on July 4. Lee described the battle at Gettysburg only in broad terms, and summed up the course and consequences of the three days of fighting by stating merely that "works on the enemy's extreme right and left were taken . . . his numbers were so great and his position so commanding, that our troops were compelled to relinquish their advantage and retire."[35]

Early in the afternoon of July 4 a heavy rain began to fall at Gettysburg that continued throughout the evening and well into the following morning. Although it made the movements to Fairfield and Cashtown slower, the bad weather did have the effect of dampening what little inclination Meade had for pushing forward vigorously from his position to see what the Confederates were up to. Consequently, the Army of Northern Virginia was able to successfully make its escape from Gettysburg, with the lead elements of its main body reaching Hagerstown by the afternoon of July 6. That same day, the members of Imboden's contingent arrived at Williamsport, but to their dismay the heavy rains of the past few days had raised the river to a point where an immediate crossing was impossible.[36]

By then the Federals had begun to stir. Meade understood that a pursuit would have to be undertaken, for not only did it make sense operationally, but the president would surely demand it. (And unbeknownst to Meade, he inadvertently aroused the president's usual anxiety on this point to a fever pitch by issuing an order to his army on July 4 congratulating it on its success and urging "greater efforts to drive from our soil every vestige of the presence of the invader.") Nonetheless, not wishing to follow "the bad example [Lee] had set me in ruining himself attacking a strong position," Meade was content on July 4 merely to push forward reconnaissances. The next morning, he learned of Lee's departure and responded by sending Maj. Gen. John Sedgwick's Sixth Corps, which was the largest corps in his army and had been lightly engaged at Gettysburg, directly in pursuit toward Fairfield Gap on the

Figure 3.3.   The Retreat from Gettysburg. Robert Underwood Johnson and Clarence Clough Buel, eds., *Battles and Leaders of the Civil War,* vol.
3 (New York: The Century Magazine, 1884–1888), 426

fifth, while cavalry probed the passes north and south of Fairfield. Although
the cavalry engaged in spirited skirmishes with the Confederates around
Monterey Pass to the south, when Sedgwick reached Fairfield, he found the
position too strong to be attacked.[37]

Meade responded by ordering Sedgwick to rejoin the rest of the Army of
the Potomac as it implemented the plan he developed to march south
through the Monocacy Valley toward Frederick and then turn west, cross
Catoctin Mountain, and advance to Middletown. As the Army of the Potomac moved south from Gettysburg, Meade instructed Maj. Gen. William
French, commander of the Union forces at Frederick that a week earlier had
been holding Harpers Ferry, to seize Turner's Gap in South Mountain so
Meade and the Army of the Potomac could use it to get at Lee's army in the
Cumberland Valley. To facilitate these movements and hinder Lee's, a cav-
alry division that had been sent back from Gettysburg to Westminster on July
2 to secure the Army of the Potomac's supply base would push through South
Mountain ahead of French to Hagerstown and Williamsport.[38]

During the afternoon of July 6, Federal cavalry units, the vanguard of Meade's
force, suddenly appeared just outside Williamsport. With Imboden and his command understanding that "if we did not repulse the enemy we should all be captured and General Lee's army be ruined by the loss of its transportation," they
put up a staunch defense that compelled the Federals to pull back. As Imboden
held off the Federal cavalry, Stuart arrived to assist his efforts. Once the Yankees
had been clearly repulsed, Stuart took his command to Hagerstown to join

Longstreet's corps, which had arrived that afternoon and gone into camp. There they were joined by Ewell's and Hill's commands the next day.[39]

In a letter to Davis from Hagerstown on July 7, Lee reported the arrival of the army "in the vicinity of this place" and once again explained his departure from Gettysburg. "Finding the enemy position too strong to be carried," he stated, "and being much hindered in collecting necessary supplies . . . I determined to withdraw to the west side of the mountains." Interestingly, while Lee made it clear that he intended to move his sick and wounded, as well as the Federal prisoners accompanying the army across the Potomac at Williamsport, he gave no indication that he intended to do more with the rest of the army than "withdraw to the west side of the mountains." This suggests he may still have been holding out some hope that his opportunity for achieving significant success north of the Potomac had not yet come to an end. It would not be surprising if this were in fact the case. After all, the previous September, it had been Lee's intention to reconcentrate his army at Hagerstown after the elimination of the garrisons at Martinsburg and Harpers Ferry and then draw the Federals into battle far from Washington in the Cumberland Valley. That plan, of course, had been upset by the fact that McClellan moved out of Washington far faster than expected and denied the Confederates any opportunity for a successful counterstroke. But now Lee was concentrated at Hagerstown, and if his army was bloodied and tired from the fighting at Gettysburg, so was Meade's. And it could be hoped that Meade might be compelled by Lincoln to push into the Cumberland Valley with greater haste than prudence, maybe even enough to create the kind of tactical opportunity the Federals had so generously offered on July 1.[40]

The first priority, however, was making sure that if the Army of Northern Virginia ended up retreating, it could do so safely. By the time the army reached Hagerstown, though, Lee advised Davis on the eighth, "a series of storms commencing the day after our entrance into Maryland" had placed the Potomac "beyond fording stage." To make matters worse, a storm that day ensured that it would be "so for at least a week." As a consequence, Lee stated, "I shall therefore have to accept battle if the enemy offers it, whether I wish to or not." Nonetheless, Lee also suggested in his message that he was not yet completely convinced that a retreat across the Potomac was necessary and urged the president to "understand that I am not in the least discouraged, or that my faith in the protection of an all merciful Providence, or in the fortitude of this army, is at all shaken." If the Federals decided they wanted another battle believing recent events would present them with a much-diminished foe, Lee was confident they would be in for a rude surprise. The condition of the Army of Northern Virginia, he advised Davis, "Though reduced in numbers by the hardships and battles through which it has passed since leaving the Rappahannock . . . is good and its confidence [is] unimpaired."[41]

Nonetheless, the ability of the army to get across the Potomac remained compromised by high waters that continued to render the river unfordable. Moreover, the pontoon bridge Ewell's men laid down a few miles downstream from Williamsport at Falling Waters in mid-June had been wrecked on July 4 by an enterprising detachment of cavalry from French's command. Consequently, as he awaited the arrival of Meade's army in the Cumberland Valley, Lee dispatched orders to his engineer battalion on July 10 to go to Falling Waters to oversee the reconstruction of the pontoon bridge. During the two days prior to this, Lee devoted much of his attention to preparing for Meade's arrival, spending most of his time on July 8 and 9 conferring with his staff and corps commanders and conducting an extensive reconnaissance of the area with them. Based on his observations and discussions with his subordinates, Lee decided to establish a defensive position that began west of Hagerstown and ran south along Salisbury Ridge to the Potomac and covered the river crossings at Williamsport and Falling Waters. With Lee playing an active supervisory role, on July 9 several staff officers went to work laying out a strong line.[42]

Fortunately, the enemy would give Lee time to complete this work. Although exhausted from the stress of assuming command barely a week before and fighting off the Confederates at Gettysburg, hampered by the fact that the Army of Northern Virginia's high command had left Gettysburg unscathed while his own had been devastated (one of his two most trusted corps commanders was dead, the other seriously wounded, as was another corps commander), and understandably anxious not to do anything to put at risk what had already been accomplished, Meade moved with admirable dispatch from Gettysburg. By nightfall on July 8, he had established his headquarters at Middletown, had two corps at Turner's Gap in South Mountain, and the following day, as Lee and his subordinates prepared their line on Salisbury Ridge, pushed a significant force over South Mountain. From there, Meade advised Halleck he intended to "move on a line from Boonsborough toward the center of the [enemy's] line from Hagerstown to Williamsport, my left flank looking to the river and my right toward the mountains."[43]

On July 10, as Meade continued pushing his army across South Mountain, Lee reported to Davis that, although almost finished ferrying the wounded and prisoners across, the Potomac remained "past fording." He also complained that he did not have any "definite intelligence of the movements or designs of the enemy." Lee then proceeded to demonstrate how inadequate the intelligence he was receiving was by stating that reports indicated only that the Federals were "reported as moving by way of Frederick . . . as if approaching in this direction"—information that was well out of date. Nonetheless, Lee deduced that it was "the intention of the enemy to deliver battle." If this were in fact true, he reported that he would have no choice "but to accept it," but once again assured Davis that although it was having trouble securing food, the Army of Northern Virginia was "in good condition, and we have a good supply of ammunition."[44]

Two days later the Army of the Potomac arrived in front of Salisbury Ridge. Fortunately, by this time Lee had finished work fortifying his position on the ridge, with Ewell's corps posted on the left, Hill's in the center, and Longstreet's on the right. Below Salisbury Ridge, the lowlands over which the Federals would have to advance if they were to make an attack had been transformed by the rains of the past few weeks into deep and muddy bogs. As they completed the line at Salisbury Ridge, Lee's men eagerly hoped the near future would bring another clash with the Army of the Potomac, this time with the roles of attacker and defender reversed. Ewell found, upon finishing work on their segment of the line, his soldiers' "spirit was never better . . . and the wish was universal that the enemy would attack." "Oh!" one officer later lamented, "how we all did wish that the enemy would come out in the open & attack us, as we had done them at Gettysburg."[45]

However much Lee may have himself been eager for another fight north of the Potomac, the time he had available to wait at Williamsport was severely limited because, as he advised Davis on July 12, "in our restricted limits the means of obtaining subsistence is becoming precarious." His only hope was that pressure from Washington would induce an otherwise prudent Meade to make a hasty, ill-prepared attack, rather than taking the time to fully exploit what Lee described as "the power he possesses of accumulating troops." If Meade were to do this, Lee advised Davis, "I should be willing to await his attack. . . . The army is in good condition and occupies a strong position."[46]

It would have come as no surprise to Lee that Meade was in fact under incredible pressure from Washington to throw his army at the Confederates at Williamsport. Lincoln's anger at Meade's congratulatory order pledging to drive the enemy "from our soil" was fully impressed upon Halleck, who urged Meade not to let the Confederates escape back into Virginia. Shortly after his men arrived in front of Salisbury Ridge on July 12, Meade informed Halleck he intended to attack the next day. The following day, however, Meade had second thoughts, further demonstrating that Lee had been correct in his assessment of him as a general who was unlikely to commit the kind of errors the Confederacy needed in order to achieve victories. Meade called to-gether his corps commanders and solicited their opinion as to the wisdom of an attack. "Five of the six," Meade later advised Halleck, "were unquali-fiedly opposed." Consequently, he told the general-in-chief that he had de-cided to conduct a more thorough "examination of the enemy's position, strength, and works. . . . with the expectation of finding some weak point, upon which . . . I shall hazard an attack." Lincoln by this point was beside himself with anxiety that what he perceived as a golden opportunity would be missed. His success at impressing his concerns upon Halleck was evident in the general-in-chief's brusque response to Meade on the evening of July 13. "You are strong enough to attack and defeat the enemy before he can ef-fect a crossing," Halleck insisted and bluntly directed Meade, "Call no council of war. It is proverbial that councils of war never fight. . . . Do not let the enemy escape."[47]

As Meade cautiously reconnoitered the Confederate line on July 13, mak-ing it clear that if he was going to make an attack it would be carefully pre-pared, Lee decided he could "await an attack no longer." That day, the bridge at Falling Waters had been completed, the river had finally dropped enough at Williamsport to be fordable, and sufficient boats were now available to fa-cilitate a crossing. Moreover, with his army pinned against the Potomac, there was the possibility that, instead of making a direct attack on Salisbury Ridge, the Federals might push into Virginia somewhere lower on the Po-tomac and turn Lee's position. These factors, as well as the difficulty he was having procuring sustenance for his troops in their fixed position, led Lee to conclude on July 13 that nothing more could be accomplished north of the Potomac. Late in the afternoon he directed Stuart to position his cavalry so they could occupy the defenses along Salisbury Ridge and cover the with-drawal of Ewell's corps to the fords at Williamsport and of Longstreet's and Hill's to the bridge at Falling Waters.[48]

As Meade prepared to advance a strong reconnaissance in force at 7:00 a.m. on the fourteenth, employing four of his corps, the Army of Northern Virginia spent the stormy night of July 13–14 evacuating their defenses and moving to the Potomac. "It was another awful night," one officer later wrote, "groping and pulling through the mud, a few feet at a time . . . marching all night in awful roads, in mud and dark, and in hard rain." By 8:00 a.m. on the fourteenth, Ewell was across, but the large number of vehicles that could only cross at the bridge prevented Longstreet from completing his crossing before nine. He was then followed across by Hill, who prior to reaching the river made a point of posting a division a little over a mile from the bridge to serve as a rear guard. Shortly before noon, there was a brief skirmish between this

force and some Federal cavalry at Falling Waters in which a brigade commander was mortally wounded and a few hundred members of the rear guard
were captured, but otherwise the entire Army of Northern Virginia was back
on the Virginia shore of the Potomac by 1:00 p.m. Of the approximately seventy-five thousand men Lee had led across the Potomac, more than twenty-
seven thousand had fallen in the course of the campaign, while Federal losses
came to about thirty thousand.[49]

Once his army was back in Virginia, Lee issued orders directing it to continue
its march southward. Hill's and Longstreet's commands, he directed, would
commence their march early on the fifteenth, move up the Shenandoah Valley to Mill Creek, and go into camp on either side of the village of Bunker
Hill, while Ewell's followed and halted its march a few miles north at the
hamlet of Darkesville. Upon reaching Bunker Hill and establishing headquarters there on the fifteenth, Lee sat down to write a letter to his wife.
"The army has returned to Virginia," he informed her, "rather sooner than I
had originally contemplated, but having accomplished what I purposed on
leaving the Rappahannock, viz., relieving the Valley of the presence of the
enemy and drawing his army north of the Potomac. . . . I hope we will yet be
able to damage our adversaries when they meet us and all will go right. . . .
We are all well."[50]

Lee was undoubtedly sincere in the assessment he provided his wife. Yet
even he had to understand that his effort to carry the war into Pennsylvania
had failed to do anything to arrest the unmistakable decline in Southern fortunes that had made it necessary. Only a loss of Northern will to continue the
war could save the Confederacy in 1863, and the only way to bring this about
was to achieve decisive success on the battlefield. Lee went into Pennsylvania
in order to feed the only army that so far had demonstrated an ability to
achieve those successes and in search of an opportunity for another, understanding that this course of action also carried with it the risk of placing the
Army of Northern Virginia in a situation where there was not only a real
prospect of a tactical or operational setback, but of an outright catastrophe.
(Indeed, when the risks the Confederate army ran during Gettysburg Campaign came up in a postwar conversation with Lee, one man recalled being told
by the general that: "Everything was risky in our war. He knew oftentimes that
he was playing a very bold game, but it was the only *possible* one."[51]) It only required prudent management and good sense on the Federal side to make the
odds against Lee achieving the sort of victory he needed insurmountable,

which Hooker and Meade provided. By doing so, they not only denied Lee any opportunity to achieve the victory on which his hopes for arresting the inexorable decline in the South's military fortunes rested, but also significantly hastened the fall of the Confederacy.

Notes

1. In addition to Coddington, *Gettysburg Campaign*, 153–574; Sears, *Gettysburg*, 123–508; Woodworth, *Beneath a Northern Sky*, 36–219, Bowden and Ward, *Last Chance for Victory*, 140–525, and the works cited in the bibliographic essay and notes below, the treatment of the events covered by this chapter has been influenced by Brooks D. Simpson's insightful essay, "'If Properly Led': Command Relationships at Gettysburg," in *Civil War Generals in Defeat*, edited by Steven E. Woodworth (Lawrence: University Press of Kansas, 1999), 161–89, 228–30.

2. Marshall, *Lee's Aide-de-Camp*, 218; Ewell to Chilton, ——, 1863, OR, vol. 27, pt. 1: 443; Early to Pendleton, August 22, 1863, ibid., 466.

3. Marshall, *Lee's Aide-de-Camp*, 218–19; Lee to Cooper, July 31, 1864, OR, vol. 27, pt. 2: 307; James Longstreet, "Lee's Invasion of Pennsylvania," *Battles and Leaders*, vol. 3: 249–50.

4. Lee to Cooper, January 20, 1864, in *Wartime Papers*, eds. Dowdey and Manarin, 574; Lee to Ewell, June [29], 1863, ibid., 534–35.

5. George Cary Eggleston, *A Rebel's Recollections* (Cambridge: The Riverside Press, 1875), 145–46.

6. Halleck to Meade, June 27, 1863, OR, vol. 27, pt. 1: 61; Meade to Halleck, June 28, 1863, ibid., 61–62.

7. Meade to Halleck, June 28, 29, 1863, ibid., 64–65, 66–67; Halleck to Meade, June 27, 28, 1863, ibid., 61, 63; Meade to Thomas, October 1, 1863, ibid., vol. 27, pt. 1: 114.

8. Rodes to Pendleton, ——, 1863, ibid., pt. 1: 552; Early to Pendleton, August 22, 1863, ibid., 467–68; Johnson to Pendleton, September 20, 1863, ibid., 503; Hill to Chilton, November ——, 1863, ibid., 606–07; Longstreet to Chilton, July 27, 1863, ibid., 358; Freeman, *R.E. Lee*, vol. 3: 62–63.

9. Heth to Starke, September 13, 1863, OR, vol. 27, pt. 1: 637; Hill to Chilton, November ——, 1863, ibid., 607; Ewell to Chilton, ——, 1863, ibid., 444; Early to Pendleton, August 22, 1863, ibid., 467–68.

10. Hill to Chilton, November ——, 1863, ibid., 607; Heth to Jones, June 1877, *SHSP*, vol. 4: 157.

11. Stanton to Meade, June 30, 1863, OR, vol. 27, pt 3: 69; Orders, Hdqrs. Army of the Potomac, June 30, 1863, ibid., vol. 27, pt. 1: 416; Circular, Hdqrs. Army of the Potomac, June 30, 1863, ibid., 416–17; Meade to Halleck, July 1, 1863, ibid., 71; Circular. Hdqrs. Army of the Potomac, July 1, 1863, ibid., pt. 3: 458–49; Henry J. Hunt, "The First Day at Gettysburg," *Battles and Leaders*, vol. 3: 274.

12. The first day of battle at Gettysburg on July 1 is exhaustively chronicled in David G. Martin, Gettysburg, July 1 (Conshohocken, PA: Combined Books, 1995), and Harry W. Pfanz, Gettysburg—The First Day (Chapel Hill: University of North Carolina Press, 2001). The essays in Gary W. Gallagher, ed., The First Day at Gettysburg: Essays on Confederate and Union Leadership (Kent, OH: Kent State University Press, 1992) offer excellent accounts and analysis of particular aspects of the day's events, although Alan T. Nolan's essay on "R.E. Lee and July 1 at Gettysburg," (1–29, 144–46), while it raises a number of good points, is characterized by an excessively harsh assessment of Lee, his generalship on July 1, and his decisions leading up to the battle. Walter H. Taylor Paper, September 1877, SHSP, vol. 4: 126; Freeman, R.E. Lee, vol. 3: 66–67.

13. Ewell to Chilton, ———, 1863, OR, vol. 27, pt. 2: 444.

14. Terry L. Jones, ed., Campbell Brown's Civil War: With Ewell and the Army of Northern Virginia (Baton Rouge: Louisiana State University, 2001), 204-05; Sears, Gettysburg, 184–85; Ewell to Chilton, ———, 1863, OR, vol. 27, pt. 2: 444.

15. Ewell to Chilton, ———, 1863, ibid., 444; Freeman, R.E. Lee, vol. 3: 68–70; Henry Heth, The Memoirs of Henry Heth, edited by James L. Morrison (Westport, CT: Greenwood Press, 1974), 175.

16. Lee to Cooper, January 20, 1864, in Wartime Papers, eds. Dowdey and Manarin, 576; Arthur J.L. Fremantle, Three Months in the Southern States: April–June, 1863 (New York: John Bradburn, 1864), 254–56; Hill to Chilton, November 1863, OR, vol. 27, pt. 2: 607.

17. Lee to Cooper, January 20, 1864, in Wartime Papers, eds. Dowdey and Manarin, 576; Gary W. Gallagher, "Confederate Corps Leadership on the First Day at Gettysburg: A.P. Hill and Richard S. Ewell in a Difficult Debut," in The First Day at Gettysburg, ed. Gallagher, 45–47.

18. Longstreet, "Lee in Pennsylvania," 421.

19. Gary W. Gallagher offers an excellent focused examination of Lee's thinking as he determined whether to resume the offensive the evening of July 1, the factors that shaped it, and historical opinion on the matter in "'If the Enemy Is There, We Must Attack Him': R.E. Lee and the Second Day at Gettysburg," in The Second Day at Gettysburg: Essays on Confederate and Union Leadership, edited by Gary W. Gallagher (Kent, OH: Kent State University Press, 1993), 1–32.

20. Sears, Gettysburg, 252–57; Freeman, R.E. Lee, vol. 3: 86–92; Lee to Chilton, January 1864, in Wartime Papers, eds. Dowdey and Manarin, 577.

21. Jay Luvaas, "A Prussian Observer with Lee," Military Affairs 21 (Fall 1957): 108.

22. Meade to Thomas, October 1, 1863, OR, vol. 27, pt. 1: 114–15.

23. Fremantle, Three Months in the Southern States, 259–60. Excellent examinations of particular aspects of the second day of battle at Gettysburg are provided in Gallagher, ed., The Second Day at Gettysburg, while definitive treatments of the fighting on both ends of the field on July 2 can be found in Harry W. Pfanz, Gettysburg—The Second Day (Chapel Hill: University of North Carolina Press, 1987); and Gettysburg—Culp's Hill

and Cemetery Hill (Chapel Hill: University of North Carolina Press, 1993). Troy D. Harman offers a provocative analysis of Lee's conduct of the battle on July 2 and 3 in *Lee's Real Plan at Gettysburg* (Mechanicsburg, PA: Stackpole Books, 2003).

24. Meade to French, July 3, 1863, OR, vol. 27, pt. 3: 501; Meade to Couch, July 3, 1863, ibid., 502

25. Jones to McClellan, July 30, 1864, ibid., pt. 2: 752.

26. Stuart to Chilton, August 20, 1863, OR, vol. 27, pt. 2: 692–97; Lee to Cooper, January 20, 1864, in *Wartime Papers*, eds. Dowdey and Manarin, 580.

27. Bowden and Ward, *Last Chance for Victory*, 422–23; Stuart to Chilton, August 20, 1863, OR, vol. 27, pt. 2: 697.

28. W.W. Blackford, *War Years with Jeb Stuart* (New York: Charles Scribner's Sons, 1945), 230–31.

29. Lee to Cooper, January 20, 1864, in *Wartime Papers*, eds. Dowdey and Manarin, 578–79; Ewell to Chilton, ———, 1863, OR, vol. 27, pt. 2: 447.

30. Lee to Cooper, January 20, 1864, in *Wartime Papers*, eds. Dowdey and Manarin, 578–79; Longstreet to Chilton, July 27, 1863, OR, vol. 27, pt. 2: 359; Ewell to Chilton, ———, 1863, ibid., 447–48. Jeffry D. Wert, *Gettysburg: The Third Day* (New York: Simon & Schuster, 2001), offers a full account of July 3 at Gettysburg, while there is also much of value in the essays in Gary W. Gallagher, ed., *The Third Day at Gettysburg and Beyond* (Chapel Hill: University of North Carolina Press, 1994).

31. Lee to Cooper, January 20, 1864, in *Wartime Papers*, eds. Dowdey and Manarin, 578–79; Longstreet to Chilton, July 27, 1863, OR, vol. 27, pt. 2: 359.

32. Alexander, *Fighting for the Confederacy*, 266; Freeman, *R.E. Lee*, 129–30; Fremantle, *Three Months in the Southern States*, 267–69. Earl J. Hess, *Pickett's Charge: The Last Attack at Gettysburg* (Chapel Hill: University of North Carolina Press, 2001) is the most recent and fullest account of the grand charge.

33. Robert G.H. Kean, *Inside the Confederate Government: The Diary of Robert Garlick Hill Kean*, edited by Edward Younger (New York: Oxford University Press, 1957), 79; Ulysses S. Grant, *Personal Memoirs of U.S. Grant* (1885; Lincoln: University of Nebraska Press, 1996), 327–33; Lincoln to Halleck, [July 7, 1863], in *Works of Lincoln*, ed. Basler, vol. 6: 319.

34. Ewell to Chilton, ———, 1863, OR, vol. 27, pt. 2: 448; Longstreet to Chilton, July 27, 1863, ibid., 360; Hotchkiss, *Make Me a Map of the Valley*, 157–58; Lee to Imboden, July 4, 1863, in *Wartime Papers*, eds. Dowdey and Manarin, 537–38; Hdqrs. Army of Northern Virginia, General Orders No. 74, ibid., 539–40. The authoritative account of operations from Gettysburg to Williamsport and Falling Waters is Brown's wonderfully detailed *Retreat from Gettysburg*.

35. Lee to Davis, July 4, 1863, in *Wartime Papers*, eds. Dowdey and Manarin, 538–39.

36. Lee to Cooper, January 20, 1864, ibid., 581–82.

37. Hdqrs. Army of the Potomac, July 4, 1863, OR, vol. 27, pt 3: 519; Lincoln to Halleck, July 6, 1863, ibid., 567; Meade to Smith, July 5, 1863, ibid., 539; Meade to Thomas, October 1, 1863, ibid., pt. 1: 117–18.

38. Circular, Hdqrs. Army of the Potomac, July 5, 1863, ibid., pt. 3: 532; Meade to Halleck, July 6, 1863, ibid., pt. 1: 80–81; Meade to Thomas, October 1, 1863, ibid., 117–18.

39. John D. Imboden, "The Confederate Retreat from Gettysburg," *Battles and Leaders*, vol. 3: 426–28; Stuart to Chilton, August 30, 1863, OR, vol. 27, pt. 2: 701–03; Longstreet to Chilton, July 27, 1863, ibid., 361; Ewell to Chilton, ——, 1863, ibid., 448; Hill to Chilton, November ——, 1863, ibid., 609.

40. Lee to Davis, July 7, 1863, in *Wartime Papers*, eds. Dowdey and Manarin, 541.

41. Lee to Davis, July 8, 1863, ibid., 543–44.

42. French to Williams, October 1, 1863, OR, vol. 27, pt. 1: 489; Hotchkiss, *Make Me a Map*, 159–60; Brown, *Retreat from Gettysburg*, 287, 293–95, 320–22.

43. Itinerary of the Army of the Potomac and co-operating forces, June 5–July 31, 1863, OR, vol. 27, pt. 1: 145–46; Meade to Halleck, July 9, 1863, ibid., 86–87.

44. Lee to Davis, July 10, 1863, in *Wartime Papers*, eds. Dowdey and Manarin, 545–46.

45. Meade to Thomas, October 1, 1863, OR, vol. 27, pt. 1: 118; Ewell to Chilton, ——, 1863, ibid., pt. 2: 448; Edward Porter Alexander, *Fighting for the Confederacy: The Personal Recollections of General Edward Porter Alexander*, edited by Gary W. Gallagher (Chapel Hill: University of North Carolina Press, 1989), 271.

46. Lee to Davis, July 12, 1863, in *Wartime Papers*, eds. Dowdey and Manarin, 548.

47. John Hay, *Inside Lincoln's White House: The Complete Civil War Diary of John Hay*, edited by Michael Burlingame and John R. Turner Ettlinger (Carbondale: Southern Illinois University Press, 1997), 61–62; Meade to Halleck, July 12, 13, 1863, OR, vol. 27, pt. 1: 91–92; Halleck to Meade, July 13, 1863, ibid., 92.

48. Lee to Cooper, January 20, 1864, in *Wartime Papers*, eds. Dowdey and Manarin, 582; Lee to Stuart, July 13, 1863, ibid., 549–50.

49. Circular, Hdqrs. Army of the Potomac, July 13, 1863, OR, vol. 27, pt. 3: 675; Meade to Thomas, October 1, 1863, ibid., pt. 1: 118; Alexander, *Fighting for the Confederacy*, 272; Lee to Cooper, January 20, 1864, in *Wartime Papers*, eds. Dowdey and Manarin, 582–83; Ewell to Chilton, ——, 1863, OR, vol. 27, pt. 2: 449; Longstreet to Chilton, July 27, 1863, ibid., 361–62; Hill to Chilton, November 1863, ibid., 609.

50. Circular, Hdqrs. Army of Northern Virginia, July 14, 1863, in *Wartime Papers*, eds. Dowdey and Manarin, 582–83; Lee to his wife, July 15, 1861, ibid., 551.

51. Allan, "Memoranda," 17.

CHAPTER FOUR

Waltzing with General Meade

Although he had managed to get safely across the Potomac and felt secure enough at Bunker Hill to proclaim the Army of Northern Virginia "all well," in fact Lee and his army were by no means out of danger on July 15, 1863. By moving up the Shenandoah Valley to Bunker Hill, Lee left the Loudoun Valley east of the Blue Ridge open to the Army of the Potomac. By pushing into the Loudoun Valley, Meade could cover Washington and possibly cut the Army of Northern Virginia off from Richmond by seizing the passes in the Blue Ridge. Recognizing that a move into the Loudoun Valley might enable him to satisfy his superiors' demands to inflict further damage on the rebels, Meade moved promptly, albeit with his usual prudent good sense, to do so.

The week-long race for the Blue Ridge passes that ensued proved to be the opening phase of a season of campaigning that would see much marching and maneuvering, but relatively little actual fighting. This was to Lee's short-term operational advantage, as it facilitated his efforts to repair as best he could the heavy damage his army had suffered during the first seven months of 1863. Strategically, however, Lee understood that time remained his enemy. Nothing had occurred to change the fact that the Confederacy had reached the point where losses in manpower and material could never be fully made up, while the enemy not only was able to do this, but growing stronger every day. Although acutely aware of the need to conserve the South's military resources, with the odds against Confederate success growing longer every day, Lee still deemed a defensive mind-set and seeking only to maintain an operational stalemate unacceptable.

Only by maintaining the initiative and an aggressive mind-set, Lee believed, could he avoid getting caught in another Chancellorsville or Gettysburg-type set-piece engagement that, regardless of its tactical results, would inflict losses in manpower and material he could not afford. By employing maneuver and remaining aggressive in the late summer and fall of 1863, Lee hoped he could induce his Federal counterpart to make mistakes and place his army in disadvantageous operational and tactical situations that would make it possible for the Army of Northern Virginia to achieve significant successes without exhausting itself in the process. This would allow Lee to preserve his own resources, and thus slow the arrival of the day where Northern material superiority became in itself decisive. Moreover, only by such a course of action did Lee believe he could negate whatever negative effects the events of July 1863 might have had on Southern morale, and depress Northern morale to the point that the effects of defeats at Gettysburg and elsewhere would be nullified. As if the challenge Lee faced after Gettysburg of husbanding his resources while also trying to create and seize opportunities for operational and tactical success in Virginia were not enough, during the second half of 1863 his efforts would be complicated as they had never been before by events in the West.

This new phase of the war certainly opened inauspiciously for the Army of Northern Virginia, for in the week after Williamsport, prudent, methodical George Meade very nearly stole a march on Robert E. Lee. Within twenty-four hours after finding Lee had evacuated his defenses at Williamsport and returned to Virginia, Meade had his army moving east toward and through South Mountain and was soon pushing across the Potomac at Sandy Hook and Berlin into the Loudoun Valley. Just as McClellan had the previous November, Meade intended to advance roughly in two wings south through the Loudoun Valley toward the Manassas Gap Railroad, with its right wing and cavalry attempting to seize the gaps in the Blue Ridge, and then toward Warrenton and Culpeper. By nightfall on July 18, Meade had four corps across the Potomac with one division of cavalry having seized Snicker's Gap and another under orders to push south on the nineteenth and "take possession of the gaps as far as Chester Gap."[1]

While Meade was moving into the Loudoun Valley, Lee was learning of the fall of Vicksburg and informing President Davis on July 16 of his intention to rest his army at Bunker Hill. "I learn that the enemy has thrown a pontoon bridge over the Potomac at Harper's Ferry." He added, "Should he follow us in this direction, I shall lead him up the Valley and endeavor to attack him as far from his base as possible. . . . The men are in good health and spirits, but want shoes and clothing badly. I have sent back to endeavor to procure a supply of both, and also horseshoes. . . . As soon as these necessary articles are obtained we shall be prepared to resume operations." Two days later, though, reports reached Lee that the Federals were in the Loudoun Valley, had seized Snicker's Gap, and were moving to take Ashby's Gap. Lee responded by asking Stuart to find out whether in fact the Federals were at the gaps and if so, "the exact condition of things, whether this force is simply cavalry, or whether the enemy's infantry is moving in that direction." If these reports were true, Lee understood that he was in real danger, for if Meade got possession of the gaps in the Blue Ridge he could seal up the Army of Northern Virginia in the Shenandoah Valley and cut its communications with Richmond.[2]

On July 19, as Meade finished crossing the Potomac, Lee determined he had no choice but to resume operations even though the task of resupplying his army at Bunker Hill had not been completed. He ordered Longstreet to take his corps to Millwood, located just west of Ashby's Gap, and then "should nothing occur to arrest your progress or render it advisable for you to . . . occupy Ashby's Gap, I request you to proceed next day to Front Royal, cross the mountains at Chester Gap and take some position at the headwaters of the Rappahannock." Hill's corps would follow on the twenty-first to join Longstreet, unless it appeared the enemy was advancing directly on Richmond, in which case Lee instructed Longstreet he was to push east and establish a position behind the Rapidan River.[3]

Longstreet left Bunker Hill early on the twentieth and reached Millwood, only to find that the Federals had secured Ashby's Gap and advanced through it to the Shenandoah River. Longstreet immediately reported this to Lee and marched south the following day, hoping he could reach Manassas and Chester Gaps before the Federals. Meanwhile, Lee instructed Ewell on July 20 to move south toward Berryville and Millwood and "be prepared to vacate the Valley if pressed by superior numbers or to join me as circumstances may require." In his letter to Ewell, Lee also expressed concern that his route to Chester Gap might be cut off and laid out an alternate route through the Blue Ridge should that happen. Recognizing the importance of his mission, though, Longstreet marched to Front Royal on the twenty-first and pushed his lead brigade across the Shenandoah River to secure the gaps. When they reached the Blue Ridge, Longstreet's men found Union forces at

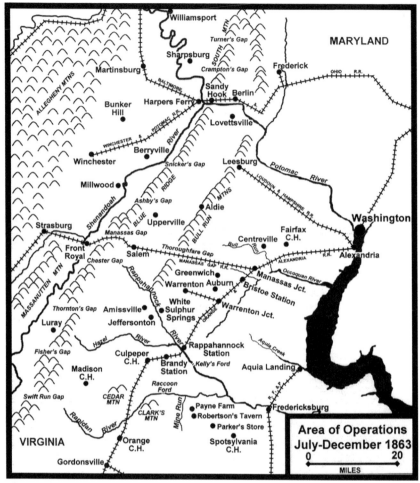

Figure 4.1.   Area of Operations.

Manassas Gap that were too strong to be driven off but not strong enough that they could not be contained, while managing to secure Chester Gap just before the Federals arrived.[4]

By that point, Meade had pushed a substantial portion of his army nearly to the Manassas Gap Railroad at the southern end of the Loudoun Valley, was aware that Lee was moving up the Shenandoah Valley, and was determined to do all he could to complicate Confederate efforts to push through the Blue Ridge. On July 22 Meade ordered Maj. Gen. William H. French's corps to link up with a contingent of cavalry that had secured Manassas Gap the day before. Shortly before midnight, French's lead division arrived at the gap but found a division from Longstreet's corps blocking a push into the Shenandoah Valley. The rest of French's command arrived on the morning of the twenty-third, but not before a brigade from Hill's corps had arrived at Manassas Gap to take the place of Longstreet's men and allow the First Corps to push through Chester Gap, safe passage through which had been secured by the dispersal of the Union cavalry at its eastern exit the previous day.[5]

Fortunately for Hill's men, by the time French managed to get his command organized for an attack, two divisions from Ewell's corps reached Manassas Gap after making an ill-conceived attempt, ordered by Lee, to destroy a small Federal force defending the section of the Baltimore and Ohio Railroad that passed through the Shenandoah Valley. Hill's and Ewell's men then spent much of July 23 fighting off determined attacks by French that ended at nightfall with the Federals too exhausted to push through the gap. Meanwhile, Longstreet's corps moved through Chester Gap toward Culpeper Court House, which it reached at noon on the twenty-fourth. That day Hill's command resumed its march toward Culpeper, while Ewell, believing the entire Army of the Potomac would soon be in front of him, ordered his two divisions at Manassas Gap to pull back to Front Royal. From there, he determined it would not be prudent, given the proximity of Meade's army, to follow Hill and Longstreet through Chester Gap and directed the two divisions at Front Royal to march south up the Page Valley to Thornton's Gap. Ewell ordered his other division, which was then at Winchester and "much jaded" as a result of the fruitless lunge after the Federals on the twenty-second, to move up the Shenandoah Valley from Winchester, cross Massanutten Mountain at New Market Gap, and then move across Page Valley to Fisher's Gap in the Blue Ridge. Once they had passed through the Blue Ridge, Ewell directed his command to reassemble at Madison Court House, a task that was completed by July 29.[6]

Lee himself had reached Culpeper five days earlier with Longstreet's command and advised Richmond of his decision to abandon the Shenandoah Valley and his intention "if practicable, to give the army a few days' rest." Then, while awaiting the completion of his army's movements through the Blue Ridge, he took advantage of the pause at Culpeper to respond to letters from family members in which his growing concern regarding the enemy's material superiority was clear. He complained to his wife that "our enemies . . . pleasure seems to be to injure, harass and annoy us as much as their extensive means enable them" and confided to her and a cousin, "I knew that crossing the Potomac would draw them off, and if we could only have been strong enough we should have detained them. But God willed otherwise." "The army," he added, "did all it could. I fear

I required of it impossibilities. But it responded to the call nobly and cheerfully, and though it did not win a victory it conquered a success. We must now prepare for harder blows and harder work."[7]

As the last of Ewell's command finished their march to Madison Court House on the twenty-ninth, Lee wrote again to Davis to report that scouts had determined that Meade was concentrating his army around Warrenton and that the Federal army had been "much reduced in numbers." Based on these reports and Meade's "feeble operations since" Gettysburg, Lee advised Davis that, "although our loss has been heavy . . . I believe the damage to the enemy has been as great in proportion." Nonetheless, he remained concerned that "their means are greater than ours and . . . when they move again they will much outnumber us." As to what Meade's intentions were, Lee could not discern what they were, but doubted they included taking the Army of the Potomac to Fredericksburg. If he did, Lee stated he did not think the proper move would be to take up again the Army of Northern Virginia's former positions "in rear of Fredericksburg, as any battle fought there excepting to resist a front attack would be on disadvantageous terms, and I therefore think it better to take a position farther back."[8]

Meade had indeed concentrated his army at Warrenton but, although thwarted in his attempt to trap Lee in the Valley, was by no means ready to end his push south. On July 28, he informed Halleck that he was planning to cross the Rappahannock, then advance along the Orange and Alexandria Railroad toward Culpeper "and as far beyond as the enemy's position will permit." On August 1, a division of Federal cavalry commanded by Brig. Gen. John Buford crossed the river at Rappahannock Station and managed to drive Stuart's cavalry back until it was within two miles of Culpeper. At that point, though, Buford encountered infantry from Hill's corps that Lee had ordered to Stuart's assistance and decided to pull back beyond Brandy Station to a point where he could be supported by infantry that had followed him across the Rappahannock.[9]

The Federals were content on August 2 to maintain the bridgehead they had secured over the Rappahannock, while Lee spent the day trying to determine whether Buford's activities were the prelude to an advance on Gordonsville or merely intended to cover a rumored movement to Fredericksburg. Lee also received a message that day from Davis suggesting, "it would seem to me more advisable to take a position farther to the rear. . . . [M]y recollection of the topography is that a strong position may be taken on the south side of the Rapidan, where this bank commands." With Davis's counsel in mind, unable to find "any field in Culpeper offering advantages for battle," and wishing to put his army in a position from which it could respond to a Federal advance against Gordonsville or Fredericksburg quickly, Lee concluded he had no choice but "to unite the army south of the Rapidan." On August 3, he ordered Longstreet and Hill to leave Culpeper and cross to the south side of the Rapidan. The following day, the three corps of the Army of Northern Virginia were finally reunited behind the Rapidan.[10]

Meade would not actually press forward to occupy Culpeper for several weeks, leaving the area between the Rappahannock and Rapidan to Stuart's cavalry. His hesitance to push further south was motivated in large part by a lack of confidence in the logistical network upon which such a move would be dependent. Indeed, when he initially advised Washington of his intention to cross the Rappahannock in July, he proclaimed that such a move would "test the question which has been raised of the capacity of the Orange and Alexandria Railroad to supply the army and the practicability of maintaining open such a long line of communications." As if this were not enough, during this time Meade was also compelled to send a significant contingent of troops north to New York to help restore order to the city after it experienced three days of horrible riots in mid-July that were fueled by outrage over the draft. This development and the concurrent expiration of many short-term enlistments eroded the strength of the Army of the Potomac to the point that Lincoln asked Halleck to make it clear to Meade that the administration was not pushing him to seek a "general engagement" with the Confederates and recognized that if "he could not safely engage Lee at Williamsport, it seems absurd to suppose he can safely engage him now, when he has scarcely more than two thirds of the force he had at Williamsport."[11]

As the Army of Northern Virginia settled into its positions behind the Rapidan, an exhausted Lee sent a message to Davis on August 8. Clearly shaken by the setback in Pennsylvania and the tense weeks in which he had barely kept one step ahead of disaster, Lee proposed to "Your Excellency the propriety of selecting another commander for this army." He lamented that he had "seen and heard of expression of discontent in the public journals at the result of the expedition [into Pennsylvania]" and that although he had not detected any discontent within the army, he presumed it did exist and that "no matter what may be the ability of the officer, if he loses the confidence of his troops disaster must sooner or later come." Lee also reported, "I sensibly feel the growing failure of my bodily strength. I have not yet recovered from the attack I experienced in the spring . . . and am prevented from making the personal examinations and giving the personal supervision to the operations in the field which I feel to be necessary. I am so dull that in making use of the eyes of others I am frequently misled. Everything, therefore points to advantages to be derived from a new commander."[12]

When Lee's message reached Richmond three days later, Davis immediately replied that he agreed with his general's statement that a commander who had lost the confidence of his command should be replaced, but "when I read the sentence I was not at all prepared for the application you were about to make." Davis then made it clear that there was no way he was going to accept Lee's proposal for a change of commanders. He expressed regret at the "criticisms of the ignorant" and stated that he was "truly sorry to know that you still feel the effects of the illness you suffered last spring," but assured Lee that "practice" would do much to help him make use of "the eyes of others." He then asked his "dear friend" that even if he were to accept all of the points in Lee's letter, "where am I to find that new commander who is to possess the greater ability which you believe to be required? . . . My sight is not sufficiently penetrating to discover such hidden merit, if it exists." Davis then ended whatever thoughts Lee might have still had that his application for relief from command would be accepted by kindly, but bluntly, stating, "To ask me to substitute you by some one in my judgment more fit to command, or who would possess more of the confidence of the army, or of the reflecting men of the country is to demand an impossibility."[13]

Davis's letter reached Lee at his headquarters at Orange Court House on August 22. Lee replied that although disappointed at the president's refusal to accept his application for relief from command, "I shall not continue the subject, but beg that whenever in your opinion the public service will be advanced . . . that you will act upon the application before you." While he awaited Davis's response to his request, Lee had focused his energy on getting his army back into a condition that would enable it to once again take the offensive. To staunch a flood of desertions, he instituted a system of furloughs and expressed concern that a recent proclamation offering amnesty to returning soldiers was, contrary to his and Davis's expectations, making the situation worse. He also carefully monitored reports regarding the movements of the enemy and hoped the hot weather and trouble finding forage for his horses would quickly be alleviated. "Nothing," he advised Richmond on August 24, "prevents my advancing now but the fear of killing our artillery horses." Seven days later, he wrote to Longstreet from Richmond urging him to "use every exertion to prepare the army for offensive operations. . . . I can see nothing better to be done than to endeavor to bring General Meade out and use our efforts to crush his army." On September 3, despite a severe cold and an extremely painful attack of rheumatism in his back, Lee ascended

Clark's Mountain, which offered a magnificent view of the region north of the Rapidan, to look at the enemy. "He has spread himself over a large surface and looks immense," he advised his wife the next day, "but I hope will not prove as formidable as he looks. . . . [T]his past week he has been very quiet and seems at present disposed to continue so."[14]

If matters were quiet along the Rapidan, the situation was far different elsewhere. Vicksburg, of course, had fallen on July 4, with the last Confederate post along the Mississippi, Port Hudson, surrendering only a few days later, allowing the "Father of Waters," in Lincoln's words, to "flow unvexed to the sea." In addition, the Federals were making a determined joint attack on Charleston, South Carolina. By September, Confederate forces led by P. G. T. Beauregard still held the city, but Federal efforts had smashed Fort Sumter into rubble and closed the port. Then, on August 29 Rosecrans resumed his operations in Tennessee. After forcing Bragg back to Chattanooga in July, Rosecrans spent several weeks resisting intense pressure from Washington to be less meticulous in preparing his next move and his doing so was once again vindicated. Thanks to the solid logistical foundation he established in the weeks following the capture of Tullahoma, Rosecrans was able to once again boldly maneuver his army and compelled Bragg to decide on September 6 he had no choice but to abandon Chattanooga. Making matters worse, in late August another Union force, commanded by Ambrose Burnside, began advancing toward Knoxville and was able on September 2 to liberate the loyal population of that town.[15]

It was to discuss what could be done to salvage the rapidly crumbling situation elsewhere in the Confederacy that brought Lee to Richmond for several private meetings with President Davis in late August and early September. Finally, as Burnside took possession of Knoxville, which placed him on the railroad that most directly connected Virginia with the western Confederacy, and it became clear that Rosecrans was advancing in strength on Chattanooga, Davis decided on September 2 that it was necessary to send a considerable body of troops from Lee's army elsewhere. Over Lee's objections, Davis ordered two brigades from the Army of Northern Virginia to Charleston and decided the bulk of Longstreet's First Corps would go west to help Bragg. Lee immediately made arrangements and issued orders for the movement of Longstreet's troops and, before leaving Richmond, discussed the possibility of going west with his troops to Tennessee. Lee made clear that he was cool to the idea and expressed his sentiments in such a manner that he felt compelled on September 6 to assure Davis that he appreciated that the president had a far better understanding of the entire situation and sought "merely to express the opinion that the duty could be better performed by the officers already in that department." Longstreet, though, enthusiastically endorsed Davis's decision. "If it should become necessary to retire as far as Richmond temporarily," he advised Lee, "I think we could better afford to do so than we can to give up any more of our western country." In addition to his enthusiasm for the whole enterprise, Longstreet was eager to personally go to Tennessee. Consequently, Lee was able to fend off Davis's suggestion that he go to Tennessee as well. By September 9, Longstreet's men were on the march from the Rapidan to begin their journey, with Lee understandably anxious about the move and how it would compromise his own efforts. "If I was a little stronger," he informed Davis on September 11, "I think I could drive Meade's army under cover of the fortifications of Washington. . . . I may be forced back to Richmond. The blow at Rosecrans should be made promptly and Longstreet returned."[16]

As Lee feared, the Union high command detected Longstreet's departure from the Rapidan almost as soon as it began. On September 13, Meade received intelligence that something was up and decided to order his cavalry, backed by a corps of infantry, to cross the Rappahannock. The Federals then managed to drive Stuart back across the Rapidan and secure possession of Culpeper Court House. In the process, they gleaned information that enabled Meade to inform Halleck on the fifteenth, "I have no doubt Longstreet's corps has gone south." The following day, the rest of the Army of the Potomac advanced to Culpeper and the Rapidan. After a careful reconnaissance of Lee's formidable position south of the Rapidan, Meade developed a plan to cross the river and try to turn or envelop the Confederate position. On September 22, Buford's cavalry division crossed the Rapidan well above Lee's position and conducted a successful reconnaissance in force. By the time the ink was dry on Buford's report on the operation, though, whatever hopes Meade might have had of doing something more were in the process of being dashed. Early on the morning of September 24, Meade received directions to send two corps to Washington, which the Lincoln administration intended to send to Rosecrans, who had just experienced a spectacular reversal in fortune.[17]

Although forced to abandon Chattanooga, Bragg had pulled his army back to north Georgia determined to find an opportunity to strike at Rosecrans. Bragg's eagerness to do this was bolstered by Richmond's decision to send him assistance from the Army of Northern Virginia and Rosecrans's pushing his maneuvers to the point where he presented the Army of Tennessee with a golden opportunity. At a place in north Georgia called McLemore's Cove on September 9–10, one of Rosecrans's corps found itself separated from its comrades and unaware that a far stronger segment of

Bragg's army was nearby and under orders to fall upon and destroy it. Unfortunately for the Confederacy, this fantastic opportunity would be missed, due to insubordination on the part of Bragg's subordinates.

A few days later, Bragg's and Rosecrans's armies found themselves engaged in a desperate battle along Chickamauga Creek. There the dysfunctional command climate within the Army of Tennessee once again led to opportunities for truly decisive results being missed, although the timely arrival of Longstreet's command on the field on September 20 enabled Bragg to achieve a decisive tactical victory that compelled Rosecrans to abandon the field and take refuge in Chattanooga. Bragg posted his army on high ground outside the town and threatened to starve the Army of the Cumberland to death. The Lincoln administration quickly responded to the crisis by ordering Ulysses S. Grant to Chattanooga to take charge of the situation, and deciding he would be assisted in his efforts by two corps from Meade's army.[18]

Within days after Washington's decision, Lee was aware that Meade had lost the services of two corps. This came as an immense relief to Lee, as Meade's push across the Rappahannock had exacerbated his intense anxiety over Longstreet's absence and fears that he had "lost the use of troops here where they are much needed, and that they have gone where they will do no good." News of the victory at Chickamauga arrived the day after Buford's reconnaissance; however, it did little to alleviate Lee's discontent with Davis's decision to weaken the Army of Northern Virginia. Indeed, he mainly saw in Bragg's success the opportunity to begin the process of returning Longstreet's force to Virginia. "No time ought now to be wasted," he advised Richmond upon learning of Bragg's victory. "Everything should be done that can be done at once, so that the troops may be speedily returned to this department. . . . [T]hey will not get here too soon."[19]

With the weakening of Meade's army, though, Lee believed the situation had been transformed and that the Army of Northern Virginia should take the offensive. The first evidence of Meade's diminution reached Lee on September 27. Although all reports indicated they were leaving to reinforce Rosecrans, Lee advised Davis that he was concerned "they might be intended to operate on the Peninsula as a diversion to Meade's advance." In fact, on September 18, Meade had advocated such a demonstration by the troops already on the Peninsula to support a move by his own army to Fredericksburg. Fortunately for Lee, Lincoln and Halleck did him the great favor of vetoing Meade's proposal. By doing so, they preserved for Lee a favorable operational situation. As Meade pointed out to his superiors, due to the terrain on the south side of the Rapidan, he could not hope to assault Lee's position with much prospect of success. Further complicating Meade's operations was the fact that following Lincoln's and Halleck's mandate that he base his operations on the Orange and Alexandria Railroad meant that his army would be dependent on a long supply line that required a significant body of troops to protect it. Moreover, being tied to the railroad on this line of operations could render the Army of the Potomac vulnerable to enemy turning movements—just as John Pope's army had been the previous year. And no one could forget how Lee had responded to Pope's occupation of the region between the Rapidan and Rappahannock by initiating a series of turning movements that ultimately set the stage for the humiliating Union defeat at Second Manassas. In contrast, Lee not only had a strong tactical position behind the Rapidan, but a good, short, and relatively secure line of communication back to Gordonsville, and from there to supply bases in the Shenandoah Valley and Richmond.[20]

It was the felicity of his position for offensive operations, though, that immediately seized Lee's imagination when reports that Meade's army was being weakened arrived. By October 1, Lee was able to report to Richmond, "I consider it certain that two corps have been withdrawn from General Meade's army to re-enforce General Rosecrans." Although he recognized that Meade had lost only "two of [his] smallest and most indifferent corps," within a week after confirming their departure Lee had decided he would take the offensive. On October 3, he met with his corps commanders on top of Clark's Mountain and shortly thereafter began making active preparations for an offensive campaign. Lee decided that, as he had the previous August, he would attempt to turn the Union position at Culpeper by swinging west and north around Meade's right.[21]

Five days after the conference on Clark's Mountain, Lee ordered Stuart's cavalry, which was to screen the movement, west across the Rapidan River to Madison Court House. On October 9 and 10, Ewell's and Hill's corps moved to Madison Court House, accompanied by Lee, who was compelled to ride in an ambulance for much of the movement due to a bad attack of rheumatism in his back. As Ewell and Hill finished their marches to Madison Court House on the tenth, Stuart pushed forward toward Culpeper and for the next two days engaged in spirited fighting with the Federals. Lee's "hope of getting an opportunity to strike a blow" at Meade at Culpeper, however, came to naught, for as his infantry approached the town on the eleventh, it was discovered that Meade had pulled back to the Rappahannock.[22]

Although he had regained the land between the Rappahannock and Rapidan, Lee was by no means satisfied as he halted his army near Culpeper on October 11 and, despite the great pain he still felt in his back, was determined to keep pressing forward. The following morning, the army was once again on the march, with Ewell's corps marching to Jeffersonton and then crossing the Rappahannock at White Sulphur Springs, while Hill's command was directed to push to Amissville and then follow Ewell across the river. From there, the two corps would converge on Warrenton and then push to the Orange and Alexandria Railroad with the objective of getting on Meade's line of supply and cutting him off from Washington. By doing this, or at least threatening to do this, Lee might be able to force Meade's army into an engagement when it was off balance and in a position where the Army of Northern Virginia's demonstrated superiority at maneuver warfare could produce decisive results at an acceptable cost. First, however, Stuart had to clear the route to the Rappahannock, a task that took up much of the day on October 12. The next day, Ewell and Hill pushed across the Rappahannock and reached Warrenton.[23]

Meade quickly picked up evidence of what the Confederates were doing and what Lee's objective was. Unlike Pope the previous summer, though, Meade had made no proclamations about letting lines of retreat take care of themselves. Thus, he smartly turned his army around and ordered it to pull back toward Washington, following the Orange and Alexandria Railroad, in two columns. As Lee finished concentrating his forces at Warrenton on the thirteenth, Meade established "the seizure of the Centreville Heights in advance of the enemy" as his objective and issued orders that evening for completion of the army's concentration at Centreville on the fourteenth. If, once this movement was complete and the Army of the Potomac was firmly established in a good defensive position, Lee wished to bring on an engagement, Meade was more than willing to oblige him.[24]

During the afternoon of the thirteenth, Lee learned Meade was marching hard for the Bull Run crossings, and that evening decided to push east toward the Orange and Alexandria with the objective of reaching it near Bristoe Station. Ewell's corps would advance from Warrenton to Greenwich, while Hill's command would move first to New Baltimore and then to Greenwich. Lee then spent much of the night of October 13–14 worrying about Stuart, whose cavalry was reported to be trapped at Auburn with a column of Federal infantry between it and Warrenton, which compelled Lee to initially divert Ewell's advance toward Auburn on the morning of the fourteenth.[25]

Shortly after the Confederate infantry began its march from Warrenton on October 14, Stuart reached Lee and informed him that his command was no longer in danger. Unfortunately for Lee, this was in part a consequence of the fact that the Union movement toward the Bull Run crossings was so well advanced that there was little between Auburn and Warrenton. Nonetheless, Lee was determined to try and strike some portion of the Army of the Potomac before it was entirely across Bull Run. Thus, the march to Bristoe Station continued. After a brief skirmish with the Union rear guard near Auburn, Ewell's command proceeded to Greenwich. There it was determined that the Army of Northern Virginia would advance toward the railroad, with Hill on the left taking the direct road from Greenwich to Bristoe Station, while Ewell on the right would advance over farm roads and reach the railroad south of Bristoe Station. When Hill's and Ewell's commands began their advance, Lee had before him an opportunity to achieve a decisive success. Although the bulk of the Army of the Potomac was nearly at Centreville, on the afternoon of October 14 there was still a Union corps moving along the railroad that had yet to reach the crossings of Bull Run. If Lee's superior force could deliver an effective attack against this corps, it could severely mangle, if not completely annihilate it, which would severely hamper any attempt by Meade to undertake significant offensive operations for months.[26]

Unfortunately, October 14 would bring defeat instead of decisive success. Lee accompanied Ewell's column as it advanced toward the railroad and consequently was absent when an overzealous Hill blundered into the skillfully posted and handled Federal corps at Bristoe Station. Upon hearing the sound of battle coming from Hill's advance, Lee immediately rushed over to the Third Corps's position and learned that a rashly delivered attack had resulted in its receiving a bad mauling from the Federals. Some of Ewell's forces managed to reach the railroad shortly after Hill's setback and attack the Federals near Kettle Run, but were too late and found the enemy too strongly positioned to redeem the day. That night, the Federals finished crossing Bull Run, and Meade posted his army in a strong position around Centreville. A visibly angry Lee met with Hill early in the evening of October 14 and received a verbal description of what had happened that afternoon. The following morning, as a cold rain fell, Lee went over the ground around Bristoe Station where so many of his men had fallen and once again encountered Hill. When the Third Corps commander attempted again to explain what had happened, Lee coldly cut him off. "Well, well, General," Lee remarked, "bury these poor men and let us say no more about it."[27]

Lee spent the rest of October 15 digesting reports that the Federals were fortifying their position on the other side of Bull Run. He quickly determined that neither a direct assault against Meade's position nor another at-

Figure 4.2.   Lieutenant General Ambrose P. Hill, Confederate, c. 1864. National Archives

tempt to turn it would produce results commensurate with the effort. Lee then briefly flirted with the idea of moving west to the Loudoun Valley in hopes of keeping the Federals near Washington and possibly threatening another move into Maryland that might force Meade north of the Potomac. Indeed, Lee advised his wife on October 19 that if his army was "properly provided with clothes I would certainly have endeavored to have thrown them north of the Potomac." But a lack of essential supplies made the thought of moving into Loudoun County and asking his troops to march "over the rough roads of that region, at a season, too when frosts are certain and snows probable" unacceptable. Nor could he maintain a position so far north in light of the fact that the area between Bull Run and the Rappahannock River was "entirely destitute" of supplies and the Federals had damaged the Orange and Alexandria Railroad during their retreat. Consequently, on October 17, Lee advised Davis: "I can see no benefit to be derived from remaining where we are, and shall consequently return to the line of the Rappahannock." The following day, Lee's infantry fell back to the Rappahannock, while Stuart's cavalry had a spirited fight with some poorly led enemy cavalry in which the Federals were so badly routed that the episode became known as the "Buckland Races." By the nineteenth, Lee's infantry was once again south of the Rappahannock. Left behind was a railroad so thoroughly wrecked that one man informed his family, "But for the grading and bent iron you would not know that there ever was a railroad along here." This, Lee hoped, "may prevent another advance of the enemy in this direction this season."[28]

Although they may not have produced a dramatic battle, by not falling into the same trap Pope had the year before, Meade's actions during the Bristoe Station campaign materially advanced the Union war effort. To be sure, Lee had won a few weeks' breathing space by his maneuvers, but these by no means offset the losses at Bristoe Station. Moreover, Meade had denied Lee any opportunity to achieve the sort of dramatic victory the Confederate cause needed and ensured that there would be no slackening in the North's determination to continue its effort to crush the Confederacy through exhaustion. Nonetheless, when Meade reported that Lee was retreating, but that it was not clear whether the Confederates were pulling back to the Rappahannock or moving west to the Loudoun Valley, he received a decidedly chilly response from Washington. "Lee is unquestionably bullying you," wrote Halleck on the eighteenth. "If you cannot ascertain his movements, I certainly cannot. If you pursue and fight him you will find out where he is." An understandably furious Meade immediately wrote back to demand that he be "spared the infliction of such truisms in the guise of opinions" and offered his resignation from command of the Army of the Potomac "if my course . . . does not meet with approval."[29]

Meade advanced across Bull Run on October 19, anticipating that he would encounter Lee's army in the vicinity of Warrenton. A few days earlier, Meade had exclaimed to his staff that if Lee was willing to "fight me, man to man, I will do it this afternoon." But, of course, Lee was too good a general to remain north of the Rappahannock or place his army anywhere else it might have to fight at a tactical or operational disadvantage. When it was

Figure 4.3.   Major General George G. Meade, Union, 1864. National Archives

clear Lee would not fight at Warrenton, and that keeping the Orange and Alexandria as the line of operations held out no more prospect of decisive success now than it ever had, Meade again proposed shifting his army to Fredericksburg and basing his operations on the Richmond, Fredericksburg, and Potomac Railroad. "I do not see the practicability," he reported to Washington on October 21, "of an advance on this line. . . . The Orange and Alexandria Railroad has been destroyed from Bristoe Station to Culpeper Court House. To repair and put in working order the road . . . will require the use of a considerable part of this army for guards and working parties." By moving to Fredericksburg, Meade could turn Lee's position and gain a much shorter line of communications. Despite the potential advantages to be gained from such a move, which Meade once again presented to them in early November, abandoning the line of operations along the Orange and Alexandria Railroad remained unacceptable to Lincoln and Halleck. "[T]he President," Halleck advised Meade, "does not see that the proposed change of base is likely to produce any favorable result. . . . I have fully concurred in the views he has heretofore communicated on this subject. Any tactical movement to turn a flank or threaten a communication is left to your own judgment; but an entire change of base under existing circumstances, I can neither advise nor approve."[30]

As Meade debated operational courses of action with the Lincoln administration, an event of profound significance took place in the Northern states. Lee's strategic vision rested on an assumption that the South's only chance for victory rested in achieving battlefield successes that would drive the costs in blood and treasure and sow war weariness in the North to a point where its people would replace the Lincoln government with one willing to end the war and recognize the Confederacy. In November 1863, the people of the North had an opportunity to let their position be known in state and local elections. The most closely watched races were the more than half a dozen gubernatorial contests, the most critical of which were in Ohio and Pennsylvania, two states where the governors had been stalwart supporters of the Lincoln administration and linchpins of the whole Union war effort. The stakes could not be clearer, as the Democrats nominated candidates associated with the wing of the party that advocated seeking other means than war for restoring the Union. When the voters of the North went to the polls during the first week of November, though, they made clear that they fully shared Lincoln's determination to crush the Confederacy. The Republicans won every statewide race of any consequence, in many cases by overwhelming majorities, and claimed sweeping victories in Ohio and Pennsylvania. In the process, the people of the North did as much in November as their armies had earlier in the year in Mississippi, Tennessee, Virginia, and Pennsylvania to lengthen the odds against which Lee would have to contend if he was to prevent the fall of the Confederacy—and demonstrate just how long those odds were. Shortly thereafter, Lincoln went to Gettysburg and delivered a speech in which he laid out the stakes involved in the war and the nobility of the Union cause with such power and eloquence that he set a high bar for anyone who might wish to challenge the notion that the Confederacy must be crushed.[31]

However effectively Lincoln was executing his responsibilities as the leader of the Republican Party and spokesman for the Union cause, his performance as commander in chief of the armed forces continued to be a source of exasperation to Meade. Although dismayed by the administration's mandate that he maintain a line of operations along the Orange and Alexandria that offered little prospect for achieving a truly decisive victory, Meade was not so cautious a general as to be unable to seize opportunities for a tactical success when they appeared. He quickly pushed south from Centreville toward the Rappahannock with his men laying down railroad track, one of Lee's men wrote in amazement, "as fast as we pulled it up."[32]

As he approached the Rappahannock, Meade immediately saw an opportunity for a tactical success due to the presence north of the Rappahannock of fortified bridgeheads Lee had left behind at Rappahannock Station and Kelly's Ford. Lee later explained to Davis that he had established these hoping they would deter Meade from advancing much beyond Warrenton Junction before winter. Shortly after receiving Halleck's note rejecting his plan to advance to Fredericksburg, however, Meade decided to attack the Confederate positions as the first step in an effort to force a crossing of the Rappahannock. On November 7, he ordered three Union corps to take the Confederate position at Kelly's Ford, while two attacked the Confederates at Rappahannock Station. Shortly after nightfall, the Federals attacked. Taken almost completely by surprise, the Confederate defenders at both places were quickly overwhelmed, with the Federals taking nearly two thousand prisoners and pushing forward to secure a lodgment on the south side of the river at both places.[33]

With the Federals in complete possession of the high ground on the north side of the Rappahannock, Lee could not hope to maintain a position along its south side. Thus, during the night of November 7–8, he ordered his command to pull back to a line between Culpeper and Brandy Station as a heavy fog settled over the area. This fog impeded Meade's efforts to push his army across the Rappahannock and follow up his victory. Then, when it became clear the Federals were going to advance toward him in strength, Lee once again decided on November 8 that the lack of good defensible terrain made a stand north of the Rapidan too risky and chose to withdraw to the south side of that stream. With the assistance of a snowstorm on the ninth, Lee was able to make his escape without too much trouble, and on November 10 reported to Richmond that the army was safely occupying "about the same position as before the recent advance" to Bristoe Station. Meade followed south until he reached Culpeper, where he received a rare message of praise from Lincoln, and as his advanced elements began taking up positions at the Rapidan, work continued on repairs to the railroad behind them.[34]

Despite poor weather that indicated the time for active campaigning was rapidly becoming short and the fact that from his observation post on Clark's Mountain Lee could observe just about anything he attempted to do, Meade began planning another offensive as soon as he reached Culpeper. A direct assault on Lee's position on the high ground south of that river was out of the question, so Meade conceived a plan for a quick crossing of the river down-stream from Lee's position in front of Orange Court House, followed by an immediate push south to the Orange Turnpike and Orange Plank Road. If he was successful in this endeavor, Meade then planned to swing west and advance "rapidly toward Orange Court House, thus turning the enemy's works, and compelling him to give battle on ground not previously selected or prepared," while hoping to "so cripple him as to render more certain the success of the final struggle." If this should prove unattainable, Meade would then have the option of moving west to Fredericksburg to place his army on the line he had been begging for weeks for permission to take.[35]

Meade set the commencement of this movement for November 23, the same day Grant began in earnest his effort to avenge the Union defeat at Chickamauga. After arriving in Chattanooga and replacing Rosecrans with Maj. Gen. George Thomas on October 23, Grant had ordered a successful effort to open a new supply line for the besieged forces in the town. Shortly thereafter reinforcements arrived in the form of troops from his old Army of the Tennessee, now commanded by his good friend Maj. Gen. William T. Sherman, and the two corps that had been dispatched from the Army of the Potomac and were operating under the overall command of Joe Hooker. Then, on November 23, Grant began his offensive against Bragg by ordering Thomas's Army of the Cumberland to drive the Confederates off a hill known as Orchard Knob. This was followed the next day by a dramatic attack by Hooker that seized Lookout Mountain, and on November 25 by an assault by Sherman's and Thomas's commands on Bragg's position. These engagements broke the Confederate line on Missionary Ridge and crushed whatever hope Chickamauga and the presence of Longstreet's command had inspired that the Union tide of victory in the west might somehow be arrested.[36]

Lee, of course, knew little of what exactly was occurring out west, except that it continued to deny him the services of a corps commander and troops whose absence he badly regretted. And he would have little time to dwell on it, or the pain he still felt in his back, for on November 26 news arrived that Meade was moving toward the Rapidan fords south and east of Culpeper. He then fired off a message to Richmond reporting this development and that the Army of Northern Virginia would immediately be put on the march from its positions near Orange Court House, and asked that troops around the capital be sent north to Hanover Junction to assist him.[37]

On the evening of November 26, Lee's army began moving, but not toward Spotsylvania Court House. Instead, Lee ordered the Second Corps, which was operating under the direction of Maj. Gen. Jubal Early due to Ewell's being too ill to command, to push east along the Orange Turnpike and Raccoon Ford Road, while to the south Hill's corps advanced east along the Orange Plank Road. A division of cavalry under Stuart's supervision screened the advance, which Lee hoped would enable him to fall upon the Federal flank and rear if Meade tried to push toward Richmond. If Meade, however, turned west with the intention of striking the Confederate flank, Lee hoped not only to thwart this effort, but to bring the Federals to battle when they were on the march and deliver a decisive blow of his own.[38]

Fortunately for Lee, Meade's attempt to quickly cross the Rapidan was anything but smoothly executed. One of the Federal corps commanders was late in beginning his march on November 26 and once across the Rapidan had problems figuring out the road network. Consequently, instead of the entire Army of the Potomac reaching Robertson's Tavern on the Orange Turnpike by the evening of the twenty-sixth as Meade intended, only one corps was at the tavern by the twenty-seventh. During the morning of that day, Lee's cavalry began skirmishing with that lone Union corps, with infantry taking over the engagement shortly before noon. Meanwhile, a Union corps that was supposed to be at Robertson's Tavern by then once again became confused over the route it was to take. By the time it had gotten itself straightened out, however, Maj. Gen. Edward Johnson's division from Early's corps was moving toward its position near the Payne Farm. At around four in the afternoon, Johnson launched an assault that drove the Federals back but quickly lost momentum due to superior Federal numbers, thick woods that made it impossible to maintain a solid battle line, and the inability of Confederate troops to replenish their empty cartridge boxes after nightfall.[39]

After digesting news of the fight at Payne's Farm and reports regarding the movements of the rest of Meade's army, Lee decided on the evening of November 27 to go on the defensive by pulling back to a position on the west side of Mine Run. Upon reaching this position, Lee's men immediately began fortifying it, as one wrote in his journal, "with that energy and determination which only a soldier can muster up when the enemy is fronting him. By night they had up works almost as strong as the original walls of Fort Sumter." As Lee's men dug in, Meade pushed his army, the concentration of which was finally completed just before daylight on the twenty-eighth, west astride the Orange Turnpike. Through a driving rainstorm, the Army of the Potomac spent the afternoon of November 28 pushing Lee's pickets across Mine Run. Then, however, they found out just how good the

Army of Northern Virginia had become at selecting and quickly fortifying a defensive position. "A reconnaissance of the enemy's position showed it to be extremely formidable," Meade later wrote. "The western bank of Mine Run, with an elevation of over 100 feet, had a gentle and smooth slope to the creek, averaging over 1,000 yards of cleared ground. The summit, on which was the enemy's line of battle, was already crowned with infantry parapets, abates, and epaulements for batteries. The creek itself was a considerable obstacle, in many places swampy and impassable."[40]

After briefly harassing the Confederates with artillery fire, Meade spent November 29 probing Lee's position and learned that one of his own corps commanders, Maj. Gen. Gouverneur Warren, thought he had found a position from which he could successfully attack Lee's right. Meade then ordered Warren to take his command and two divisions from another corps to the position he had identified and make an attack the next morning, while the rest of the Army of the Potomac would support him by pressing against the rest of the Confederate line. Lee, for his part, spent November 29 awaiting events and pushing his men to continue improving their defensive position behind Mine Run. Lee had not, however, resigned himself to a purely defensive stance. During the night of November 28, he had instructed Stuart to take a division of cavalry on a raid against the Union rear area. Stuart managed to reach all the way to Parker's Store on the Orange Plank Road on the twenty-ninth, where he successfully attacked a small party of Union cavalry and captured some Federal military stores. Then, however, as it became clear that Meade was intending to make a major attack on November 30, Stuart broke off his raid and pulled back to Mine Run. Convinced that Meade would make an attack, Lee decided he would wait for it from behind his strong position and then seize any opportunity that might present itself for a successful counterattack.[41]

As a bitterly cold November 30 dawned, the Army of the Potomac prepared to gratify Confederate hopes that Meade would be so foolish as to shatter his army in a futile attack against the Mine Run entrenchments. Shortly after reaching the jump-off point for the attack he had proposed the previous evening, however, Warren was stunned to find Lee's position was much more formidable than he anticipated and, he later wrote, "at once decided not to attack, and so informed General Meade." Although initially dismayed at Warren's decision, Meade was too prudent to do what the enemy wanted him to do by making an attack that had little chance of success. And to the great good fortune of the soldiers in his army and the Union cause in general, Meade possessed the moral courage to act on his judgment even though he knew that to do so would surely bring the wrath of his superiors in Washington on his head. At the same time, Meade was not willing to go so far as to defy Lincoln and Halleck on a point on which they had made themselves crystal clear by remaining south of the Rapidan and Rappahannock River and pushing east to Fredericksburg. Had Meade acted on his own judgment and moved to Fredericksburg, Lee might have had little choice but to give up the line of the Rapidan and the vital railroad junction at Gordonsville and take up a position south of Fredericksburg behind the North Anna River. Fortunately for Lee, a frustrated Meade made the only decision Washington's restrictions allowed and ordered his army to recross the Rapidan and pull back to Culpeper.[42]

Lee was surprised and undoubtedly dismayed that November 30 brought only some minor skirmishing and occasional exchanges of artillery fire but no major attack. Lee then decided he would wait another day and if the Federals did nothing, would take the offensive himself on December 2. When December 1 passed with the Federals doing little besides bolstering their position on the Plank Road, Lee issued orders for an advance the following morning. He instructed Hill to extend the Mine Run line further south and told him "to concentrate [Maj. Gen. Richard H.] Anderson's and [Maj. Gen. Cadmus M.] Wilcox's divisions on my extreme right with a view to making the attack" on December 2. Lee's intention was that while the rest of the army continued to hold Meade in position, those two divisions and Stuart's cavalry would assail the Federal left and rear. Lee's eagerness to strike a blow was vividly impressed upon a member of Stuart's staff who made his way to army headquarters early on the morning of December 2. During their interview, Lee paced anxiously in front of a warm fire, repeatedly slapping his palm with the back of a hairbrush and exclaiming, "Captain, if they don't attack us today we must attack them! . . . We must attack them, sir! . . . And you young men must exert yourself! You must exert yourselves, sir." To Lee's disappointment, when his men pushed forward on December 2 they found the Army of the Potomac was gone. Still eager to strike a blow at his retreating foe, Lee immediately ordered a pursuit, but this effort was impeded by the dense forest through which Meade's columns had retreated and by the time the lead elements of the Army of Northern Virginia reached the Rapidan, the Federals were safely across.[43]

Lee was immensely frustrated that his hopes of attacking the Army of the Potomac and delivering a destructive blow while it was in the open and separated from its railroad supply line by the Rapidan had come to naught. When it was clear Meade was beyond his grasp, Lee exclaimed in front of his staff and subordinates, "I am too old to command this army; we should never have permitted those people to get away." The withdrawal of the Army of the

Potomac across the Rapidan, Lee understood, had denied him a chance (however slim, given the cautious nature of Meade's generalship) to create an opportunity for a victory on the battlefield that might discourage the North in its effort to persist in what few could deny in late 1863 was an increasingly effective effort to exhaust the Confederacy. "I am greatly disappointed at his getting off with so little damage," Lee wrote his wife as his army returned to its previous positions behind the Rapidan, but hopefully added, "we do not know what is best for us, and I believe a kind God has ordered all things for our good."[44]

And so the campaign season of 1863 came to a close with Lee and the Army of Northern Virginia securely behind the Rapidan and continuing to inspire confidence in the Southern people that their bid for independence could succeed in the face of increasingly evident Northern material superiority. Yet 1863 had clearly been a bad year for the cause of Southern independence. Northern armies had secured control of the entire Mississippi River and liberated the loyal population of East Tennessee, developments that boosted Northern morale and determination to continue striving for victory—as evident in the results of the 1863 election. Moreover, in combination with the ever-tightening blockade, the establishment of greater efficiency in the mobilization and administration of Northern resources, and the losses suffered by the Confederacy on the battlefield, these developments had further tipped the balance of resources in favor of the North.

Even for the stalwart Army of Northern Virginia, there was more cause for concern than celebration when its commander and men looked back at the end of 1863. To be sure, given the disadvantage in resources they constantly labored under and the tremendous risks they had consistently been compelled to take by the strategic and operational situations they faced, Lee and his men could take no small degree of pride in the fact that the army was still in existence. Nonetheless, whatever the victory at Chancellorsville might have done to depress the North's confidence in ultimate victory and willingness to continue making awesome sacrifices in pursuit of that victory, it was by no means enough to compensate for the terrible losses Lee's army had suffered during that battle. This had then been followed by the expedition into Pennsylvania, which although undertaken on the basis of sound assumptions regarding the Confederacy's strategic and operational needs, had produced a costly battle in which there was no question that the Army of Northern Virginia had suffered a terrible defeat—and had been exceedingly fortunate to avoid a completely catastrophic one. The elaborate waltz Lee and his army had engaged in with Meade and the Army of the Potomac during the months that followed the armies' return to Virginia had bought time, but did little to arrest the steady erosion of the Confederacy militarily. The only thing that could do this was military victories that would lead the North to give up its effort to crush the South—if this was possible—and the 1863 elections demonstrated that the North's will to continue the war remained strong.

Moreover, Lee was well aware that the victory at Chancellorsville had been a near-run thing, with what success he had achieved coming largely as a consequence of enemy mistakes and the ability of his army to exploit them, which by the end of 1863 was clearly declining. Meanwhile, with the exception of Hooker's troubles at Chancellorsville, the performance of the Army of the Potomac high command throughout the year had been solid and competent. Considering the constant stream of troubles and restrictions Washington had been imposing, it was probably too much to hope for spectacular leadership from a Union general in Virginia in any case. But given the fact that time and resources were on the North's side, solid leadership was all that was really needed to ensure that 1863 would advance the cause of the Union in Virginia. And this Hooker and Meade had provided.

That 1863 had been a good year for the Union cause and that Northern confidence in the ultimate fall of the Confederacy was strong was evident in an action President Lincoln took on December 8. That day, in his annual message to Congress, Lincoln held out an olive branch to the people of the South, offering fairly liberal terms of amnesty and for the reorganization of loyal state governments in the Southern states. Lincoln did this not from a position of weakness, but from one of strength rooted in recent political successes and a sense that the course of the war must be making it evident to the people of the South that they were engaged in a pointless endeavor—a sentiment Lincoln believed holding out a lenient policy for reconstruction would further encourage.[45] Just as the advance of the Union armies was steadily grinding down the military capacity of the South, Lincoln hoped his plan would accelerate an erosion of Southern will to continue the war. But if that will remained so strong that Northern victories in 1863 and Lincoln's terms were not enough to bring about its evaporation by the spring of 1864, so be it. After Mother Nature finished taking her toll on Lee's ill-supplied army over the winter of 1863–1864, Lincoln would once again send his armies southward to break it.

Notes

1. Circular, Hdqrs. Army of the Potomac, July 14, 17, 1863, OR, vol. 27, pt. 3: 695, 718; Meade to Halleck, July 16, 18, 1863, ibid., pt. 1: 95, 96; Itinerary of the Army of the Potomac and co-operating forces, June 5–July 31, 1863, ibid., 147–48.

2. Lee to Davis, July 16, 1863, in *Wartime Papers*, eds. Dowdey and Manarin, 552; Lee to Stuart, July 18, 1863, ibid., 553–54.

3. Lee to Longstreet, July 19, 1863, ibid., 554; Lee to Cooper, January 20, 1864, ibid., 583–84.

4. Longstreet to Chilton, July 27, 1863, OR, vol. 27, pt. 2: 362; Lee to Ewell, July 20, 1863, in *Wartime Papers*, eds. Dowdey and Manarin, 555–56.

5. Itinerary of the Army of the Potomac and co-operating forces, June 5–July 31, 1863, OR, vol. 27, pt. 1: 149; Norton to Meade, July 21, 1863, ibid., pt. 3: 733–34; Meade to Thomas, October 1, 1863, ibid., pt. 1: 118; French to Williams, October 1, 1863, ibid., 490; Hill to Chilton, November ——, 1863, ibid., pt. 2: 609; Longstreet to Chilton, July 27, 1863, ibid., pt. 2: 362.

6. Ewell to Chilton, ——, 1863, ibid., 449–50; French to Williams, October 1, 1863, ibid., pt. 1: 490; Hill to Chilton, November ——, 1863, ibid., pt. 2: 609; Longstreet to Chilton, July 27, 1863, ibid., 362; Lee to Cooper, January 20, 1864, in *Wartime Papers*, eds. Dowdey and Manarin, 584.

7. Lee to his wife, July 26, 1863, ibid., 559–60.

8. Lee to Davis, July 24, 29, 1863, ibid., 558–59, 564; Lee to Stuart, July 26, 1863, ibid., 561.

9. Meade to Halleck, July 28, 1863, OR, vol. 27, pt. 1: 103; Buford to Alexander, August 2, 1863, ibid., 932.

10. Davis to Lee, August 2, 1863, ibid., vol. 51, pt. 2: 750; Lee to his wife, August 2, 1863, in *Wartime Papers*, eds. Dowdey and Manarin, 567; Lee to Davis, July 31, August 1, 1863, ibid., 566; Lee to Cooper, August 4, 1863, January 20, 1864, ibid., 568, 584.

11. Meade to Halleck, July 28, 1863, OR, vol. 27, pt. 1: 103; Lincoln to Halleck, July 29, 1863, in *Works of Lincoln*, ed. Basler, vol. 6: 354.

12. Lee to Davis, August 8, 1863, in *Wartime Papers*, eds. Dowdey and Manarin, 589–90.

13. Davis to Lee, August 11, 1863, OR, vol. 29, pt. 2: 639–40.

14. Lee to Davis, August 22, 17, 24, 1863, in *Wartime Papers*, eds. Dowdey and Manarin, 593; Lee to Longstreet, August 31, 1863, ibid., 594; Lee to his wife, September 4, 1863, ibid., 595.

15. Shea and Winschel, *Vicksburg Is the Key*, 203–04; Woodworth, *Six Armies in Tennessee*, 47–66.

16. Freeman, *R.E. Lee*, vol. 3: 163–66; Lee to Davis, September 6, 9, 11, 1863, in *Wartime Papers*, eds. Dowdey and Manarin, 596, 596–97, 599; Longstreet to Lee, September 5, 1863, OR, vol. 29, pt. 2: 699.

17. Meade to Halleck, September 13, 14, 15, 1863, ibid., 175, 177–78, 179–80, 187–88; Meade to Thomas, December 6, 1863, ibid., pt. 1: 9; Buford to Pleasonton,

September 23, 1863, ibid., 141; Halleck to Meade, September 24, 1863, ibid., pt. 1: 147–48.

18. Woodworth, *Six Armies in Tennessee*, 67–128, 136–38, 141–52.

19. Lee to Davis, September 14, 23, 1863, in *Wartime Papers*, eds. Dowdey and Manarin, 600, 603.

20. Lee to Davis, September 28, 1863, OR, vol. 29, pt. 2: 753–54; Lee to Elzey, September 28, 1863, ibid., 754; Meade to Halleck, September 18, 1863, ibid., 201; Halleck to Meade, September 19, 1863, ibid., 206–07; Lincoln to Halleck, September 19, 1863, ibid., 207–08.

21. Lee to Davis, October 1, 3, 1863, ibid., 766, 769; William D. Henderson, *The Road to Bristoe Station: Campaigning with Lee and Meade, August 1–October 20, 1863* (Lynchburg, VA: H.E. Howard, 1987), 69–71.

22. Stuart to Chilton, February 13, 1864, OR, vol. 1: 439–41; Lee to Seddon, October 11, 1863, in *Wartime Papers*, eds. Dowdey and Manarin, 607; Lee to Cooper, October 23, 1864, ibid., 612.

23. Lee to Cooper, October 23, 1864, ibid., 612–13.

24. Meade to Thomas, December 6, 1863, OR, vol. 29, pt. 1: 10; Circular, Hdqrs. Army of the Potomac, October 13, 1863, ibid., pt. 2: 304, 306–07.

25. Stuart to Chilton, February 13, 1864, ibid., pt. 1: 447–48; Lee to Seddon, October 13, 1863, in *Wartime Papers*, eds. Dowdey and Manarin, 608; Lee to Cooper, October 23, 1863, ibid., 613.

26. Freeman, *R.E. Lee*, vol. 3: 177–80; Pfanz, *Richard S. Ewell*, 338–39.

27. Freeman, *R.E. Lee*, vol. 3: 180–83.

28. Walter Battle to his mother, October 18, 1863, Civil War Letters of George Boardman Battle and Walter Raleigh Battle, edited by Hugh Buckner Johnston, bound vol. 85, FSNMP; Lee to Davis, October 17, 1863, in *Wartime Papers*, eds. Dowdey and Manarin, 609; Lee to Lawton, October 19, 1863, ibid., 610; Lee to his wife, October 19, 1863, ibid., 611; Lee to Cooper, October 23, 1863, ibid., 613–14.

29. Meade to Halleck, October 18, 1863, ibid., pt. 2: 345, 346, 354, 361; Halleck to Meade, October 18, 1863, ibid., 346.

30. Theodore Lyman, *Meade's Headquarters, 1863–1865: Letters of Colonel Theodore Lyman from the Wilderness to Appomattox*, edited by George R. Agassiz (Boston: Atlantic Monthly, 1922), 31; Meade to Halleck, October 19, 21, November 2, 1863, OR, vol. 29, pt. 2: 354, 361, 409–10; Halleck to Meade, November 3, 1863, ibid., 412.

31. Phillip Shaw Paludan, *The Presidency of Abraham Lincoln* (Lawrence: University Press of Kansas, 1994), 226–31; Donald, *Lincoln*, 454–66.

32. Old to Catherine, October 25, 1863, John N. Old Letters, bound vol. 138, FSNMP.

33. Lee to Davis, November 10, 1863, in *Wartime Papers*, eds. Dowdey and Manarin, 620; Meade to Thomas, December 6, 1863, OR, vol. 29, pt. 1: 10–11.

34. Lee to Davis, November 10, 1863, in *Wartime Papers*, eds. Dowdey and Manarin, 620; Lincoln to Meade, November 9, 1863, in *Works of Lincoln*, ed., Basler, vol. 7: 7; Meade to Thomas, December 6, 1863, OR, vol. 29, pt. 1: 11.

35. Meade to Thomas, December 7, 1863, ibid., 13.

36. Ibid.; Woodworth, *Six Armies in Tennessee*, 153–202.

37. Lee to Davis, November 26, 1863, in *Wartime Papers*, eds. Dowdey and Manarin, 626; Lee to Cooper, November 26, 1863, ibid.

38. Lee to Cooper, April 27, 1864, ibid., 633.

39. Meade to Thomas, December 7, 1863, OR, vol. 29, pt. 1: 14–15; Johnson to Brown, February 2, 1864, ibid., 847.

40. Lee to Cooper, December 2, 1863, in *Wartime Papers*, eds. Dowdey and Manarin, 629; entry for November 28, 1863, Charles T. Furlow Journal, Yale University Archives, New Haven, CT, copy in bound vol. 376, FSNMP; Meade to Thomas, December 7, 1863, OR, vol. 29, pt. 1: 15–16.

41. Ibid., 16–17; Lee to Cooper, April 27, 1864, in *Wartime Papers*, eds. Dowdey and Manarin, 635; Stuart to Chilton, April 30, 1864, OR, vol. 29, pt. 1: 899–900.

42. Edwards to his father, December 3, 1863, Leroy S. Edwards Letters, bound vol. 334, FSNMP; Warren to Williams, December 3, 1863, ibid., 698; Meade to Thomas, December 7, 1863, ibid., 17–18.

43. Hill to Chilton, January 27, 1864, ibid., 896; Lee to Cooper, December 1, 2, 3, 1863, in *Wartime Papers*, eds. Dowdey and Manarin, 628, 630–31; Blackford, *War Years with Jeb Stuart*, 245–46.

45. Donald, *Lincoln*, 471–73.

CHAPTER FIVE

Winter Quarters and
a New Foe

Before winter had fully gripped central Virginia in December 1863, Lee once again found himself engaged in discussions with officials in Richmond about his playing a major role in reversing Confederate fortunes elsewhere in the South. After the defeat at Chattanooga, Davis had no choice but to accept Bragg's request for removal from command of the Army of Tennessee and did so while Lee was engaged in the Mine Run Campaign. However, there was no successor for Bragg within the Army of Tennessee, which was then encamped at and around Dalton, Georgia, whom Davis deemed acceptable. Consequently, on December 9, Lee found himself en route to Richmond to talk with Davis. Two days earlier, he had received a message from Davis asking if he would be willing "to consistently go to Dalton" and immediately replied that he could "see no good that will result" from traveling to Georgia—unless it was to assume permanent command of the Army of Tennessee. This, Lee made clear, was something he had no desire to do. "I fear that I would not receive cordial cooperation," he protested, "have not that confidence either in my strength or ability as would lead me of my own option to undertake the command in question . . . [and] think it necessary if I am withdrawn from here that a commander for this army be sent to it. Genl Ewell's condition I fear is too feeble to undergo the fatigue and labor incident to the position."[1]

Nonetheless, it was with some gloom that Lee departed from the Army of Northern Virginia on December 9, as he no doubt believed there was a strong possibility that he would not be returning to it. By the time he left Richmond on December 21, however, Lee had managed to talk Davis out of sending him west. Although the first man he suggested as Bragg's replacement, Beauregard, proved unacceptable to Davis, Lee undoubtedly had an effect on the president's decision to order Gen. Joseph E. Johnston to take over the Army of Tennessee. After returning to Orange County a few days before Christmas and establishing his headquarters in a location convenient to his lookout post on Clark's Mountain, Lee threw himself into the task of getting his army ready for the 1864 campaign season.[2]

Although the winter of 1863–1864 saw limited action in Virginia, it was not a good time for Lee or the Confederacy. Dwindling resources and difficulties getting them to the troops rooted in a badly strained transportation system and problematic management in Richmond constantly wore on Lee's mind. In early January, he complained to Richmond about a lack of meat that compelled him to reduce rations while others, he heard, were not required to make such sacrifices. "I am mortified," he wrote to Richmond in early January, "to find that when any scarcity existed this was the only army in which it is found to reduce the rations. . . . I have never heard of any reduction in the meat ration issued to troops in and about Richmond, Petersburg, Wilmington, Savannah, Mobile, or in the Southwest. . . . Many of them could with propriety, I think, be placed on lighter diet than troops in the field."[3]

The problem remained so bad a few weeks later, that on the same day he issued an order advising the men of the need for a reduction in rations, he warned the secretary of war that the situation was having a "bad effect upon the men, both morally and physically. Desertions to the enemy are becoming more frequent, and the men cannot continue healthy and vigorous if confined to this spare diet for any length of time. Unless there is a change, I fear the army cannot be kept together." Further exacerbating the problem he faced maintaining his army's strength were manpower policies that seemed to encourage soldiers to believe they could serve where they wished without regard to the greater interests of the Confederacy, which demanded their presence in the main field armies, a matter on which Lee felt compelled to express his views to Davis and other officials on a number of occasions.[4]

Supplies of blankets, all types of clothing, and shoes also remained inadequate. Indeed, Lee's mind was so engaged on the matter that at one point he, the commanding general of the army, found himself discussing with the quartermaster general "the practice of the best makers and . . . the arrangement of nature" regarding which side of the skin of the animal shoes were made from should be turned inward. Lee's wife even got involved in the army's supply difficulties by, despite her own badly faltering health (which also weighed on Lee's mind that winter), engaging in efforts to knit socks in Richmond for the army. By May she had sent hundreds of pairs to her husband's headquarters, which Lee then forwarded to the men of the Stonewall Brigade, although they came nowhere close to meeting the need.[5]

That this was the case was due in large part to the utter collapse of the economic foundations of the Confederate war effort due to consistently wretched management of government finances and the wartime economy. Unlike the Lincoln administration, which had access to extensive domestic resources and the international marketplace, as well as men who possessed considerable financial acumen and were capable of adapting fiscal policies to the needs of the Union war effort, the Confederacy possessed few of these things. The inadequacy of taxation and the sale of bonds to produce sufficient revenue to support the Confederate war effort had led the government in Richmond to rely heavily on Treasury notes to finance the war, which had the effect of driving up prices for commodities to unsustainable levels. In April 1863 the Confederate government attempted to address the problem by passing a law imposing an income tax, new excise taxes, and a "tax in kind" of 10 percent on agricultural products. The primary effect of these measures, however, was to foment powerful and widespread resentment in the Confederacy due to the provision of exemptions for land and slaves (which would not be subjected to taxation until February 1864, by which time it was too late to mitigate bitterness the exemptions had generated). The hardships the tax in kind imposed on farm families struggling to survive with so many of their male members in the army further depressed morale in the Confederacy and confidence in the currency, as did the setbacks suffered by Confederate arms in 1863. Consequently, these measures failed to rein in inflation, nor did they generate sufficient revenue to support the war effort. By the winter of 1863–1864, the failure of Confederate economic policy, the deterioration of the South's rail network, the loss of Tennessee and access to other resource rich areas of the Confederacy, the stranglehold the increasingly effective Union blockade was imposing on the South's external trade, and incompetence of Commissary General Lucius Northrop had combined to raise serious questions about the ability of the Confederacy to sustain its armies and the people they defended.[6]

While the Confederate high command struggled to feed its armies and pay its bills, the men responsible for the Union war effort were free to focus their thinking in January and February 1864 on operations. In February they were inspired to authorize a campaign in Florida that accomplished little and culminated in a Union defeat at the Battle of Olustee on the twentieth. Much

more significant—and positive from a Unionist standpoint—was an operation that was carried out in Mississippi that same month. In this campaign,
Federal commanders implemented for the first time a new operational
method they would apply with devastating effect on the South during the
last two years of the war.

A significant set of problems had developed as Union armies liberated
large sections of the South in 1862 and 1863, namely, controlling territory
and maintaining adequate supply lines. This posed little difficulty when
Union forces could support themselves via water, but a great deal of difficulty
when they found themselves dependent on railroads for supplies, which required protection against raids by regular Confederate cavalry and Southern
irregular forces. The question of how to exhaust the Confederacy by seizing
territory that was critical to its economic, military, and political viability
without first exhausting Federal military resources was one that Grant was
compelled to give considerable thought to in 1863. By the end of the year,
he had come up with an inspired solution, although one that was only possible once the Federals had abandoned their effort to conciliate Southerners
by respecting their property in late 1862. To impress upon the Southern people the military power of the North, Grant would, writes historians Herman
Hattaway and Archer Jones, "rely heavily on raids himself rather than on the
further occupation of the enemy's country. . . . They required no communications, because the advance was temporary, and the raiding forces, usually
in motion, could live off the country. Furthermore, since the Union would
not have to hold the region permanently, it would need no additional troops
as garrisons." Unlike the relatively small cavalry forces that had been the
principal tools for conducting raids so far in the war, under Grant's scheme
these raids would be undertaken by commands of ten thousand troops or
more, many of whom would be traditional infantry. This would make the
raiding force strong enough to fight off almost any force the Confederates
might put in front of it and magnify its destructive capabilities. Just as important as the material virtues of the raiding method were its political and
psychological effects. Such operations would demonstrate to the people of
the South the impotence of the Confederate government and the entire ex-
periment in Southern independence in the face of Northern military
strength.[7]

In early February 1864, Grant gave his new method its first large-scale
test. That month he had Gen. Sherman take approximately twenty thousand
men and march east from Vicksburg to the Mississippi state capital at Jackson. From Jackson, Sherman would then push on to the strategic rail junction at Meridian, wrecking the rail network in the region through which his

army passed and destroying or consuming the military resources in the area. Once this had been accomplished, Sherman would make no attempt to maintain a presence in the area over which he had advanced, but either make his way to Mobile, Alabama, or retrace his steps back to Vicksburg with his entire force. Although pushing on to Mobile proved impractical, by the time Sherman's force had returned to Vicksburg during the first week of March, it had destroyed more than a hundred miles of railroad, and either consumed or put to the torch vast quantities of Southern war material, in the process providing compelling evidence of the efficacy of the new method of raids.[8]

As Sherman was wreaking havoc in Mississippi, Lee continued to struggle to get his forces in shape for the upcoming campaign. "You farmers must be very industrious & make heavy crops," Lee advised a family member on February 20. "You see what a distance we have now to forage, how precarious the supply must be when roads are bad & how wearing to our wagons & teams." Lee also spent the winter closely monitoring Federal activities and contemplating his own options for 1864. As always, he believed the best course of action was to take the offensive. On February 3, he advised Davis, "If we could take the initiative and fall upon them unexpectedly we might derange their plans and embarrass them the whole summer." He then offered two possible ways—indeed the only ways available to the Confederacy at the time—for doing this. First, he suggested that Longstreet's force in East Tennessee could be reinforced in order to enable it to "penetrate into Kentucky, where he could support himself, cut Grant's communications so as to compel him at least to detach from Johnston's front, & enable him to take the offensive." The second option was to bring Longstreet back to Virginia. If this were done, Lee thought he might be able to take the offensive to compel Meade to fall back to Washington or at least significantly diminish the size of the Federal host at and around Culpeper. "We are not in a condition, and never have been," Lee argued, "to invade the enemy's country with a prospect of permanent benefit. But we can alarm and embarrass him to some extent and thus prevent his undertaking anything of magnitude against us."[9]

During the week that followed this letter, Lee found himself confronted with a sudden crossing of the Rapidan River on February 6 by elements of the Army of the Potomac who were attempting to divert attention from Federal movements on the Peninsula. Neither the operations on the Peninsula nor along the Rapidan amounted to much, although there was a sharp clash at Morton's Ford involving Ewell's command on the seventh, after which the Federals withdrew back across the Rapidan. "Their loss in comparison with ours was large," Lee advised his wife on February 14. "We are all quiet again."

A few days later, Lee was again writing to Davis on the matter of Longstreet's situation in East Tennessee and restating his belief in the need to retake territory in Tennessee and "to take the initiative before our enemies are prepared to open the campaign." Lee then spent late February and early March monitoring and overseeing efforts to counter an ill-conceived Federal raid against Richmond led by Col. Ulric Dahlgren and Brig. Gen. H. Judson Kilpatrick. After documents were found that suggested the objective of the raid was the murder of Davis and his cabinet, Lee advised Richmond to publicize evidence of "the barbarous and inhuman plot" but refrain from executing Union prisoners in retaliation.[10]

As Lee continued struggling to maintain his army's material well-being and considered in consultation with his civil superiors their course in the aftermath of the Dahlgren Raid, momentous events were taking place on the other side of the lines. The most significant of these was the appointment of a new man to command all the Union armies. In February 1864, the U.S. Congress revived the rank of lieutenant general, last held formally by George Washington, and on March 9 Lincoln officially promoted Ulysses S. Grant to the new rank and made him the general-in-chief of all the Union armies. The victor of Fort Donelson, Shiloh, Vicksburg, and Chattanooga wasted no time plunging into his new duties. The very day after he received his new commission, Grant boarded a train and traveled to Brandy Station to meet with General Meade.[11]

What exactly Grant and Meade discussed regarding future operations against Lee is lost to history, but it is fairly clear that the two men brought to the problem very complementary views. Like many in the Army of the Potomac high command, Meade possessed a belief, instilled during McClellan's tenure in command, that the overland approach following the Orange and Alexandria Railroad was an operationally faulty one. It would be far preferable, Meade believed, to move to the south and east toward Fredericksburg and the Richmond, Fredericksburg, and Potomac Railroad, and he had continually petitioned his superiors in Washington unsuccessfully for permission to do this during the fall of 1863. Meade believed, however, the best course of action would actually be for the Union to eschew the overland approach and instead make a major campaign against Richmond following the James River (and Lee's constant worries that the Federals would do this suggest Meade was correct in his view on the matter).[12]

It turned out that Grant came to Washington thinking very much along the same lines. A few months after the victory at Chattanooga, Halleck had sent Grant a letter asking for his views on future operations. Grant responded with a memorandum in January that proposed taking sixty thousand men from the Army of the Potomac and sending them down the Chesapeake Bay to make an amphibious landing at Suffolk. From there, this force would move south and west toward Raleigh, North Carolina, to tear up the transportation network that linked Virginia with the rest of the Confederacy and encourage discontent with the cause of Southern independence in the region. It was a well-conceived, and eminently feasible plan. Moreover, it was one that fully complemented Meade's desire to get the Army of the Potomac off the over-land route and take it some place where it could inflict truly decisive damage on the Confederacy.[13]

Of course, the ultimate fate of Grant's plan rested with two men who for more than a year had been frustrating the wishes of Meade and like-minded officers in the Army of the Potomac to lead their command to more fruitful fields of operations. As convinced as Meade was of the pointlessness of con-tinuing to base operations on the Orange and Alexandria Railroad, so were

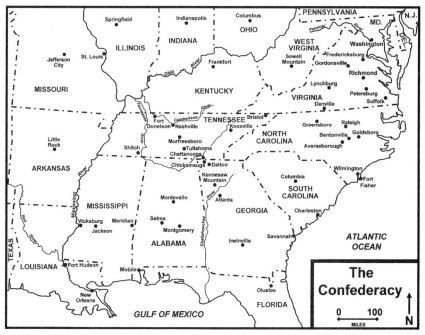

Figure 5.1.   The Confederacy.

Lincoln and Halleck of the need to keep the Army of the Potomac on that railroad in order to ensure the safety of Washington. Consequently, when Halleck responded to Grant's proposal in mid-February he made two points crystal clear: the first, of course, was that his plan was unacceptable to Washington; the second was that no plan so conceived would ever receive approval.[14]

Grant, however, had not reached the exalted rank of lieutenant general and inspired his friend Sherman to proclaim him "Washington's legitimate successor" without knowing how to work around obstacles thrown in his path—be they recalcitrant subordinates, difficult terrain, or problematic superiors. And unfortunately for the Confederacy, as Grant developed his plans during the weeks following his appointment as general-in-chief, during which time he was in frequent consultation with Meade, he demonstrated these qualities in spades. Very well, Grant decided, if Washington insisted on keeping the Army of the Potomac on the overland approach, it would be done. "Lee's army," he informed Meade on April 9, "will be your objective point. Wherever Lee goes, there you will go also."[15]

At the same time, Grant smartly took advantage of the need for political general Benjamin Butler to have a significant command in the election year of 1864 to win Lincoln's approval for a major operation along the James River. As Grant conceived it, the combined effort of Meade's Army of the Potomac and Butler's Army of the James would place Lee in a vise, with Meade at the least keeping the Army of Northern Virginia so engaged that it could not prevent Butler from delivering a decisive blow against the Confederate cause by wrecking Lee's army through the seizure of its capital and base of operations. "My first object being to break the military power of the rebellion and capture the enemy's important strongholds," Grant later wrote, "made me desirous that General Butler should succeed in his movement against Richmond, as that would tend more than anything else, unless it were the capture of Lee's army, to accomplish this desired result in the East." Indeed, Grant placed so much importance on Butler's operations that he briefly considered having Meade open the 1864 campaign season by moving west in order to lure Lee in that direction. This, Grant thought, would facilitate Butler's ability to achieve the objectives Grant had identified in the plan he proposed to Halleck in January—namely, the destruction of Lee's logistical and political bases of support—only with the much richer prize of Richmond, rather than Raleigh, as the target of operations. However, Grant sensibly ended up following Meade's script from the previous fall. He would cross the Rapidan to try to turn Lee's right flank and catch the Confederates at a tactical disadvantage. If this did not produce a decisive victory over Lee,

Grant would then follow the plan Meade had tried in vain to win approval for from Washington, namely of then moving the Army of the Potomac south and east to a line of operations based on the Richmond, Fredericksburg, and Potomac Railroad, while ensuring he would have the option of ultimately pushing to the James to link up with Butler. Not surprisingly, given the chilly reception his January proposal had received, there is no evidence that Grant explicitly spelled out these elements of his plan for the 1864 campaign to either Halleck or Lincoln.[16]

Lee and his army were, in Grant's mind, the Confederate center of gravity, and the entire Union war effort must be oriented around destroying that force, the "one common centre" as Grant phrased it, whose defeat was "the first great object." This would be achieved quickly, Grant hoped, through sound execution of the plans he conceived for Meade's and Butler's forces. But failing that, Lee would be defeated gradually by the cumulative effect of the efforts of the armies operating directly against his army and the exhaustion of Confederate resources by Union armies operating in the Shenandoah Valley and Georgia. If crushing Confederate armies on the battlefield proved unachievable or insufficient to quickly break the South's will to continue the fight, the method of raiding that had tested so well in the Meridian Campaign would wear it down while exhausting the South's ability to fight. In the Shenandoah Valley, forces under Maj. Gen. Franz Sigel were assigned the task of pinning down Confederate forces there and denying its rich agricultural resources to Lee, while Grant instructed the Union commander in Georgia, Sherman, that he was "to move against Johnston's army, to break it up, and to get into the interior of the enemy's country as far as you can, inflicting all the damage you can upon their war resources." These were all, though, supporting movements. "Lee, with the capital of the Confederacy, was the main end to which all were working," wrote Grant, ". . . the capture of Johnston and his army would not produce so immediate and decisive a result in closing the rebellion as would the possession of Richmond, Lee and his army."[17]

Lee, of course, was hopeful that he could frustrate whatever plans Grant was developing and prevent the fall of the Confederacy in 1864, although he must have been quite pessimistic regarding the prospects for success. The winter of 1863–1864 was a hard one for the Army of Northern Virginia and the entire Confederacy, with widespread shortages and Union soldiers in occupation of much of the South's richest and most valuable territory. If this were not enough to foster gloom at the Army of Northern Virginia headquarters, it was clear Grant was carefully marshaling Union military power with the intention of delivering hard blows against the rebel armies while denying the Confederates any opportunity for a decisive battlefield success. With the prospect of yet another year battling against heavy odds and a man in charge of the Union war effort whose record of success gave no reason to expect any let up in the application of the North's over-whelming material superiority on the battlefield, what hope could Lee have for the cause of Confederate independence as he contemplated the future during the cold early months of 1864?

The answer to this question, of course, rested, as it always had in Lee's mind, on the will of the Northern public to continue the war. The only way to avoid seeing the Confederacy crushed under the weight of Union power was to achieve successes on the battlefield. Optimally, these would be in the form of tactical victories that would destroy Northern armies in the field; however, experience had demonstrated that, short of extreme good fortune, this was beyond Lee's means even when his army was much stronger than it would be when the campaign season opened in 1864. Still, even if Northern armies could not be destroyed, they could be outmaneuvered and placed in compromising operational and tactical situations where they would be vul-nerable. If Lee could create and take advantage of such opportunities, he might win victories that would sow frustration in the North and might un-dermine the Northern public's faith in ultimate victory to the point that they would seize on the opportunity presented by the presidential election of 1864 to replace the government in Washington with one that would stop the bleeding and recognize Confederate independence.

Although Lee and the Confederacy were so weak in comparison with their foes that the only real hope for victory was to reach the November elections with their armies strong and defiant enough to push Northern frustration to the breaking point, it did not follow that the proper stance in 1864 was to abandon an aggressive operational and tactical mind-set in fa-vor of conducting a passive defense where Lee would merely await the en-emy's blows and attempt to repulse them. Such a mind-set would concede the initiative to the Federals, and the war had demonstrated over and over again that this was a dangerous thing, for it would diminish Lee's control over the situation and his ability to create and exploit opportunities for tac-tical success.

As Lee often pointed out to Davis during the winter of 1863–1864, the best course of action would be to seize the operational initiative and go on the offensive before the Federals could, for it would frustrate the ability of the Union high command to thoroughly marshal their forces and force them to react. This, of course, proved impracticable due to resource constraints. But if forced to open the 1864 campaign season on the defensive and concede the initial moves to the Federals, there was no reason to continue to cede the initiative to the Federals once they were in the field and, as always, it made sense to be aggressive and conduct an active defense in which Lee would constantly seek opportunities to take the offensive himself. A passive defense would allow the Federals to dictate the terms of any engagement and follow their preference for methodically conducted set-piece engagements in which superior firepower and numbers could be applied. By conducting an active defense, the Confederates could disrupt Federal preparations, throw them off balance, create opportunities for decisive tactical success, bleed the Federal army, and win victories that would boost Confederate and depress Northern morale.

The strategic balance and the fact that the November elections were so close further argued for an aggressive mind-set and a mentality that focused on short-term operational possibilities, throwing everything the Confederacy had into the fight in 1864, and dismissing those who argued for husbanding Southern resources for the long haul. To hold back on the battlefield would result in missed opportunities for success and whatever chance existed in 1864 for producing a revolution in the North. Moreover, there was little point in preserving resources for whatever might happen after November 1864. If the political revolution the Confederacy needed in the North did not happen that month, Lee and his cause were doomed anyway to destruction at the hands of a Lincoln administration that was armed with comparatively infinite resources and totally unwilling to relent in its effort to crush the Confederacy.

Throughout the late winter of 1863–1864, Lee regularly endured the brutal cold and wind to ascend Clark's Mountain for a look at his foe, while also relying on information from a network of scouts and spies north of the Rappahannock, in an effort to glean the intentions of the new Union general-in-chief and plot his own course. Initially, Lee thought Grant might prefer to initiate operations where he had previously been successful by making his first effort against Johnston's or Longstreet's forces. By the end of March, however, reports in Northern newspapers regarding Grant's personal movements led Lee to change his mind about this. Unclear to Lee, though, was whether reports that the Union Ninth Corps was going to be transferred from East Tennessee to Annapolis, Maryland, were accurate and, when this was confirmed, what that unit's role in the 1864 campaign would be. Regardless, Lee remained sure of what the South's best course of action was. "If a good move could be made before they are ready to execute their plans," he proclaimed in letters to Longstreet and Davis, "we would confound their schemes and break them up. . . . Energy and activity on our part, with a constant readiness to seize any opportunity to strike a blow, will embarrass, if not entirely thwart the enemy in concentrating his different armies, and compel him to conform his movements to our own." "The great obstacle everywhere," he added, "is scarcity of supplies. That is the controlling element to which everything has to yield."[18]

While continuing to complain about his supply situation, Lee spent the first half of April 1864 becoming increasingly convinced that the Federals intended to concentrate a strong force in central Virginia with which to attack the Army of Northern Virginia "as soon as the weather is settled." The only point of doubt was whether the Ninth Corps would be joining the Army of the Potomac in this effort or operating on the Peninsula. At the latter place, Lee deduced, they would operate alongside Federal forces that had operated unsuccessfully against Charleston in 1863. Either way, it was clear to Lee that he needed the First Corps back from Tennessee. In part, this was because he wanted Longstreet on hand in case poor health should compel a change at the head of the Army of Northern Virginia, something that weighed heavily on Lee's mind in early April when he complained to his son: "I feel a marked change in my strength since my attack last spring and am less competent for duty than ever." Finally, on April 11, Longstreet received orders to leave Bristol, Tennessee, where his command had been posted so that it could move to Lee or Johnston depending on circumstances, and report to Lee. If enough forces could be concentrated at Richmond from the forces now released from the defense of Charleston to defend the capital from the east, Lee proposed to Davis on April 15 that when Longstreet had arrived, the Army of Northern Virginia might "move right against the enemy on the Rappahannock. Should God give us a crowning victory there, all their plans would be dissipated, and their troops now collecting on the waters of Chesapeake will be recalled to the defense of Washington."[19]

Lee then instructed Longstreet to have his corps take up a position in and around Gordonsville and shortly after their arrival went over to see the First Corps, which one South Carolina colonel advised his wife, was "glad to get back to the Army of Va." The bond between Lee and his men was powerfully in evidence when the general reviewed the First Corps on April 29. It was, that same colonel wrote his wife the next day, "A gala day for our Corps. Our venerable military father, Genl. Lee, did us the compliment to come down and review us. It was the most imposing pageant we have ever witnessed. . . . the shouts and tossing up of hats of the armed multitude. We all feel better after a sight of our grand chieftain. No one can excite their enthusiasm as he does."[20]

In addition to visiting with the First Corps, Lee spent the last week of April puzzling over why the Army of the Potomac had not begun its advance yet. That same week scouts resolved the mystery of what role the Ninth Corps would play in Virginia by reporting that corps's movement through Washington and Alexandria and then south along the Orange and Alexandria Railroad to relieve the units from the Army of the Potomac that had previously been guarding the road. Then, on May 2 Lee called his corps and division commanders together on Clark's Mountain and predicted the Federals would once again attempt to turn their right flank by crossing the Rapidan downstream from where they were standing.[21]

Finally, on May 4, reports reached Lee that the Army of the Potomac had broken camp and was heading toward the Rapidan crossings at Germanna and Ely's Fords. Lee immediately ordered Ewell and Hill to move east along the Orange Turnpike and Orange Plank Roads respectively to reoccupy their former position behind Mine Run, which was accomplished by nightfall on the fourth. Meanwhile, Longstreet's corps moved forward from its camps around Gordonsville and covered sixteen miles by nightfall. "Genl Meade is in motion," Lee advised Richmond from his new headquarters at Verdiersville, "whether with the intention of attacking, or moving towards Fredericksburg, I am not able to say. But it is apparent that the long threatened effort to take Richmond has begun."[22]

Grant's plan was to have one corps cross the Rapidan at Ely's Ford, while the rest of the Army of the Potomac, followed by the Ninth Corps, crossed further west at Germanna Ford. The two wings of the army would then quickly push south through the aptly named Wilderness where Hooker had been brought to grief the previous year and reach the open ground to the south. If successfully executed, this march would put the Union army between Lee and Richmond and give Grant and Meade the ability to then swing west to engage Lee on ground of their own choosing.[23]

The danger that the Federals might do this was a consequence of the fact that Lee was forced to let the Federals make the first move in 1864 and it was something Lee wished to prevent. As soon as he learned of the Federals breaking camp, Lee hoped to attack them while their ability to respond effectively was complicated by the fact that Lee's line of march was perpendicular to their own and by the thick woods and limited number of roads in the Wilderness. Spirits were high among the 62,000 men in the Army of Northern Virginia as they moved toward the 120,000 man force Grant was leading into the Wilderness on May 4. "All nature seems smiling on this spring morn," wrote one member of the Stonewall Brigade. "What a grand sight is the Army of Lee in motion. The whole brigade is all life, seems as though they are never to be conquered."[24]

Fortunately for Lee, when night fell on May 4, the Federals had yet to clear the Wilderness and were compelled to spend the evening there. Hoping to hit them before they could reach open ground and fully bring to bear their superior numbers and firepower, Lee directed Ewell and Hill to push east to occupy the lines at Mine Run early on May 5 and instructed Longstreet to continue moving forward to join the rest of the army. Although he clearly hoped to engage the Federals in the Wilderness, Lee wanted his attack to be a heavy one and made a point of telling Ewell that he "preferred not to bring on a general engagement before General Longstreet came up."[25]

Evidence of Lee's approach quickly reached the Union high command and led to the dispatch of Maj. Gen. Gouverneur K. Warren's Fifth Corps west along the Orange Turnpike toward Mine Run. When Warren confirmed reports that a large Confederate force was moving toward him, Meade and Grant immediately put an end to the effort to push through the Wilderness. "If there is to be fighting this side of Mine Run," Meade remarked, "let us do it right off."[26]

Notes

1. Davis to Lee, December 5, 1863, OR, vol. 29, pt. 2: 861; Lee to Davis, December 7, 1863, in *Wartime Papers*, eds. Dowdey and Manarin, 642.

2. Lee to Davis, December 3, 1863, ibid., 641; Lee to his wife, December 22, 1863, ibid., 643–44; Freeman, *R.E. Lee*, vol. 3: 218.

3. Lee to Davis, January 2, 1864, in *Wartime Papers*, eds. Dowdey and Manarin, 646–47; Lee to Northrop, January 5, 1864, ibid., 647–48.

4. Hdqrs. Army of Northern Virginia, General Orders No. 7, January 22, 1864, in *Wartime Papers*, eds. Dowdey and Manarin, 659; Lee to Seddon, January 22, 1864, ibid., 659–60; Lee to Davis, January 13, 27, 1864, ibid., 650–51, 662.

5. Lee to Lawton, January 30, 1864, ibid., 664; Lee to his wife, March 19, 20, 30, May 2, 1864, ibid., 680, 681, 687, 707.

6. James M. McPherson, *Ordeal by Fire: The Civil War and Reconstruction* (New York: McGraw-Hill, 2003 ed.), 220–22; Mark Grimsley, "Surviving Military Revolution: The U.S. Civil War," in *The Dynamics of Military Revolution, 1300–2050* (Cambridge, UK; New York: Cambridge University Press, 2001), 86–87, 89.

7. Hattaway and Jones, *How the North Won*, 491–93.

8. Ibid., 506–10.

9. Lee to Charles Carter Lee, February 20, 1864, Lee Papers, WL; Lee to Davis, February 3, 1864, in *Wartime Papers*, eds. Dowdey and Manarin, 666–67.

10. Lee to his wife, February 14, 1864, ibid., 671; Lee to Davis, February 18, 1864, ibid., 674–75; Lee to Cooper, February 29, 1864, ibid., 675; Lee to Johnson, March 2, 1864, ibid., 677; Lee to Seddon, March 6, 1863, ibid., 678.

11. Grant, *Memoirs*, 403–04.

12. Ethan S. Rafuse, *George Gordon Meade and the War in the East* (Abilene, TX: McWhiney Foundation Press, 2003), 27–30, 103.

13. Grant to Halleck, January 19, 1864, OR, vol. 33, pt. 1: 394–95.

14. Halleck to Grant, February 17, 1864, ibid., vol. 32, pt. 2: 411–13.

15. Sherman to Grant, March 10, 1864, in *Sherman's Civil War: Selected Correspondence of William T. Sherman, 1860–1865*, edited by Brooks D. Simpson and Jean V. Berlin (Chapel Hill: University of North Carolina Press, 1999), 603; Grant to Meade, April 9, 1864, OR, vol. 33: 827–28.

16. Grant to Stanton, July 22, 1865, ibid., vol. 36, pt. 1: 17; Grant, *Memoirs*, 408, 411–17.

17. Grant, *Memoirs*, 415, 419, 423; Grant to Sherman, April 4, 1864, OR, vol. 32, pt. 3: 246.

18. Lee to Davis, March 25, 30, 1864, in *Wartime Papers*, eds. Dowdey and Manarin, 683–84, 687–88; Lee to Longstreet, March 28, 1864, ibid., 684–85.

19. Lee to his son, April 9, 1864, ibid., 695–96; Lee to Davis, April 8, 12, 15, 1864, ibid., 693–94, 698, 699–700; Longstreet to Taylor, March 23, 1865, OR, vol. 36, pt. 1: 1054.

20. William D. Rutherford to his wife, April 14, 30, 1864, William D. Rutherford Letters, bound vol. 374, FSNMP.

21. Lee to Longstreet, April 20, 1864, Lee Papers, WL; Lee to Bragg, April 16, 1864, in *Wartime Papers*, eds. Dowdey and Manarin, 701; Lee to Davis, April 25, 29, 30, 1864, ibid., 705, 706–07, 708–09; Ewell to Taylor, March 20, 1865, OR, vol. 36, pt. 1: 1070.

22. Longstreet to Taylor, March 23, 1865, ibid., 1054; Lee to Bragg, May 4, 1864, in *Wartime Papers*, eds. Dowdey and Manarin, 718; Lee to Davis, May 4, 1864, ibid., 719.

23. Andrew A. Humphreys, *The Virginia Campaign of 1864 and 1865: The Army of the Potomac and the Army of the James* (New York: Charles Scribner's Sons, 1883), 18–22.

24. "Memoirs of James L. McCowen . . . April 2–August 4, 1864," *Rockbridge County News*, February 12, 1953, copy in bound vol. 16, FSNMP.

25. Lee to Seddon, May 5, 1864, in *Wartime Papers*, eds. Dowdey and Manarin, 721–22; Lee to Ewell, May 5, 1864, OR, vol. 36, pt. 2: 952; Longstreet to Chilton, March 23, 1865, ibid., vol. 36, pt. 1: 1054; Ewell to Taylor, March 20, 1865, ibid., 1070.

26. Rafuse, *George Gordon Meade and the War in the East*, 122.

CHAPTER SIX

The Furnace of 1864

Like Meade, Robert E. Lee was eager for a test of strength between their two armies on the morning of May 5, 1864. Although Longstreet's command was still a day's march away, Lee could not let the Army of the Potomac push through the Wilderness without a fight. If the Federals were able to do this, Lee's position would be turned and he would have no choice but to try to dislodge them from open ground where their superior numbers and firepower would be even more difficult to overcome. Fortunately for Lee, Grant and Meade agreed on May 5 to accept his challenge and responded to news of the approach of the Army of Northern Virginia along the Orange Turnpike by ordering Warren to seek out the enemy along that road. As it became clear that the Federals would fight in the Wilderness, Lee was unable to contain his delight that Grant, a staff officer later wrote, "had not profited by General Hooker's Wilderness experiences, and that he seemed inclined to throw away to some extent the immense advantages which his great superiority in numbers in every arm of the service gave him."[1]

The weeks that followed would see Grant's and Lee's forces engage in a campaign characterized by a level of sustained, brutal combat that has led one recent historian to proclaim it "more in common with Verdun"—the great 1916 battle that claimed over a half million casualties and became known to its participants as "the furnace"—than with almost any other battle in American military history. The American furnace of May–June 1864, if it did not match Verdun in terms of duration and overall casualties, nonetheless left both armies exhausted and left Grant facing accusations of

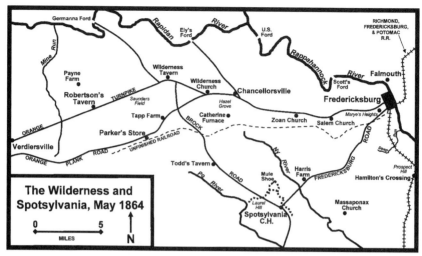

Figure 6.1.   The Wilderness and Spotsylvania.

having engaged in an exercise of wasteful and unimaginative butchery. However, by transferring the central front in the war in Virginia from the Rapidan to the James River, the Overland Campaign decisively put Lee and the Confederacy on the road to final defeat.[2]

The campaign began in earnest when Warren complied with Meade's and Grant's orders to advance down the Orange Turnpike. The enemy force in Warren's front turned out to be Ewell's corps, whose commander had twice been told that Lee wanted him to "regulate my march by General A. P. Hill, whose progress down the plank road I could tell by the firing at the head of his column, and . . . preferred not to bring on a general engagement before General Longstreet came up." Upon finding himself well ahead of Hill, Ewell halted his command shortly before noon and, after receiving confirmation of Lee's earlier instructions, sent orders to his advanced units not to get drawn into an engagement with the enemy but to fall back if contact was made. Ewell's men then built strong defensive works overlooking a clearing in the Wilderness known as Saunders Field, which enabled them to fight off a series of determined attacks by Warren's command that afternoon. Shortly after Ewell's command first made contact with the Federals, one of Ewell's staff officers rode over to Lee's command post to discuss the situation and reported the Second Corps commander would "fall back to Mine Run if pushed, understanding such to be his orders." Lee immediately replied that Ewell had misunderstood his earlier orders to avoid getting "entangled" with the enemy prematurely and "that he only wanted us to fall back in case we could not hold our position."[3]

Meanwhile, two of Hill's divisions, with Lee riding in its vanguard, pushed east along the Orange Plank Road toward its intersection with the Brock Road. If Lee could seize this intersection, he would block the route of the Union corps that had crossed at Germanna Ford out of the Wilderness. He would also cut off the Union corps that had crossed at Ely's Ford on the fourth and was under orders to march on May 5 to a point on the Brock Road well south of its intersection with the Plank Road. At mid-afternoon, Lee sent a division forward to the intersection, but by then a Union force had already reached it and was pushing west along the Plank Road. The Federals then, "like the wolf on the fold," one man later wrote, slammed into the lead elements of Hill's corps, and a fierce engagement erupted that continued until nightfall. As Hill battled the Federals, Lee had orders sent to Ewell to "be ready to support our right . . . and if an opportunity presents itself and you can get Wilderness Tavern ridge and cut the enemy off from the river, the general wishes it done." He also sent orders to Longstreet to make a night march and reach the field by daylight on the sixth.[4]

As Lee could see from personal observation, Hill's command took a serious beating on May 5 and was sure to face a much stronger Federal force the following day. Nonetheless, Lee and Hill denied requests from their subordinates for permission to pull back at bit and adjust their lines during the night so they could strengthen their position before engaging the Federals again. When a nervous division commander brought such a request to Hill, he was assured, "Longstreet will be up in a few hours. He will form in your front. I don't propose that your division shall do any fighting tomorrow, the men have been marching and fighting all day and are tired. I do not wish them disturbed."[5]

Lee's and Hill's hope that Longstreet's command would arrive in time to prevent this from being a fatal error ultimately proved correct, but Hill's command paid a dear price on May 6. At about five in the morning, with Longstreet still some distance from the field, the Federals renewed their advance along both the Turnpike and Plank Road. From behind his strong entrenchments, Ewell was able to fight off attacks by two Union corps along the turnpike. Hill, however, was quickly overwhelmed by a sledgehammer Federal advance and driven back along the Plank Road until it reached the open area around the Widow Tapp Farm. It was at that point that two divisions from Longstreet's corps arrived on the scene. They found Lee, one man later wrote, "in the midst of Hill's sullenly retreating troops. . . . He was a superb figure as he sat on his spirited gray with the light of battle on his face. His presence was an inspiration. The retreating columns turned their faces bravely to the front once more, and the fresh divisions went forward under his eye with splendid spirit." The first unit to arrive from Maj. Gen. Charles Field's division, which Longstreet had posted north of the Plank Road, was the Texas Brigade. Astride his warhorse Traveller, Lee greeted the Texans near the Tapp Farm, prompting a loud cheer when he shouted "Hurrah for Texas! Hurrah for Texas!" As the Texans began advancing toward the enemy, Lee followed right behind their battle line. But then the Texans cried out, "Go back, General Lee, go back. We won't go forward until you go back. . . . Lee to the rear." Not until some of the men physically blocked Lee and a sergeant grabbed Traveller's bridle rein to steer him in another direction did Lee accede to his men's wishes. The Texans and the rest of Longstreet's command then pushed forward on both sides of the Plank Road toward the exhausted Federals and not only brought their advance to a halt, but drove them back about a half mile.[6]

Lee was not satisfied just to have maintained his position. The Federals still controlled the Brock Road and had an open route out of the Wilderness. Consequently, Lee rode over to the Orange Turnpike to talk with Ewell. Having urged him the previous evening to make an attempt to crush the flank of the Union forces in his front, Lee tried again to convince Ewell to abandon a purely defensive stance. Meanwhile, shortly after 10:00 a.m. Longstreet developed a plan whereby four brigades would follow an unfinished railroad cut south of the Orange Plank Road to a position from which they could strike the Union left. As Lee made his way back to the Tapp Farm, Longstreet completed his preparations and launched his attack. Taken almost completely by surprise, the Union flank caved in under the weight of this attack and a follow-up advance by the rest of Longstreet's command along the Plank Road. However, the effort to follow up what Longstreet later proclaimed "a complete surprise and perfect success" lost vital momentum when the First Corps commander was accidentally wounded by some of his own men.[7]

By the time Lee was able to sort things out, more than three hours had passed and the Federals had rallied behind breastworks covering the Brock Road. Desperate to strike a decisive blow, Lee ordered his men forward in a series of assaults that managed to pierce the Union line in a few places, but were unable, due in part to what one officer later described as "almost impenetrable growth of wood and brush," to drive the Federals from their position. As this was occurring, at the other end of the line part of Ewell's corps launched an attack on the Union right that managed to capture a large section of Federal works, several hundred prisoners, and two generals, but was unable to produce a decisive result.[8]

Exhausted by the fighting of the previous two days (in which the Federals suffered about eighteen thousand casualties and the Confederates around eleven thousand), the two armies spent May 7 contemplating the smoldering Wilderness as Lee sifted through reports that the enemy had taken up his bridges over the Rapidan and conceded the section of the road that connected their positions with Germanna Ford. From this he deduced the Federals would next move south toward Spotsylvania Court House or east toward Fredericksburg. Thus, he directed Stuart to examine the roads beyond the southern flank of both armies. While committed at the moment to waiting to see what the Federals would do, Lee by no means ruled out taking the offensive, for he told Stuart he wanted information in case it proved "necessary for us to follow should the enemy continue his movement toward Spotsylvania Court House, or should we desire to move on his flank." By 7:00 p.m., Lee determined the time had come to leave the Wilderness and directed Ewell to prepare to follow the First Corps, now commanded by Maj. Gen. Richard H. Anderson, who had been told by Lee to "march towards Spotsylvania Court-House. I have reason to believe that the enemy is withdrawing his forces . . . and will strike us next at that point. I wish you to be there to meet him, and in order to do so, you must be in motion by 3 o'clock in the morning."[9]

Grant had in fact decided to move to Spotsylvania. In doing so, he broke the operational stalemate that had prevailed in the East since July 1863. As the abandonment of the road back to the Rapidan indicated, he would no longer let his movements be constrained by the limitations of the Orange and Alexandria line. Instead, he was moving south and east, shifting his line of supply to the Richmond, Fredericksburg, and Potomac Railroad and moving his army to a position from which it would have the option of accessing a water supply line. Grant's operational concept and the movement from the Wilderness that flowed from it were neither original nor especially inspired. After all, Meade had proposed a similar move the previous fall, only to have it vetoed by Lincoln. Grant wisely did not bother asking permission from Washington when he made his decision to move toward Spotsylvania.

Lee, of course, had no intention of letting the Federals turn his position by reaching Spotsylvania first. Yet not until after he had submitted a brief message to Richmond early on the eighth did Lee realize the Federals were in fact moving to Spotsylvania. Of course, he had already taken measures to ensure a significant contingent from his own army was on the way to Spotsylvania should that be the Federal destination on the eighth. Whether they would arrive in time and in sufficient strength to thwart the Federal move, though, was an open question on May 8.[10]

Dame Fortune, however, smiled on the Army of Northern Virginia on May 7–8 and allowed it to win the race to Spotsylvania. First, due to fires in the Wilderness where they intended to bivouac before beginning their march, Anderson decided to eschew resting his troops and instead ordered them to push on to Spotsylvania immediately. Then, the Federal movement to Spotsylvania was retarded by difficulties coordinating the movements of the infantry and cavalry. This delayed the march of the lead Union corps, commanded by Warren, long enough to enable Anderson to drive off some Federal cavalry that had reached Spotsylvania Court House and establish a strong position on Laurel Hill that blocked the road to Spotsylvania just before Warren arrived. Warren made a vigorous attempt to drive Anderson off, but could not do it. By the time another Union corps reached Warren at around five in the afternoon, Ewell's corps, accompanied by Lee himself, had arrived at Laurel Hill after what its commander described as "a very distressing march through intense heat and thick dust and smoke from burning woods." Ewell then went into position on Anderson's rights and together they repulsed an attack by the two Union corps on the scene, which brought the fighting on May 8 to an end.[11]

Grant and Lee spent much of May 9 resting their troops, gathering information, and considering their options. The breathing spell was especially welcome to Lee, because it allowed him to finish shuffling his high command to accommodate Hill's request the day before for relief from command due to illness. Lee responded to this by ordering Maj. Gen. Jubal Early to move over from the division he commanded in Ewell's corps to take Hill's place, and shuffling some units and commanders around to accommodate this move. Losing two of his three corps commanders in the span of only two days and less than a week into the campaign could hardly have been viewed as a propitious way to begin the campaign; however, Lee's dismay at this development was partially mitigated by the fact that it allowed him to expand the authority of Early, for whose abilities he had developed a high regard.[12]

Meanwhile, on May 8–9, Ewell finished posting his corps to the right of Anderson's position on Laurel Hill and fortifying their position. In an effort to secure the best possible terrain, however, the Second Corps ended up occupying a large salient, which became known as the "Mule Shoe," between Anderson's men to its left and Early's corps, which Lee posted to its right to cover the Fredericksburg Road. Despite these problems, as he assessed the course of the campaign on the ninth, Lee took comfort in a conviction that the Army of Northern Virginia had done quite well so far in the campaign. It had, he advised Davis, successfully thwarted every Federal attempt to turn its position and had been "impeding [Grant's] progress, without a general engagement, which I will not bring on unless a favorable opportunity offers. . . . Every attack upon us has been repelled and considerable damage done the enemy."[13]

Grant was no less sanguine about the results of the campaign so far and was determined to find some way to attack the Confederates in part out of a belief that an opening would eventually be found that would enable him to achieve decisive success. Even if this did not happen, he would at least keep Lee occupied and unable to do anything to help counter Butler's drive toward Richmond. By the end of the day, with the strength of the Laurel Hill position made clear by the attacks of the eighth, Grant developed a plan to turn or envelop one or both Confederate flanks. Maj. Gen. Winfield Scott Hancock's Second Corps, he decided, would cross the Po River to secure a position from which it could attack the left flank of Anderson's position on Laurel Hill on the tenth. Meanwhile, Maj. Gen. Ambrose Burnside's Ninth Corps, which after departing the Wilderness had made a wide march to the east that brought it to the Fredericksburg Road at a point well east of Spotsylvania Court House, would press the Confederate right.

Unfortunately for Grant, he found it no easier to coordinate operations at the ends of such an extended, exterior line than Lee had at Gettysburg. By dawn on the tenth, Hancock was across the Po but found the Confederates fully prepared for an attempt against their left. Burnside's command, meanwhile, found the Ny River blocking their route to the Confederate line, and it quickly became clear to Lee that he could expect little trouble on his right on May 10. Lee also saw in Grant's moves an opportunity to strike a blow of his own. Although he had put his men to fortifying a strong position, Lee had little interest in conducting a passive defense at Spotsylvania. Letting Grant probe and probe until he found a tactical opening or decided to leave Spotsylvania altogether would do nothing to advance Lee's operational or strategic goals. Moreover, by this point, Butler's army had moved up the James River to City Point and Bermuda Hundred with only a small Confederate force nearby to resist its movements. With Richmond in what the secretary of war proclaimed on May 10 to be "hot danger," there was no way Lee could be content to merely thwart Grant's assaults while the capital—his ultimate base of operations—fell to Butler. If Grant's army could be struck a decisive blow, however, that might compel it to recoil sufficiently to allow Lee to send assistance to Richmond's defense. Consequently, Lee kept a keen eye out for opportunities to deliver an effective attack of his own.[14]

On May 10, with strong fortifications and his interior lines at Spotsylvania making it possible to shift forces quickly to concentrate against a part of the enemy's force, Lee had a good position from which to strike a blow if the Federals provided him with an opportunity. Hancock's situation that morning, with the Po River separating him from the rest of the Army of the Potomac, seemed to provide one, and Lee moved quickly to seize it. He ordered one division from the Third Corps on the right (which according to Grant's plans was supposed to have its hands full dealing with Burnside, but did not) to take a position to the left of Anderson and press Hancock's front, while another of Early's divisions acted as a maneuver force that would swing around Hancock's right and strike its flank. Hancock, however, recognized the danger and received permission to pull back across the Po. During the mid-afternoon, the Confederates launched a determined attack against the last of Hancock's divisions still south of the Po that sent the Federals back across the river with more haste and less order than they had anticipated. With his attempts at maneuver frustrated, Grant then launched another series of assaults against Lee's line. These attacks, Lee reported to Richmond that night, "were easily repulsed, except in front of [Brig. Gen. George] Doles' Brigade, where they drove our men from their position and from a four-gun battery there posted. The men were soon rallied and by dark our line was reestablished."[15]

The moment of Federal success Lee alluded to in his report was a skillfully planned assault by twelve regiments led by Col. Emory Upton against the left side of the Mule Shoe. Inspired by Upton's success, Grant decided to renew the attack against the Mule Shoe using Hancock's entire Second Corps. Thus, he spent much of the day on May 11 and the following night maneuvering Hancock's command so it would be in position to strike the apex of the Mule Shoe on the morning of the twelfth.

Meanwhile, Lee spent May 11 trying to discern what Grant was doing. He also had to worry about a raid Grant had authorized Maj. Gen. Phillip Sheridan, commander of the Army of the Potomac's cavalry, to make toward Richmond on the ninth. Lee responded by dispatching Stuart and three brigades to deal with it, but Sheridan had taken advantage of his head start to reach the Confederate supply depot at Beaver Dam Station and spend the night of May 9–10 destroying it. On the eleventh, Stuart reached Yellow Tavern just north of Richmond, and Sheridan, eager for a fight, attacked his position. In the fighting that ensued, Stuart was mortally wounded and his command defeated. Sheridan's command then probed the Richmond defenses, producing, in the words of one of the capital's residents, much "consternation among the members of Congress," before pushing east to the Peninsula, tearing up railroads and bridges and stripping the region they rode through of whatever they could get their hands on.[16]

As he awaited Grant's next move during the evening of May 11, Lee met with a group of his subordinates in Spotsylvania Court House. When they let it be known that they were unimpressed with Grant's penchant, one man later wrote, "for throwing his men against our breastworks and having them slaughtered," Lee made it clear he did not share their views. "Gentlemen," he remarked, "I think that General Grant has managed his affairs remarkably well up to the present time." Lee then predicted that Grant's next step would be to pull back toward Fredericksburg that night and told his lieutenants, "I wish you to have everything in readiness to pull out at a moment's notice. . . . We must attack these people if they retreat." When two of the officers present responded to Lee's statement by calling attention to how events of the past week had provided a vivid illustration of the virtues of remaining on the defensive in a fortified position, he bluntly rejected this course of action as unsuited to the operational needs and capabilities of the Army of Northern Virginia. "This army cannot stand a siege," he remarked, "we must end this business on the battlefield, not in a fortified place."[17]

Lee's hopes that he could escape his static defensive stance at Spotsylvania and prevent the Federals from inexorably grinding down his force were kindled during the afternoon and night of May 11–12 by reports that some of Grant's forces at Spotsylvania were moving and that they seemed particularly active on the Confederate right. As he told his subordinates, Lee wrongly deduced that this meant Grant had had enough at Spotsylvania and was preparing to move toward Fredericksburg. Sensing an opportunity to strike, Lee ordered his commanders to prepare to move and, to facilitate a rapid movement, instructed Ewell to pull forces from the Mule Shoe. Ewell protested that the heavy rain that night would make moving his infantry hard on the men and managed to secure Lee's permission to keep them in their trenches. The artillery, however, would leave. Shortly after midnight, though, the commander of the division holding the Mule Shoe received reports of activity in his front and persuaded Ewell to bring back the artillery. It took several hours for the Confederate gunners to return to their former positions, and by the time they were back, Hancock's four divisions had struck the Mule Shoe. Twenty pieces of artillery fell into Federal hands, along with thousands of prisoners, and the Mule Shoe was shattered. Never before had an attack by the Army of the Potomac achieved such a spectacular tactical success. The Army of Northern Virginia was on the verge of being brutally and perhaps irretrievably broken in half.[18]

Fortunately for Lee, the attack against the right side of the Mule Shoe by Burnside's corps was ineffective, and order among the thousands of Hancock's men who had broken into the Mule Shoe quickly broke down. Riding forward toward the site of the Federal breakthrough, Lee found the commander of Ewell's reserve division, Brig. Gen. John B. Gordon, already leading his men forward. Gordon asked for directions and was told by Lee to continue executing his plan to launch a counterattack against Hancock. Then, as Gordon's men pushed forward, they saw Lee doing the same with the intention of personally leading them, just as he had less than a week earlier when faced with a similar crisis at the Tapp Farm. "Not a word did he say," one observer recounted a few weeks later, "but simply took off his hat, and as he sat on his charger I never saw a man look so noble, or a spectacle so impressive." Gordon, however, grabbed the reins of Lee's horse and exclaimed, "General, these are Virginians!—These men have never failed! They never will! Will you boys!" Gordon's men replied, "No! No! . . . General Lee to the rear; Lee to the rear! . . . Go back General Lee, we can't charge until you go back." Some of Gordon's officers then moved to physically block Lee while one man grabbed his horse and forced him to turn around.[19]

Satisfied that Lee was no longer moving into harm's way, Gordon turned to his men and ordered them to charge. Shortly thereafter, his division slammed into Hancock's disorganized command and, in cooperation with Maj. Gen. Robert Rodes's division, drove the Federals back to the outer line of the Mule Shoe. Grant and Meade responded by ordering Maj. Gen. Horatio Wright's Sixth Corps to enter the battle on Hancock's right and directing Warren to attempt yet another attack on Laurel Hill. Meanwhile, Lee rode over to Brig. Gen. Nathaniel Harris's Mississippi Brigade and called out, one man later recalled, "Men, I have sent for you. The line of the Army of Northern Virginia is broken and you must retake the works. I myself will lead you in the charge." Once again, though, one of the soldiers grabbed the reins of Lee's horse and cried out, "General Lee, you are worth all of us put together! Can't you trust us?" As he had before, Lee yielded to the entreaties of his soldiers and let them join the fight without him. Thanks in part to the efforts of Harris's Mississippians, neither Wright nor Hancock were able to regain the momentum Hancock's initial assault had achieved.[20]

Grant refused to concede defeat. Warren's attack on Laurel Hill, however, achieved nothing. Grant then directed Burnside to renew his attack against the Mule Shoe. As Burnside moved to comply, Lee happened to make his way over to that section of his line and learned that Burnside's left flank was at that moment uncovered. Immediately sensing an opportunity, Lee personally ordered two brigades from Early's corps to launch an attack, which slammed into the division holding Burnside's exposed flank just as the Federals were advancing toward the Mule Shoe and routed it. With the steam taken out of Burnside's attack, Lee, eager to find and exploit any opportunity that might exist to seize the initiative from Grant, immediately ordered a reconnaissance to see if an attack along the Fredericksburg Road might produce even greater results. To Lee's dismay, he quickly learned that even after the earlier setback, Burnside's command held positions so strong that they "would have afforded," in Early's words, "an almost insuperable obstacle to the proposed flank movement." Consequently, Lee had no choice but to accept that the Army of Northern Virginia would spend the rest of May 12 on the tactical defensive.[21]

Meanwhile, the fighting on the western side of the salient continued, reaching a truly savage character at a point in the works that became known as the "Bloody Angle," where the two sides fought at close range for about twenty hours. By keeping the Federals at bay through rains that added to the horror of sustained combat at such short range, the Confederate defenders bought Lee time to construct a shorter line at the base of the salient. This task was completed early on the morning of May 13 and was followed by orders to abandon the bloody salient. Exhausted, the Federals let Lee's men do so relatively unmolested. "I had never before imagined," wrote one observer who had witnessed a number of earlier engagements, including Gettysburg, "such a struggle to be possible."[22]

Although the Army of Northern Virginia had managed to yet again survive another crisis, it had taken a severe beating. And this was not all the bad news Lee had to digest on May 13, 1864. The evening before, news had reached him that Stuart had died of his wounds at Yellow Tavern. Lee was personally devastated and remarked to one of Stuart's staff officers that night: "I can scarcely think of him without weeping." Stuart's death made it three of four corps commanders down in only a week, although a very able successor to Stuart in command of the Army of Northern Virginia's cavalry was soon found in Wade Hampton.[23]

As if this were not enough, the only corps commanders who had been with the army since the beginning of the campaign had become a source of concern. Lee never seems to have been completely comfortable with Ewell, even though that officer's performance as commander of the Second Corps had been generally solid and at times quite impressive. Perhaps this was a consequence of the fact that before his elevation to corps command Lee did not know Ewell very well. Moreover, Ewell's best performances before and after his elevation to corps command had occurred outside Lee's direct observation. Whatever the reason, Lee's discontent with Ewell received a powerful boost during the fighting for the Mule Shoe on May 10 and 12.

Lee had expressed reservations about the Mule Shoe the moment the Second Corps laid out and began fortifying it, but acceded to keeping troops in it on receiving assurances from Ewell that the salient was defensible. Then, on the evening of May 10, after Upton's assault was repulsed, Lee felt it necessary to give Ewell detailed instructions on how to improve and manage his line. As if this were not enough, as his position crumbled under the weight of Hancock's attack on May 12, Ewell lost his head and began cursing and striking some of his men with his sword. Lee saw this and remarked, "General Ewell, you must restrain yourself; how can you expect to control these men when you have lost control yourself?" Ewell quickly regained his composure, but the episode, not to mention the fact that the only Union successes at Spotsylvania so far had come against the Second Corps, clearly exacerbated concerns Lee already had about Ewell.[24]

Fortunately for the Army of Northern Virginia, the days that followed brought heavy rains that impeded Grant's attempt to swing the two corps on his right around behind the rest of the Federal force at Spotsylvania so they could reach a position beyond the Confederate right. Lee almost immediately picked up evidence of Grant's move and shifted the bulk of Anderson's corps from the left to the right of the line on the fourteenth and fifteenth, effectively thwarting the Union attempt to turn his flank. During and after these movements the two armies remained in constant contact around Spotsylvania, with continuous skirmishing punctuated by local attacks and counterattacks combining with the constant rain and mud to wear away at both armies physically and spiritually. Lee responded to this and news that Grant was being reinforced from Washington by petitioning his government for reinforcements. However, with Butler's army menacing Richmond and significant Union forces operating in the Shenandoah Valley, there was little chance during the second week of May 1864 that the Davis administration would fulfill Lee's requests.[25]

Confederate spirits received a considerable boost, though, when news arrived of a victory on May 15 by Confederate forces in the Shenandoah Valley commanded by Maj. Gen. John C. Breckinridge at New Market. Although he badly wanted reinforcements from the Valley, Lee responded to the news by urging Breckinridge to pursue the defeated Union army and "if practicable follow him into Maryland." Soon thereafter a message from Richmond reached Lee, reporting Beauregard's victory in the Battle of Drewry's Bluff on May 16 and Butler's subsequent decision to pull his forces back to a defensive position at Bermuda Hundred, developments Lee immediately hoped would make reinforcements available for his army from that quarter. Upon learning that there would be no pursuit into Maryland, he was able to direct Breckinridge to bring his infantry to Hanover Junction, but as long as Butler was at Bermuda Hundred, Richmond was unwilling to comply with Lee's requests for assistance from that front. This prompted Lee to advise Davis on May 18, "The question is whether we shall fight the battle here or around Richmond. If the troops are obliged to be retained at Richmond I may be forced back."[26]

That same morning, Grant, thinking that Lee's efforts to counter his maneuvers of the fifteenth and sixteenth might have left the Confederate position at the base of the former Mule Shoe vulnerable, threw two corps at it.

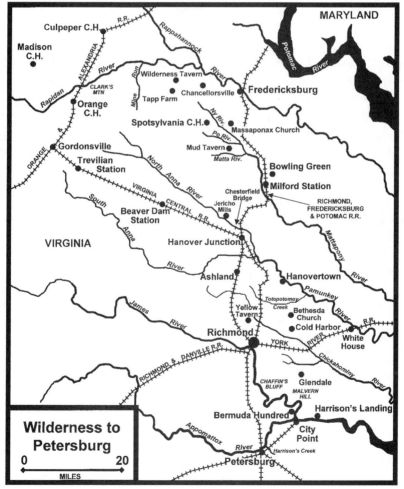

Figure 6.2.   The Wilderness to Petersburg.

With great ease, Ewell's gunners repulsed the attack and by doing so convinced Grant that the time had finally come to leave Spotsylvania. Before
the Federals could implement their commander's plan to do so, though, Lee
authorized Ewell to conduct a reconnaissance in force on the nineteenth.
Ewell moved forward from his lines with nearly his entire corps toward the
Fredericksburg Road and encountered a Federal force at the Harris Farm. A
sharp three-hour engagement ensued that ended with Ewell pulling back to
his original line, having, Lee later recalled, "lost all presence of mind" during
the battle and achieved nothing—other than lengthening the Confederate
casualty list at Spotsylvania to about ten thousand overall (Grant's command
lost about eighteen thousand), and raising further concerns about Ewell.[27]

On May 20, Grant's command was once again in motion. At approximately
ten that evening Hancock's corps set off for Massaponax Church on the
Telegraph Road, where they linked up with a small force of cavalry, and
then marched through the night to Guinea Station on the Richmond, Fredericksburg, and Potomac Railroad. Hancock's objective was Bowling Green
and Milford Station, which his corps reached at around noon on the
twenty-first. Hancock's move, Grant believed, would place the Second
Corps in a position to menace Lee's communications with Richmond,
which would induce the Confederate commander to leave his defensive position at Spotsylvania and go after Hancock in an effort to catch his command when it was isolated and vulnerable to destruction. This would, Grant
hoped, give his other three corps, which was to push south following the
Telegraph Road, a chance to catch Lee's army in the open and deliver a decisive blow.[28]

Reports reached Lee that the Federals were on the move during the night
of May 20–21. After sifting through them to try to determine what exactly
Grant was up to, Lee deduced Grant's intention was to move south and east,
with the Mattapony River between the two armies, to link up with Sheridan's cavalry for an attack against Richmond. Thus, Lee concluded that the
only good course of action available was to fall back to a position behind the
North Anna River from which he could cover Hanover Junction. He then
directed Ewell's command to evacuate its lines at Spotsylvania, march
around the rear of the rest of the army, and then push on to Mud Tavern,
which was located on the Telegraph Road just south of where it crossed the
Po River. Ewell reached Mud Tavern by dawn on May 21 and took up a position where he blocked the route Grant had intended to have Warren's

corps follow when Lee took the bait offered by Hancock. Grant responded by directing Warren to instead cross the Po east of the Telegraph Road, which cleared that road for Lee's army. On the evening of May 21–22, Ewell, accompanied by Lee himself and followed by Anderson's corps, marched south on the Telegraph Road to the North Anna, while the Third Corps, which A. P. Hill had resumed command of on the twenty-first, took another road to the west. By 5:00 a.m. on the twenty-second, Lee was able to report to Richmond that he and two corps were behind the North Anna and that he expected Hill to arrive by noon. "I should have preferred contesting the enemy's approach inch by inch," he added, "but my solicitude for Richmond caused me to abandon that plan."[29]

As Grant's forces advanced toward the North Anna the following day, Lee sent Davis a message that indicated his belief in the efficacy and desirability of offensive action had not been diminished by recent events. The Federal army, he wrote, "as far as I am able to judge, has been very much shaken. . . . Whatever route he pursues I am in a position to move against him, and shall endeavor to engage him while in motion." He also pointed out that he was now close enough to Richmond that it would be feasible to combine his and Beauregard's armies for offensive action. It was, Lee advised Davis, his understanding that Butler was in a strong defensive position, which Beauregard did not have the ability to attack with success. "On the contrary General Grant's army will be in the field," he noted, "His difficulties will be increased as he advances . . . and it seems to me our best policy to unite upon it and endeavor to crush it. I should be very glad to have the aid of General Beauregard in such a blow, and if it is possible to combine, I think it will succeed."[30]

As Lee spent the morning of May 23 entreating Richmond to send reinforcements, the Federals advanced to the North Anna. At around noon, elements from Hancock's corps began testing the Confederate redoubt covering the Chesterfield Bridge that carried the Telegraph Road over the North Anna. Then, late in the afternoon, they overran the Confederate position and forced its defenders to retreat across the river. As this was going on, Grant pushed Warren's corps across the river upstream at Jericho's Ford, which provoked a sharp fight between it and a division from Hill's corps that ended with the Federals maintaining a strong position south of the North Anna. When he learned that Hill had committed only a single division to a fight with an enemy that had a river at its back, Lee was infuriated and once again found it necessary to take a subordinate to task. "General Hill," he asked the next morning, "why did you let those people cross here? Why didn't you throw your whole force on them and drive them back as Jackson would have done?"[31]

Although frustrated at Hill's performance on the twenty-third, the situation at the North Anna brought potential opportunity for Lee. Grant had two good crossing points over the North Anna at Chesterfield Bridge and Jericho Mills. Lee and his chief engineer, Maj. Gen. Martin L. Smith, however, had posted the Army of Northern Virginia in a fortified, inverted "V" with the point on the river between the two wings of the Federal army. Hill's corps held the western leg of the "V," while Anderson's and Ewell's commands held the leg that faced to the north and east. On the morning of the twenty-fourth, Grant sent another corps across the river at Jericho Mills to support Warren and directed Hancock to push across at Chesterfield Bridge. To connect the two wings, Grant wanted Burnside's corps to cross at Ox Ford, which was located approximately equidistant from the other two crossing points. Burnside, however, found that a crossing at that point was impossible and was compelled to cross further upstream at Quarles' Ford. Late in the afternoon, one of Burnside's brigade commanders made a futile assault against the western face of the strong Confederate position. After night had fallen, Lee wrote to Richmond that the day had brought no more than "feeble attacks upon our lines. . . . They were easily repulsed."[32]

The matter-of-fact tone contained in Lee's message covered the fact that he had spent May 24 in physical and mental anguish. Grant's forces were divided, and, it was assumed, one of Lee's staff officers later wrote, "dispirited by the bloody repulses of the repeated attacks on our lines." In its presumed demoralized state and with its two wings separated by the Army of Northern Virginia, Grant's command appeared vulnerable to a counterstroke of the type Lee had been looking to deliver ever since the two armies had first tangled in the Wilderness. As the situation developed, late on May 23 Lee had issued orders to Anderson, whose corps held the center of his line, to have "everything in readiness by daybreak tomorrow to move in any direction." Unfortunately for the Confederacy, Lee's health betrayed him. More than two weeks of continuous campaigning, during which breakdowns among his corps commanders had compelled him to be more active than ever before in managing his army, had taken a heavy toll on Lee and he was unable to fight off an attack of dysentery that rendered him, one staff officer wrote a few days later, able to "attend to nothing except what was absolutely necessary for him to know and act upon." As the opportunity to strike he had long sought came and went, Lee was confined to his tent, repeatedly crying out: "We must strike them a blow—we must never let them pass us again—we must strike them a blow." Without Lee's active hand to guide the effort, there would be no counterattack at the North Anna. By nightfall on May 24, Grant's troops were entrenched, and whatever opportunity may have existed for the Confederates to deliver an effective blow was gone.[33]

After a relatively quiet May 25, Grant decided to make another attempt to turn Lee's right by moving east along the north bank of the North Anna until it came together with the South Anna to form the Pamunkey River, a tributary of the York River. The Federals would then cross the Pamunkey at Hanovertown, switching to a new base of supplies at White House. On May 26, Grant's men began their march, and by dawn on May 29, the entire army had crossed at Hanovertown. After briefly being confused by a feint by Grant to the west, Lee received reports during the night of May 26–27 that a significant Federal force had crossed the Pamunkey. He immediately dispatched cavalry toward Hanovertown to check the Federals and ordered the rest of his army to fall back toward Ashland. By the time night fell on the twenty-seventh, Lee himself was already south of Ashland and had determined that his next move would be to "get possession of the ridge between [Totopotomoy Creek] and Beaver Dam Creek, upon which sits Pole Green Church." From this position, the Army of Northern Virginia would be able to block any attempt by Grant to move directly on Richmond from Hanovertown.[34]

After making his decision to take up a position between Totopotomoy and Beaver Dam creeks, however, Lee began to have second thoughts. Only cavalry had been seen advancing from Hanovertown toward Richmond and, lacking any other decent information about the Federal army's whereabouts, Lee confided to Davis that he had begun to wonder "whether now that he finds the road open by Ashland, he may not prefer to take it" and advance on Richmond from the north, in which case he would come down in the rear of the Totopotomoy line. Consequently, Lee advised Davis that he had decided to personally "pause for a while" near Atlee's Station to see whether he should post the army on Totopotomoy Ridge or "try to intercept [the enemy] as near Ashland as I can. In either event I shall endeavor to engage him as soon as possible."[35]

As Lee's infantry marched toward Pole Green Church, on the morning of May 28 four Confederate cavalry brigades, supported by three regiments of infantry under the command of Maj. Gen. Wade Hampton, moved toward Hanovertown to gather information regarding the Union army's location and intentions. Just before reaching a place called Haw's Shop, Hampton ran into a significant body of Union cavalry, and for five hours the two sides fought a bitter battle. Although the engagement ended with the Federals getting the upper hand, Hampton was able to gather information regarding Grant's movements that assuaged Lee's concerns about his decision to post his army between Totopotomoy and Beaver Dam creeks. By mid-morning, the Second Corps, now commanded by Early, to whom a sick Ewell had relinquished command two days earlier, was in line of battle near Pole Green Church.

Figure 6.3.   Jubal A. Early, Confederate, c. 1860–1870. Library of Congress

(Lee immediately decided he wanted the change to be a permanent one. After blocking attempts by Ewell to resume command of his corps, in mid-June Lee would arrange for his assignment to command the Richmond defenses.) Shortly thereafter, Anderson's corps took up a supporting position between Hundley's Corner and Shady Grove Church. Although he conceded to Davis that he lacked "very definite information as regards [Grant's] position or numbers," by the evening of the twenty-eighth, there was no evidence that any Federals had moved or were attempting to move to the south side of Totopotomoy Creek. Consequently, Lee directed Breckinridge's force from the Valley, which had been posted at Hanover Junction during the maneuvering along the North Anna, and Hill's corps to take up positions to the west of Early that overlooked the southern bank of the Totopotomoy.[36]

Although in a good defensive position, Lee was still eager to take the offensive. The odds for success in such an endeavor would be greatly enhanced, clearly, if he and Beauregard could combine their forces. On May 29, Lee managed to secure a meeting with Beauregard to discuss this. Bolstering Lee's case was evidence that the Federals were diminishing their force at Bermuda Hundred, which they were doing due to Grant's decision to have one of Butler's corps reinforce the Army of the Potomac. Nonetheless, Beauregard still believed, as he told Davis, that to reduce his command "for the purpose of reenforcing Lee would jeopardize the safety of the part left to guard my lines and would greatly endanger Richmond itself." When he reached Atlee's Station on May 29, Beauregard gave Lee basically the same message—that none of the twelve thousand men he had under his command could be spared. Afterward, a resigned but probably not surprised Lee informed Davis of what Beauregard had said and assured him, "If Genl Grant advances tomorrow I will engage him with my present force."[37]

Notes

1. Venable, "General Lee in the Wilderness Campaign," 240–41.

2. Mark Grimsley, *And Keep Moving On: The Virginia Campaign, May–June 1864* (Lincoln: University of Nebraska Press, 2002), xv. The campaign and battles described in the following two chapters have been authoritatively chronicled by Gordon Rhea in *The Battle of the Wilderness, May 5–6, 1864* (Baton Rouge: Louisiana State University Press, 1994); *The Battles for Spotsylvania Court House and the Road to Yellow Tavern, May 7–12, 1864* (Baton Rouge: Louisiana State University Press, 1997); *To the North Anna River: Grant and Lee, May 13–25, 1864* (Baton Rouge: Louisiana State University Press, 2000; and *Cold Harbor: Grant and Lee: May 26–June 3, 1864* (Baton Rouge: Louisiana State University Press, 2002). Grimsley's

is the best one-volume treatment, while readers will find many important insights in Earl J. Hess's superb *Trench Warfare under Grant & Lee: Field Fortifications in the Overland Campaign* (Chapel Hill: University of North Carolina Press, 2007). A good focused study of Lee during the campaign can be found in Noah Andre Trudeau's "A Mere Question of Time: Robert E. Lee from the Wilderness to Appomattox Court House," in *Lee the Soldier*, ed. Gallagher, 523–38.

3. Ewell to Taylor, March 20, 1865, OR, vol. 36, pt. 1: 1070–71; Brown, *Campbell Brown's Civil War*, 247–48.

4. Marshall to Ewell, May 5, 1864, ibid., pt. 2: 953; Alexander, *Fighting for the Confederacy*, 354.

5. Heth, *Memoirs*, 184.

6. Venable, "General Lee in the Wilderness Campaign," 241; Longstreet to Taylor, March 23, 1865, OR, vol. 36, pt. 1: 1054–55; Robert K. Krick, "'Lee to the Rear,' the Texans Cried," in *The Wilderness Campaign*, edited by Gary W. Gallagher (Chapel Hill: University of North Carolina Press, 1997), 177–85.

7. Marshall to Ewell, May 5, 1864, in *Wartime Papers*, eds. Dowdey and Manarin, 721; Longstreet to Taylor, March 23, 1865, OR, vol. 36, pt. 1: 1055.

8. Charles W. Field, "Campaign of 1864 and 1865," SHSP, vol. 14: 546.

9. Lee to Seddon, May 7, 1864, in *Wartime Papers*, eds. Dowdey and Manarin, 723; Lee to Stuart, May 7, 1864, ibid.; Taylor to Ewell, May 7, 1864, ibid., 724; Hdqrs. Army of Northern Virginia, Special Orders No. 122, May 7, 1864, OR, vol. 36, pt. 2: 967; Anderson to Longstreet, [ca. May 1864], in Janet B. Hewitt et al., eds. *Supplement to the Official Records of the Union and Confederate Armies: Part I—Reports* (Wilmington, NC: Broadfoot Publishing Company, 1997), vol. 6: 656. (Hereafter cited as *OR Supplement*.)

10. Lee to Seddon, May 8, 1864, in *Wartime Papers*, eds. Dowdey and Manarin, 724.

11. Anderson to Longstreet, [ca. May 1864], *OR Supplement*, vol. 6: 656; Ewell to Taylor, March 20, 1865, OR, vol. 36, pt. 1: 1071; Lee to Seddon, May 8, 1864, in *Wartime Papers*, eds. Dowdey and Manarin, 726.

12. Hdqrs. Army of Northern Virginia, Special Orders No. 123, May 8, 1864, OR, vol. 36, pt. 2: 974–75.

13. Lee to Davis, May 9, 1864, in *Lee's Dispatches: Unpublished Letters of General Robert E. Lee, C.S.A. to Jefferson Davis and the War Department of the Confederate States of America, 1862–65*, edited by Douglas Southall Freeman and Grady McWhiney (New York: G.P. Putnam's Sons, 1957), 176.

14. Seddon to Beauregard, May 10, 1864, OR, vol. 36, pt. 2: 986.

15. Lee to Seddon, May 10, 1864, in *Wartime Papers*, eds. Dowdey and Manarin, 727.

16. Kean, *Inside the Confederate Government*, 449; Sheridan to Meade, May 13, 14, 1864, OR, vol. 36, pt. 2: 776–77.

17. Heth, *Memoirs*, 186–87.

18. Brown, *Campbell Brown's Civil War*, 253; Rhea, *Battles for Spotsylvania Court House and the Road to Yellow Tavern*, 220–21, 225–28, 232–42.

19. *Richmond Daily Dispatch*, June 2, 1864; Freeman, *R.E. Lee*, vol. 3: 318–19.

20. David Holt, *A Mississippi Rebel in the Army of Northern Virginia: The Civil War Memoirs of Private David Holt*, edited by Thomas D. Cockrell and Michael B. Ballard (Baton Rouge: Louisiana State University Press, 1995), 255.

21. Rhea, *Battles for Spotsylvania Court House and the Road to Yellow Tavern*, 295–302; Jubal A. Early, *Autobiographical Sketch and Narrative of the War Between the States* (Philadelphia: J.B. Lippincott, 1912), 357.

22. Brown, *Campbell Brown's Civil War*, 255.

23. Freeman, *R.E. Lee*, vol. 3: 327; Alexander, *Fighting for the Confederacy*, 374.

24. Hess, *Trench Warfare*, 47, 58; Lee to Ewell, May 10, 1864, in *Wartime Papers*, eds. Dowdey and Manarin, 727; Pfanz, *Richard S. Ewell*, 388–89.

25. Meade to Bowers, November 1, 1864, OR, vol. 36, pt. 1: 192; Diary of the First [Confederate] Army Corps, ibid., 1057; Lee to Seddon, May 16, 1864, ibid., pt. 2: 1011; Venable to Ewell, May 14, 1864, in *Wartime Papers*, eds. Dowdey and Manarin, 729; Lee to Davis, May 12, 13, 14, 15, 1864, ibid., 728, 729, 730.

26. Bragg to Lee, May 17, 1864, Robert E. Lee Headquarters Papers, Virginia Historical Society, Richmond, Virginia, series 7 (hereafter cited as Lee Headquarters Papers, VHS); Lee to Breckinridge, May 16, 17, 1864, in *Wartime Papers*, eds. Dowdey and Manarin, 731; Lee to Davis, May 18, 1864, ibid., 733.

27. Lee to Seddon, May 18, 1864, OR, vol. 36, pt. 2: 1019; Ewell to Taylor, March 20, 1865, ibid., pt. 1: 1073; Allan, "Memoranda," 11.

28. Grant, *Memoirs*, 482–84.

29. Rhea, *To the North Anna River*, 216–22; Venable to Ewell, May 20, 1864, OR, vol. 36, pt. 2: 801; Lee to Anderson, May 21, 1864, ibid., 814; Lee to Davis, May 22, 1864, in *Wartime Papers*, eds. Dowdey and Manarin, 746.

30. Lee to Davis, May 23, 1864, in *Wartime Papers*, eds. Dowdey and Manarin, 747–48.

31. Lee to Seddon, May 23, ibid., 749; Rhea, *To the North Anna*, 326.

32. Lee to Seddon, May 24, 1864, in *Wartime Papers*, eds. Dowdey and Manarin, 750.

33. Taylor to Anderson, May 23, 1864, in *Wartime Papers*, eds. Dowdey and Manarin, 749; Taylor to Saunders, May 30, 1864, in *Lee's Adjutant: The Wartime Letters of Colonel Walter Herron Taylor, 1862–1865*, edited by R. Lockwood Tower and John S. Belmont (Columbia: University of South Carolina Press, 1995), 164; Charles S. Venable, "The Campaign from the Wilderness to Petersburg," *SHSP*, vol. 14: 535.

34. Lee to Seddon, May 26, 1864, OR, vol. 36, pt. 3: 834; Taylor to Ewell, May 26, 1864, in *Wartime Papers*, eds. Dowdey and Manarin, 751; Lee to Seddon, May 27, 1864, ibid., 752; Taylor to Anderson, May 27, 1864, ibid., 753.

35. Lee to Davis, May 28, 1864, in *Wartime Papers*, eds. Dowdey and Manarin, 753–54.

36. Taylor to Breckinridge, May 28, 1864, ibid., 754; Lee to Seddon, May 28, 1864, ibid., 755; Lee to Breckinridge, May 28, 1864, ibid., 754–56; Pfanz, *Richard S.*

Ewell, 396–403; Diary of the First [Confederate] Army Corps, OR, vol. 36, pt. 1: 1058; Rhea, *Cold Harbor*, 96–98.

37. Grant, *Memoirs*, 490, Smith to Grant, May 28, 1864, OR, vol. 36, pt. 3: 285; Beauregard to Davis, May 29, 1864, ibid., 849; Lee to Davis, May 29, 1864, in *Wartime Papers*, eds. Dowdey and Manarin, 756.

CHAPTER SEVEN

To and Across the James

The need to engage the Federals appeared especially pressing to Lee during the last week of May 1864 due to the fact that crossing the Pamunkey River on the twenty-eighth and twenty-ninth brought the Army of the Potomac back to the York-James Peninsula and only a few short marches from the James River. For two years, Lee had benefited from the Lincoln administration's desire to keep the Army of the Potomac away from this field of set-piece operations and siegecraft where two years earlier the Confederate military had been very nearly rendered impotent. The Lincoln administration had been kind enough then to manage its handling of the war badly enough to enable Lee to save Richmond and transfer the war to fields where maneuver and boldness could negate and overcome men and material. Now, under Grant and with a far greater advantage in numbers, the Federals were back on the Peninsula and once again had the opportunity to put Lee in the position that McClellan had nearly put him two years earlier: shackled to the defense of Richmond against a foe whose firepower, skill at engineering, cautious good sense, and secure river-borne logistics made it impervious to attack and irresistible (if not especially dynamic) on the offensive.

Both commanders recognized the importance of the Federal move. Just before the 1864 campaign began, Grant had called his staff together and directed their attention to a map of Virginia. He then traced a line on it with his finger around Richmond and Petersburg and told them, one man later recalled, "When my troops are there, Richmond is mine." Lee saw the matter the same way. Never satisfied simply to fight the Federals to a tactical stalemate using defensive tactics, the threat of the Federals finally reaching the James made finding an opportunity for a successful offensive that would achieve decisive operational results a greater imperative than ever in Lee's mind. "We must destroy this army of Grant's before he gets to the James River," he told Early. "If he gets there it will become a siege, and then, it will be a mere question of time."[1]

On May 30, it appeared an opportunity had arrived. While Lee endeavored to pry reinforcements away from Beauregard, Grant moved his infantry forward from Hanovertown. Upon reaching Totopotomoy Creek, he ordered Hancock to probe the Confederate position but, after driving the Confederates back from some forward defenses, Hancock decided not to test their main battle line. Meanwhile, Grant pushed Warren's corps to the south side of the Totopotomoy during the morning of the thirtieth, and Lee saw in this move an opportunity for a decisive counterstroke. At eleven, he sent a message to Anderson stating that Warren's move indicated the Federals intended "a repetition of their former movements . . . [which] can only be arrested by striking at once at that part of their force which has crossed the Totopotomoy in General Early's front. I have desired him to do this if he thought it could be done advantageously, and have written to him that you will support him."[2]

When his skirmishers made contact with Warren's, Early also scented an opportunity, and early that afternoon advised Lee he had decided to advance a division to Bethesda Church "to see what the enemy has and, if necessary, I will send the other divisions to co-operate [in the] attack." To support his attack, Early asked Lee to have Anderson's corps take over the section of the line between Totopotomoy Creek and Beaver Dam Creek still held by the Second Corps. This would allow Early to concentrate his three divisions for the attack against Warren. He also requested, "in the event of my meeting the enemy and driving him," that Anderson be directed to push forward on the Old Church Road in support. Upon receiving Early's report, Lee immediately forwarded it to Anderson with a note attached stating, "I approve what is therein suggested and have authorized General Early to carry out what is proposed. . . . I desire you, if circumstances permit, to carry out your part."[3]

As was so often the case for both sides during the Overland Campaign, Early's attack achieved some initial success but ultimately failed to accomplish anything decisive. Reaching Bethesda Church at mid-afternoon, Maj.

Gen. Robert Rodes's division caught some Pennsylvania troops posted nearby completely by surprise and routed them. The division following Rodes then moved up to take a position on his left for an immediate pursuit north across the Old Church Road. The two divisions, however, got tangled up, which compelled Early to briefly halt their drive north to restore order. This gave Warren time to put together a line of artillery just north of Shady Grove Road that fought off Early's renewed assaults from the south and Anderson's efforts to push east to support them. By 8:00 p.m. the fight was over with nothing decisive having been achieved.

As Lee predicted, upon finding himself stymied at the Totopotomoy, Grant again set his eyes south and east, his prospects for success enhanced by the arrival at White House of a corps from Butler's command that had been ordered to join the Army of the Potomac. Lee was aware of this development and that it threatened to tip the balance of forces further, and perhaps decisively, against him. The only hope he had was if Richmond could finally pry

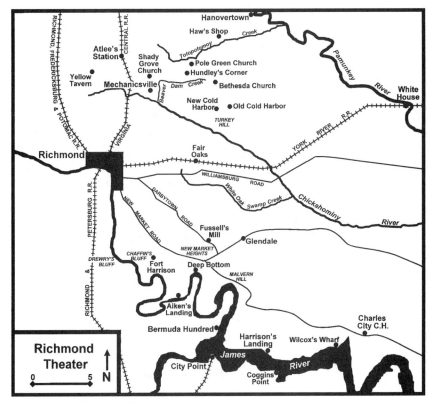

Figure 7.1.   Richmond Theater.

reinforcements away from Beauregard. Beauregard had in fact responded to the departure of a large body of troops from Butler's command by agreeing at 10:30 a.m. on May 30 to direct a division commanded by Maj. Gen. Robert F. Hoke "to hold itself ready to move at a moment's notice." Beauregard, however, was unwilling to release Hoke until he received direct orders from Richmond to do so, which drove Lee to complete exasperation by nightfall on May 30, when he fired off a message to Davis bluntly stating that if reinforcements were delayed any further, "the result . . . will be disaster." Shortly thereafter, Beauregard, just before orders to do so arrived from Davis, changed his mind about waiting for explicit orders and advised Richmond, "General Lee having called on me for re-enforcements. . . . I have ordered Hoke's division to report to him."[4]

As Lee awaited Hoke's arrival the following morning, cavalry from both armies were active, with Sheridan endeavoring to secure the route for another attempt to swing around the Confederate right, while Confederate cavalry commanded by Maj. Gen. Fitzhugh Lee attempted to counter his efforts. The key point on the map in all of this was a crossroads known as Old Cold Harbor. Lee's Confederates managed to reach it first during the morning of May 31 and promptly established a defensive position just to the east. During the afternoon, the lead brigade of Hoke's division arrived on the scene to bolster Fitz Lee's line. Soon after it arrived, however, Sheridan's forces attacked in overwhelming strength and drove the Confederates back through Old Cold Harbor, although upon seeing a second brigade from Hoke's command arrive, Sheridan deemed it necessary to relinquish control of the crossroads at the end of the day.[5]

Recognizing that letting the enemy have unfettered control of Cold Harbor would endanger his southern flank, Lee decided on the thirty-first to send more infantry to the scene. During the afternoon, he directed Anderson to pull his corps out of its position at the Totopotomoy, move south to Cold Harbor, take personal command of the situation there, and attack the Federals. If successful, a staff officer later remembered, Lee hoped Anderson would then "wheel around to the left and come down on the flank and rear of Grant's whole fortified line." Grant, of course, saw the potential danger if a Confederate move to Cold Harbor in strength went unchecked, and the opportunity that might be created if he were to overmatch the rebels in that sector. Thus, during the evening of May 31 he had orders sent to Wright directing him to immediately "move to Cold Harbor. . . . The cavalry are directed to hold on until your arrival, and it is of the utmost importance you should reach the point as soon after daylight as possible."[6]

By dawn on June 1, Anderson's lead division had reached its comrades near Cold Harbor and formed a battle line with Hoke's command that advanced toward the crossroads at around eight that morning. Sheridan's cavalry, however, was able to hold them off until by mid-afternoon Wright's entire corps was posted in breastworks covering the Old Cold Harbor crossroads and awaiting the arrival of Maj. Gen. William F. Smith's Eighteenth Corps, the unit that had been sent from Butler's command. The appearance of Wright's infantry was enough to throw Anderson on the defensive and put his men to work fortifying their own position. When Smith arrived, he went into position alongside the Sixth Corps, and together the two corps launched an attack shortly before nightfall. Although they managed to briefly penetrate the Confederate line, June 1 ended with Anderson's line still intact. Believing that one more good push would bring a decisive victory at Cold Harbor, Grant ordered Hancock to "get one division of his corps . . . to Wright before daylight, and the whole corps as soon as possible." Anticipating they would have more than enough strength to crush Anderson's command in the morning, Grant and Meade instructed Hancock, Wright, and Smith to attack at once upon the Second Corps's arrival. Fortunately for Lee, although the head of Hancock's command managed to reach their comrades at Cold Harbor early on the second, it was after a grueling night march, following a guide who did not know his business as well as he thought he did, that left the corps exhausted. Consequently, Grant and Meade ended up postponing the attack until June 3 to give Hancock's men time to recuperate and enable Smith to resupply his command with ammunition.[7]

After personally reaching Cold Harbor during the early evening of June 1, Lee first sought to secure his position there by getting troops on the high ground known as Turkey Hill, located between Anderson's right and the Chickahominy River. For this task, he ordered Breckinridge's command (which arrived on the second, but not until after Lee had to personally ride over to Mechanicsville to direct it to the battlefield) to move south. As evidence continued to mount that the Federals were concentrating for a strong attack at Cold Harbor, Lee ordered two of Hill's divisions to leave their position on the far left and help Breckinridge drive off an enemy force that had occupied Turkey Hill.[8]

At the same time he was improving his defensive position at Cold Harbor on the second, Lee demonstrated he was, one officer later wrote, "if possible, more on the alert than ever for some chance, or some weak spot to strike." Thinking Grant might have shifted so much of his force to Cold Harbor that his northern flank was now vulnerable, Lee instructed Early's corps, which along with a division from Hill's corps now held the Confederate left, "to endeavor to get upon the enemy's right flank and drive down in front of our line." Early promptly complied and conceived a plan whereby one division would press the front of the force holding the Union right, Burnside's Ninth and Warren's Fifth corps, while one hit its flank and another worked around to its rear. The well-conceived assault initially achieved some success, driving part of the Federal line back. Early, however, simply did not have enough strength to sustain the momentum of his attack, and Burnside and Warren were able to rally their men and hold on despite having lost several hundred prisoners.[9]

The fighting between Early and the Federals on June 2 did nothing to lead Grant to alter his plan to attack at Cold Harbor the following morning. Lee's men, of course, had taken advantage of the delay in the launching of the Federal attack to construct strong fortifications all along their line. Early on June 3 the Federal artillery opened up a short preliminary bombardment that failed to achieve much, and when the Union infantry charged they immediately began taking heavy casualties. Within an hour, it was clear that the assault had failed, although, encouraged by a very brief penetration of Breckinridge's position that was quickly repaired, Meade continued to press the offensive until the afternoon. Even though his line was too thinly stretched for him to give any serious thought to following up his success with a counterattack, Lee could not help but be content with the events of June 3, 1864. That afternoon and evening, he informed Richmond, "every attack of the enemy has been repulsed. . . . The only impression made on our line was at a salient of Genl Breckinridge's position, where the enemy . . . was immediately driven out with severe loss. . . . Our loss today has been small, and our success, under the blessing of God, all that we could expect."[10]

Even though his army had won a relatively easy and decisive victory the previous day, Lee was anything but satisfied with his situation on June 4. During the fighting on the third, he told a member of Davis's cabinet that had come out from Richmond to observe the fighting that his troops were suffering badly due to "exhaustion and the want of vegetables." When asked what he had in reserve in case the Federals broke through his lines, Lee replied, "Not a regiment. . . . And that has been my condition ever since the fighting commenced on the Rappahannock. If I shorten my lines to provide a reserve he will turn me; if I weaken my lines to provide a reserve, he will break them."

Lee then spent the following day worrying about whether the Federals were "preparing to leave us tonight, and . . . cross the Chickahominy." To watch for signs of such a move, Lee had sent Fitz Lee's cavalry south of that stream two days earlier, and, in a message to Anderson during the early evening of June 4, indicated he was hopeful a Federal move to the Chickahominy might re-create the opportunity he believed McClellan's crossing of that same stream two years earlier had provided to deliver a decisive blow. "The best course for us to pursue," he advised Anderson, "would be to move down and attack him with our whole force, provided we could catch him in the act of crossing. I wish you would keep your pickets on the alert tonight . . . and should you discover that he is abandoning his position be prepared to move your whole corps."[11]

Meanwhile, the question of what to do about the men who had been wounded in the attacks of June 3 had become a matter of concern. Two days after the battle, Grant sent a message to Lee seeking his agreement to letting each side send men out "bearing litters to pick up their dead and wounded without being fired upon." Lee, however, insisted upon a formal flag of truce to cover such activities, which it was generally understood to be the defeated party's responsibility to ask for. The two men went back and forth on this until Grant finally decided on June 7 to ask for a suspension of hostilities. Adding a surreal quality to the fighting at Cold Harbor was the fact that less than two years earlier the bloody battle of Gaines' Mill had been fought on nearly the very same ground and, one Mississippi soldier later wrote, "All around lay the shallow graves of those who had fallen in the former [battle]. . . . At night these old graves would shine with a phosphorescent light most spooky and weird, while on the surface of the ground, above the ghastly glimmering dead, lay thousands of dead that could not be buried."[12]

Although it condemned the men caught between the lines to an awful ordeal, costing many of them their lives, the dispute between Grant and Lee over the wounded Federals was not simply a silly exercise involving military protocol. Lee and Grant understood that the state of morale and the sustenance of political will to continue the war on both sides, which were inextricably tied to perceptions of victory or defeat in the field, would ultimately determine the outcome of the contest between their two countries. For Grant to publicly concede, after all the high expectations his arrival in Washington had inspired and all the casualties both sides had endured since the Wilderness, that he had still been unable to defeat an army he had proclaimed to be "really whipped" just a few days earlier in a dispatch to Washington would hardly inspire confidence in victory in the North. Indeed, the very day Lee and Grant finally came to terms at Cold Harbor, the Republican Party opened their national convention in Baltimore. Although they once again selected Lincoln as their presidential candidate, a steady stream of bad news from the battlefields of Virginia ensured that the party faithful would leave the convention with a profoundly pessimistic outlook on the future.[13]

While Lee haggled with Grant and kept an anxious eye out for a Federal move across the Chickahominy, problems elsewhere demanded his attention. After Sigel's defeat at New Market, Washington had given the task of organizing and leading another advance up the Shenandoah Valley to Maj. Gen. David Hunter on May 21. With Breckinridge and much of the force that had defeated Sigel with Lee at Cold Harbor, the Confederacy could only scrape together a force of about five thousand men to confront Hunter's command. Lee advised nervous commanders in the region to try to augment their forces by getting "out your reserves," while assuring them he would return "Genl. Breckinridge as soon as I can." Hunter, however, moved too quickly for Lee and the southern commanders in the region to effectively respond and, after routing a Confederate force at Piedmont on June 5, was able to seize Staunton. On June 6, Lee informed Davis that he had put two of Breckinridge's brigades in reserve and come to the conclusion that he had no choice but to send them back to the Valley.[14]

In that same letter, Lee also expressed concern that Grant was preparing to move, and indeed might already be moving, across the Chickahominy. Unbeknownst to Lee, Grant had in fact decided to push south from Cold Harbor. His objective, though, was not merely to get to the south side of the Chickahominy. Instead, Grant intended to carry out what he proclaimed on June 5 had been "My idea from the start . . . [to] move the army to the south side of the James River. . . . Once on the south side of the James River I can cut off all sources of supply to the enemy, except what is furnished by the [James River] canal. If Hunter succeeds in reaching Lynchburg that will be lost to him also."[15]

To distract Lee, Grant ordered Sheridan to take two divisions of cavalry and swing around the Confederate northern flank to the Virginia Central Railroad. Sheridan would then follow the railroad west, wrecking it as he went, in an attempt to reach a point where he could make contact with Hunter's forces and coordinate their efforts to destroy the Confederate logistical network west of Richmond. On June 7, Sheridan departed with his immediate objective being to reach Trevilian Station on the Virginia Central. By the evening of the eighth, Lee had received reports of Sheridan's departure and forwarded the news to Richmond. Suspecting correctly, as he wrote Davis, that Sheridan's "object is to cooperate with Genl Hunter and endeavor to reach the James, breaking the railroads & c., as he passes," Lee sent

Figure 7.2.   Lieutenant General Ulysses S. Grant, Union, 1864.
National Archives

two divisions of cavalry under Hampton north to intercept the Federals. On June 11, Sheridan's and Hampton's commands clashed at Trevilian Station in a fierce fight that ended with the Federal commander deciding to break off his raiding efforts and return east.[16]

That same day, Grant completed preparations for the move to the James. On the evening of the twelfth, Smith's men headed back to White House to board transports that would return them to Bermuda Hundred, while the Army of the Potomac began crossing the Chickahominy. Accompanied by cavalry, Warren's corps then pushed west to Glendale, while the other three headed for the James. When sunrise on June 13 revealed the Federals had left Cold Harbor, Lee sent Hill's corps south of the Chickahominy to find them. Hill's skirmishers soon clashed with Union pickets from Warren's command and by dark had driven them a couple of miles from Glendale. By then, Anderson's corps had crossed the Chickahominy and taken up a position on Hill's right, while Confederate cavalry secured possession of Malvern Hill. Grant, however, had so effectively covered his march that by noon on the fourteenth, Lee was uncertain as to where he was headed.[17]

Making matters worse for the Confederate chieftain was the situation in the Valley. On June 11, Hunter had reached Lexington and burned the Virginia Military Institute before turning east toward Lynchburg. With Hunter's force augmented by the arrival of a Union column commanded by Brig. Gen. George Crook, it seemed clear that the return of Breckinridge's command would still not give the Confederates sufficient force to resist it effectively. Lee wrote to Davis on the eleventh that he acknowledged "the advantage of expelling enemy from the Valley. The only difficulty with me is the means. It would [take] one corps of this army. If it is deemed prudent to hazard the defense of Richmond, the interests involved by thus diminishing the force here, I will." Lee also warned that he thought Grant intended to move to the James, which he believed would be fatal to his own army and Richmond and could only be prevented by striking a decisive blow against his forces. With the three corps on hand, every attempt to do this so far had failed; with only two, the odds against success would be so long as to make almost any offensive action completely unfeasible. Thus, just as it had in the summer of 1862, the fact that the Army of the Potomac was east of Richmond and near the James left Lee without any operational options that did not carry serious risks. And this time, the Lincoln administration would not do him the favor of taking away the threat of the Army of the Potomac moving to the James. This is not to say it did not make an effort. When Grant crossed the Pamunkey and it was clear that he was eyeing the James as a destination for his army, Halleck made a vigorous attempt to get him to abandon this course of action. Instead, he urged Grant to stay between Washington and Richmond and base his operations on the railroads north of the Confederate capital. Unfortunately for Lee, Grant sensibly rejected this advice.[18]

However, it was by no means clear to Lee how strong Grant's commitment to operating on the James really was. Nor was it evident that the Union general-in-chief had the ability to resist pressure to change his course should events give the Lincoln administration cause to act on its aversion to seeing the Army of the Potomac on the James. Lacking the means to take the offensive against Grant with any real prospect of success, it made sense to see whether taking the offensive in the Valley to arouse the anxieties of the Lincoln administration would lead it to do to the threat posed by Grant what it had done two years earlier to the one posed by McClellan. Taking the offensive in the Valley, of course, had been on Lee's mind since at least mid-May, when he urged Breckinridge to push into Maryland after New Market. Yet Breckinridge had lacked the means to carry out Lee's wishes then, while the attrition his command suffered during the fighting near Richmond, and the reinforcement of Hunter's force after Piedmont, made it unrealistic to expect it to be able just to hold its own. Thus, by the second week in June the argument for reducing the force defending Richmond to reinforce the effort to defeat Hunter was too compelling to resist. The combination of his own demonstrated impotence against the Army of the Potomac in the campaign of position warfare that was developing, and the menace and opportunity presented by Hunter, finally led Lee on June 12 to order Early's corps to move toward Lynchburg. Lee told Early his mission was, the latter wrote after the war, "to strike Hunter's force in the rear, and, if possible, destroy it; then to move down the Valley, cross the Potomac . . . and threaten Washington."[19]

Lee, of course, understood that the diminishment of his forces and the number of potentially good operational options available to his opponent meant that, if he was to thwart Grant's next move after crossing the Chickahominy, he would need more than his fair share of good fortune. Fortunately for him and the Confederacy, he got it. During the afternoon of June 14, Lee speculated in a letter to Davis that it might be Grant's intention, after crossing the Chickahominy, to reach the location of McClellan's old camp on the James at Harrison's Landing, but also feared "he may be sending troops up the James River with the view of getting possession of Petersburg." A few hours later, Lee advised Davis that reports had arrived placing Grant near the James below Harrison's Landing and that he had shifted Hoke's command to a point near Drewry's Bluff so he would be in position to respond to a Federal crossing of the James. Nonetheless, until he was absolutely certain that Grant's intention was not in fact to advance against Richmond north of the James, Lee did not dare move the two corps still with him in any way that might expose the capital to such a move.[20]

In fact the following morning, Federal engineers completed a pontoon bridge across the James to enable wagons to follow the infantry, which had begun crossing the river on the fourteenth. "Our movement from Cold Harbor to the James River has been made with great celerity," Grant advised Washington on

June 14. "The enemy show no signs yet of having brought troops to the south side of Richmond. I will have Petersburg secured, if possible, before they get there in much force." To this end, Grant ordered Smith's corps to cross the Appomattox River from Bermuda Hundred early on the fifteenth and move directly on Petersburg, which he was to attack with the first of Meade's corps to cross the James, Hancock's, supporting his efforts.[21]

As Smith's and Hancock's forces moved toward Petersburg, Lee ordered Hoke's division and a brigade to cross the James and assist Beauregard, who had only about two thousand men when Smith's corps arrived at the eastern face of the fortified Dimmock Line that surrounded Petersburg on the fifteenth. Smith, however, conducted his operations very cautiously, and although able to overrun a significant section of the Dimmock Line during the late afternoon, decided not to press his advantage—much to the relief of Beauregard, who later proclaimed, "Petersburg at that hour was clearly at the mercy of the Federal commander." When Hancock arrived that evening, Smith turned over control of the situation to him. Hancock then decided to wait for morning before renewing the assault, which gave Beauregard time to patch together a new defensive line behind Harrison's Creek. From this position Beauregard spent the morning anxiously watching Hancock reconnoiter his position. Meanwhile, Meade arrived to take personal direction of the offensive against Petersburg and let Hancock persuade him to await the arrival of the Ninth Corps before attempting a full-scale attack.[22]

At around two in the morning of the sixteenth, Lee received a message from Beauregard reporting that he was abandoning his works north of the Appomattox to concentrate his command for the defense of Petersburg. Lee immediately ordered Anderson to take two divisions south of the James to occupy Bermuda Hundred and accompanied them as they crossed the river. Shortly before 10:00 a.m., Lee sent a message from Drewry's Bluff to Beauregard asking for information, and, within an hour, a message arrived from that officer stating: "The enemy is pressing us in heavy force. Can you not send forward the re-enforcements asked for this morning?" Lee replied, "I do not know the position of Grant's army, and cannot strip north bank of James River. Have you not force sufficient?" To Lee's relief, Beauregard replied that he thought he might "have force sufficient to hold Petersburg." At three, Lee wrote back that he hoped Beauregard would be able to "drive the enemy" and that he had yet to hear "of Grant's crossing the James River." Beauregard then advised Lee that more than fifty transports had been seen on the James on the fourteenth and fifteenth. In response to a message from Lee speculating that those transports belonged to Butler and asking specifically whether Meade's forces had actually been seen, around seven that evening Beauregard advised, "No satisfactory information yet received of Grant's crossing James River. Hancock's and Smith's corps are however in our front." He also advised Lee, almost as an afterthought: "There has been some fighting to-day, without result. Have selected a new line of defenses around city, which will be occupied to-morrow . . . hope to make it stronger than the first."[23]

In fact, the Federals had renewed their offensive at Petersburg shortly before dark, but Beauregard's defenses behind Harrison's Creek were just strong enough to frustrate Meade's efforts to break them. In addition, Butler made an effort that day to take advantage of Beauregard's withdrawal from Bermuda Hundred to venture forward from his defenses, an effort that was blunted by the arrival of Anderson's men. Although quite fortunate that June 16 had not brought catastrophe, as night fell Lee was frustrated that he was unable to secure sufficient information about the enemy and complained to Davis that "I have not learned from Genl Beauregard what force is opposed to him in Petersburg, or received any definite account of operations there, nor have I been able to learn whether any portion of Grant's army is opposed to him."[24]

When dawn rose on June 17, although pleased with Anderson's success at Bermuda Hundred, Lee remained exasperated at his lack of solid information about Grant's movements and intentions. Consequently, at 6:00 a.m., he sent a telegram to Beauregard congratulating him on his successful repulse of the Federal attack the night before and asking, "Can you ascertain anything of Grant's movements?" Beauregard replied a few hours later that he knew there were two Federal corps in front of him, but had nothing positive regarding Grant's movements, and asked for reinforcements. As the Federals prepared another attack on Petersburg, Lee wrote back at noon that, lacking definite information on Grant's movements, he "did not think it prudent to" further weaken the forces north of the James. Finally, that afternoon two messages arrived from Beauregard forwarding information gleaned from prisoners that Grant was in fact in front of Petersburg with three corps, and two more were moving to join him. Lee responded by ordering Hill to move his corps from Glendale to Chaffin's Bluff and be prepared to cross the James there if ordered, but as night fell was still unsure of the wisdom of moving to Petersburg.[25]

Fortunately for Lee, affairs on the Federal side of the lines in front of Petersburg had been badly managed that day. After initial attacks by the Ninth Corps drove part of Beauregard's line back, the effort to follow up this success fell to an incompetently led division that was overwhelmed by a sudden Confederate counterattack that captured nearly fifteen hundred prisoners. Understandably frustrated by two days of disjointed and ineffectual attacks against Petersburg, Meade ordered a single coordinated attack by three corps at first light on June 18. Sensing the power the Federals possessed would be too much for him to handle, Beauregard shot a message to Lee reporting that he felt compelled to pull back to a shorter and more defensible line, but that "without reinforcements, I may have to evacuate the city shortly." Upon receipt of this message, Lee immediately ordered Hill to get his command on the march within five hours, so it could cross the James and reach a position from which it could then move to Petersburg, and directed Maj. Gen. Joseph Kershaw's division from Anderson's corps to move to Petersburg in the morning.[26]

As officers from Beauregard's staff arrived during the late evening of the seventeenth and early morning of the eighteenth to brief Lee on the events of the past three days at Petersburg, the sense of urgency in the general's movements dramatically increased. He directed the superintendent of the Richmond and Petersburg Railroad to do what he could to facilitate the effort "to get troops to Petersburg without delay." Lee also sent a message to Early advising him of the situation and directing him to "strike as quick as you can, and, if circumstances authorize, carry out the original plan, or move upon Petersburg without delay." He then advised Davis that Grant's crossing to the south side of the James was "pretty certain," that he had directed the two corps of the Army of Northern Virginia to the Petersburg front, and was personally heading to Petersburg.[27]

Following Anderson's men as they rushed to Beauregard's aid, Lee arrived at Petersburg late in the morning of June 18 and learned that Beauregard had foiled the Federal attempt to break his lines at first light by pulling back to a shorter line behind Poor Creek. The Federals, however, remained determined to have Petersburg and, after adjusting to the change in Beauregard's position, Meade ordered an afternoon assault. Even then, the Federal high command still could not get its act together and during the afternoon it launched a series of disjointed attacks that Beauregard, aided by Anderson's divisions, was able to repulse so easily that one Confederate officer later recalled, "On the whole, we did not recognize the fighting on the 18th as . . . a first class battle. . . . soldiers and our generals alike, considered it as only a day of demonstrations and reconnaissances." By the next morning, Lee's army was firmly established in formidable fortifications defending Petersburg. Recognizing his great opportunity was gone, Grant ordered his men to dig in as well. A much relieved Lee wrote to Davis on the nineteenth that although skirmishers and artillerists continued to exchange fire, "No attack has been made since my arrival." At the same time, Lee understood he and his army faced a difficult future and that a Richmond newspaper correspondent in Petersburg was indulging in wishful thinking when he crowed on June 20: "The time of our peril has passed, and the hour for congratulation and felicitation" had arrived. "The enemy's left now rests on the Jerusalem Plank Road," Lee had advised Davis the day before. "My greatest apprehension at present is the maintenance of our communications south. It will be difficult, and I fear impracticable to preserve it uninterrupted."[28]

Although he made his fair share of mistakes in the course of the Overland Campaign, given the severe disadvantages under which he labored, Lee's performance was more than commendable and his accomplishments were not insignificant. While driven from central Virginia to the James and Appomattox and badly bloodied (total Confederate losses for the campaign came to about thirty-six thousand), the Army of Northern Virginia was still intact physically and morally. Moreover, Lee's ability to preserve his army shattered expectations for a quick victory that Grant's assumption of command had inspired in a Northern populace that had difficulty seeing beyond the heavy cost in life (Federal casualties in the campaign came to around sixty-three thousand overall) and treasure to appreciate what had been accomplished. Although a considerable measure of credit for that was due to enemy blunders, Lee nonetheless merited credit for handling his army well despite terrible losses and breakdowns among the members of his high command. He fought off nearly every assault made against his position and wisely maintained an aggressive mind-set in which he always kept a watch out for opportunities to seize the initiative through offensive action. That the offensives Lee attempted during the campaign did not achieve more was testimony to the tremendous power of the Federal army and its leadership. Although it blunted their offensive effectiveness, the cautious mind-set of Grant's subordinates paid dividends in how they responded to Lee's counterattacks. Comfortable with position warfare, appreciative of the advantage in numbers and firepower they possessed, and conscious that support from their comrades was nearby, Union commanders kept their heads when confronted with one of Lee's counterstrokes and did not let tactical setbacks have serious operational consequences.

Although unable to destroy Lee's army or seize Richmond, Grant had significantly advanced the Union war effort in Virginia in the course of the Overland Campaign. Although his forces had suffered significantly more casualties than Lee's had, the North could replace its losses; the Confederacy could not. Moreover, he had gotten the Army of the Potomac off the Orange and Alexandria line of operations and onto one based on the James River.

That Federal operations did not achieve more and were only able to achieve what they did by accepting an awful price in casualties was a consequence of several factors: the skill and determination with which the Confederates had fought, the fact that Grant had to bow to the headquarters doctrine in beginning the Army of the Potomac's campaign in central Virginia, and the failure of Butler's offensive to fulfill Grant's hopes of crippling Lee's logistical base at the outset of the campaign. Nonetheless, Grant had broken the stalemate that the headquarters doctrine had imposed on the war in Virginia and led the Army of the Potomac to the banks of the James where it could achieve truly decisive results.

Notes

1. Horace Porter, *Campaigning with Grant* (1897; New York: Da Capo, 1986), 37; J. William Jones, *Personal Reminiscences, Anecdotes, and Letters of Gen. Robert E. Lee* (New York: D. Appleton, 1875), 40.

2. Lee to Anderson, May 30, 1864, in *Wartime Papers*, eds. Dowdey and Manarin, 757–58.

3. Early to Lee, May 30, 1864, OR, vol. 36, pt. 3: 854; Lee to Anderson, May 30, 1864, ibid., 851.

4. Beauregard to Bragg, May 30, 1864, ibid., vol. 51, pt. 2: 971–72; Lee to Davis, May 30, 1864, in *Wartime Papers*, eds. Dowdey and Manarin, 758–59; Beauregard to Bragg, May 30, 1864, OR, vol. 36, pt. 3: 857.

5. Fitz Lee to Robert E. Lee, May 31, 1864, OR, vol. 36, pt. 3: 858; Sheridan to Humphreys, May 31, 1863, ibid., 411.

6. "Diary of the First [Confederate] Army Corps," OR, vol. 36, pt. 1: 1058; Alexander, *Fighting for the Confederacy*, 398; Meade to Wright, May 31, 1864, OR, vol. 36, pt. 3: 404.

7. Alexander, *Fighting for the Confederacy*, 400; Wright to Humphreys with endorsement by Grant, June 1, 1864, OR, vol. 36, pt. 3: 457; Meade to Hancock, June 1, 1864, ibid., 441–42; Meade to Hancock, June 1, 1864, ibid., 458; Meade to Smith, June 1, 1864, ibid., 468; Hancock to Asst. Adjt. Gen., Army of the Potomac, September 21, 1865, ibid., pt. 1: 344; Dana to Stanton, June 2, 1864, ibid., 87.

8. Freeman, *R.E. Lee*, vol. 3: 378–79; Reagan, *Memoirs*, 193; Lee to Seddon, June 2, 1864, in *Wartime Papers*, eds. Dowdey and Manarin, 762.

9. Alexander, *Fighting for the Confederacy*, 397, 401; Lee to Seddon, June 2, 1864, in *Wartime Papers*, eds. Dowdey and Manarin, 762; Rhea, *Cold Harbor*, 296–306.

10. Lee to Davis, June 3, 1864, in *Wartime Papers*, eds. Dowdey and Manarin, 763; Lee to Seddon, June 3, 1864, ibid., 764.

11. Reagan, *Memoirs*, 192–93; Lee to Davis, June 3, 1864, in *Wartime Papers*, eds. Dowdey and Manarin, 763; Lee to Anderson, June 4, 1864, ibid., 765.

12. Grant to Lee, June 5, 6, 7, 1864, OR, vol. 36, pt. 3: 600, 638, 638–39, 666, 667; Lee to Grant, June 5, 6, 7, 1864, ibid., 600, 638, 639, 667; Holt, *Mississippi Rebel in the Army of Northern Virginia*, 276.

13. Grant to Halleck, May 26, 1864, ibid., pt. 1: 206.

14. Lee to Imboden, May 25, 1864, Lee Headquarters Papers, VHS, series 7; Lee to Davis, June 6, 1864, in *Wartime Papers*, eds. Dowdey and Manarin, 767.

15. Grant to Halleck, June 5, 1864, OR, vol. 36, pt. 3: 598.

16. Lee to Seddon, June 8, 1864, in *Wartime Papers*, eds. Dowdey and Manarin, 769; Lee to Davis, June 9, 1864, ibid., 771.

17. Hill to Taylor, June 15, 1864, OR, vol. 51, pt. 2: 1017; Lee to Davis, June 14, [13], 1864, in *Wartime Papers*, eds. Dowdey and Manarin, 777, 780.

18. Lee to Davis, June 11, 1864, in *Wartime Papers*, eds. Dowdey and Manarin, 774–75; Halleck to Grant, May 24, 27, 1862, OR, vol. 36, pt. 3: 145, 245–46.

19. Early, *Autobiographical Sketch and Narrative*, 371.

20. Lee to Davis, June 14, 1864, in *Wartime Papers*, eds. Dowdey and Manarin, 777–79; Lee to Bragg, June 14, 1864, ibid., 779; Lee to Seddon, June 14, 1864, ibid., 780.

21. Grant to Halleck, June 14, 1864, OR, vol. 40, pt. 2: 18–19; Grant, *Memoirs*, 512, 514–15. The First Petersburg Offensive is effectively examined in Thomas J. Howe, *The Petersburg Campaign: Wasted Valor: June 15–18, 1864* (Lynchburg, VA: H.E. Howard Inc., 1988).

22. Lee to Seddon, June 15, 1864, in *Wartime Papers*, eds. Dowdey and Manarin, 781–82; Lee to Davis, June 15, 1864, ibid., 783; Beauregard, "Four Days of Battle at Petersburg," *Battles and Leaders*, vol. 4: 541.

23. Beauregard to Lee, June 15, 16, 1864, OR, vol. 40, pt. 2: 657; ibid., vol. 52, pt. 2: 1078, 1078–79; Lee to Davis, June 16, 1864, in *Wartime Papers*, eds. Dowdey and Manarin, 785–86; Lee to Beauregard, June 16, 1864, ibid., 784, 785.

24. Lee to Davis, June 16, 1864, ibid., 786.

25. Lee to Beauregard, June 17, 1864, ibid., 787, 788; Beauregard to Lee, June 17, 1864, OR, vol. 51, pt. 2: 1079, 1080; Lee to Hill, June 17, 1864, in *Wartime Papers of R.E. Lee*, eds. Dowdey and Manarin, 789.

26. Beauregard to Lee, June 17, 1864, quoted in Alexander, *Fighting for the Confederacy*, 430; Lee to Hill, June 17, 1864, in *Wartime Papers*, eds. Dowdey and Manarin, 790; Lee to Beauregard, June 17, 1864, ibid.

27. Lee to Gill, June 18, 1864, ibid., 791; Lee to Early, June 18, 1864, ibid.; Lee to Davis, June 18, 1864, ibid., 791–92.

28. Alexander, *Fighting for the Confederacy*, 432; *Richmond Daily Dispatch*, June 22, 1864; Lee to Davis, June 19, 1864, in *Wartime Papers*, eds. Dowdey and Manarin, 794.

CHAPTER EIGHT

A Mere Question of Time

The operations that commenced with Grant's crossing of the James River have often been labeled the "siege of Petersburg" even though it is more accurate to describe the campaign around Petersburg and Richmond during the nine months between the arrival of Grant's forces and the fall of the city as, in General Meade's words, a "quasi-siege." After the failure of the initial offensive against the Cockade City, Grant did not follow the time-tested method in siege operations of digging forward from his fortified lines in order to get close enough for a successful assault on the enemy's defenses. Rather, he sought to complete his investment of the city by seizing control of the system of roads and railways south of the Appomattox. Once this had been accomplished, Petersburg, the army defending it, and the Confederate capital would be doomed. Given the power of the forces Grant had at his disposal and the security they enjoyed by basing their operations on the James, Lee was under no illusions about the difficulties he faced and well aware that the challenge of preserving his communications to the south might prove insurmountable.[1]

Lee's approach to the difficult operational problem Grant presented him with and preventing the fall of the Confederacy that would surely follow the loss of Petersburg and Richmond was grounded in a number of premises. The first was that he could not conduct a defensive campaign. Only by achieving local successes that would delay Grant's efforts to achieve his operational goals could Lee raise Northerners' levels of frustration with the war to the point that a "political revolution" would take place in November that would bring to power leaders willing to recognize Confederate independence. And if a political revolution in the North fueled by frustration over setbacks on the battlefield did not happen in 1864, it never would in time to prevent the fall of the Confederacy. It was clear, given the degree to which the Confederacy's resources for waging war could be expected to have deteriorated by that point, that if the North's will to preserve the Union remained strong through the fall, it would be a question of when, rather than whether the total collapse of the Confederate war effort and nation would occur. Thus, the argument for conserving manpower for the long term by eschewing offensive tactics made little sense. Offensive tactics held the only possibility for achieving battlefield successes that could produce the short-term operational and strategic benefits the South needed. In any case, from an operational standpoint, a passive defense around Petersburg and Richmond was simply suicidal. "Something more is necessary than adhering to lines and defensive positions," Lee proclaimed to one of his subordinates in June, for Grant could not be allowed to take "such positions as he chooses. If he is allowed to continue that course we shall at last be obliged to take refuge behind the works of Richmond and stand a siege, which would be but a work of time. You must be prepared to fight him in the field, to prevent him from taking positions such as he desires."[2]

To be sure, Grant's advantages in manpower and firepower, strong fortifications, and secure logistics denied Lee much hope of seizing the initiative. Yet, if Grant wished to complete his investment of Petersburg in an expeditious manner, Union forces would at some point have to leave the security of their trenches and move in the open, where they would be vulnerable to counterattacks that might achieve decisive local successes and blunt their efforts. For Lee the challenge was to respond to enemy moves quickly enough to catch the Federals outside their fortifications and at a tactical disadvantage, then deliver a strong blow that would inflict severe damage and prevent them from securing their operational objectives. Conducting an active defense, Lee believed—and quite soundly—offered the best prospects for maintaining Southern control of Petersburg's transportation network as long as possible, while denying Federals tangible signs of progress around Petersburg that would ameliorate frustration in the North over what appeared on the surface to be a stalemate in Virginia.

Lee's vision was not, however, confined to his immediate front. Rather, he viewed the Virginia theater as a whole, which led him to ground much of his hope for success during the second half of 1864 on events in the Shenandoah Valley. There it was hoped that Early could get a chance to arouse, in the words of one Confederate officer, "the well known but very absurd apprehensions of the Federal executive and War Department for the safety of Washington." If Early could achieve success in the Valley, it was hoped this would throw Lincoln and his government into the "state of almost terror into which they seemed to be thrown by every threat of a Confederate attack" and that the Union president would then, as he had two years earlier, weaken the forces on the James in order to secure Washington from threats real and imagined.[3] In addition to relieving the pressure on Petersburg and Richmond, if a political revolution in the North driven by frustration over events on the battlefield was the only hope for relief from Union military power, the combination of yet another failure in the Valley and retardation of Grant's ability to achieve sufficient successes around Petersburg and Richmond would certainly enhance the possibility that such a revolution could occur.

Yet even as he grappled with the overwhelming problems he faced in Virginia, Lee could not ignore what was happening elsewhere in the faltering Confederacy. The same day Grant had crossed the Rapidan, three Union armies operating under the direct command of Maj. Gen. William Tecumseh Sherman had begun offensive operations in Georgia against a Confederate army under Gen. Joseph Johnston that was as badly overmatched in terms of numbers as Lee was in Virginia. In the weeks that followed, Sherman and Johnston engaged in a campaign of maneuver that by the third week of June had driven the Confederates back to a mountain range barely thirty miles from Atlanta. Although Sherman had not been able yet to achieve a decisive victory, his ability to penetrate so deep into the interior of Georgia was a source of no little concern for the Confederacy.[4]

Meanwhile, on June 21–22 Lee received his first opportunity to test his method of conducting an active defense to thwart Union efforts to seize the rail lines supporting Petersburg. With Grant's approval, Meade pulled the Second and Sixth corps out of his lines in front of Petersburg, which then extended from the Appomattox River to the Jerusalem Plank Road. After crossing the latter road, these corps were instructed to advance west to extend the Union line as far as they could, securing at least the Petersburg and Weldon Railroad, before pushing north toward Petersburg. On June 21, the Federal offensive began. At his headquarters on the lawn of Violet Bank, a plantation house just north of the Appomattox, Lee almost immediately picked up evidence of the Federal move and quickly had elements from Hill's corps preparing a counterstroke. During the afternoon of the twenty-second, with Lee providing personal direction, Brig. Gen. William Mahone's division moved into a gap that opened between the two Union corps, reached a position on the left flank of the Second Corps, and then delivered a crushing attack that, Mahone later wrote, "rolled it up like a scroll." More than fifteen hundred prisoners were taken and, menaced by another division that had moved into the widening gap between it and the Second Corps, the Sixth Corps had little choice but to give up a foothold it had gained on the Weldon Railroad and pull back to the Jerusalem Plank Road. There the two Union corps prepared strong fortifications, having extended the Union line slightly but with the Weldon Railroad still in Lee's possession. As if this were not bad enough for Grant, a raiding force led by Brig. Gen. James Harrison Wilson and Brig. Gen. August V. Kautz returned to Union lines on July 1, having fallen far short of the objectives the Union high command had set for it.[5]

One bright spot for the Federal commander, however, came in the immediate aftermath of the setback at the Jerusalem Plank Road. Eager as always to seize potential opportunities to take the offensive, desperate to relieve the pressure against Petersburg, and hopeful that Grant's shifting of forces to the south might make him vulnerable at the other end of his line, Lee decided to make an attack against the Union position along the Appomattox. Execution of the attack was delegated to Beauregard, in deference to the fact that the area of operations was technically in his department. The plan was for two divisions to follow up a vigorous artillery bombardment on June 24 from high ground north of the Appomattox against the section of the Federal lines with a strong attack to seize the section of the Union line along the river, and then sweep south with the goal, one officer later wrote, of "rolling up the Federal right and compelling General Grant to battle in the open field at a disadvantage." Lee's hope that, as one division commander later wrote, "the enemy had grown careless," proved in vain, though. Even though some his men were able to reach the enemy works on the morning of the twenty-fourth, they did not do so in enough strength to hold them, much less continue the attack as intended, which compelled Lee to order his men back to their own works.[6]

If Lee was frustrated with the failure of this attack, he nonetheless had reason to take a degree of satisfaction as June 1864 came to an end. After all, the defeat at Cold Harbor, the failure to take advantage of the brilliant movement across the James, the defeat at Jerusalem Plank Road, and failure of the Wilson-Kautz Raid had made June a month of great frustration for Grant and the North as well.

Worse was to come for the Union in July, as Lee's hopes that something could be done in the Shenandoah Valley to help alleviate the serious strategic and operational problems he faced were fulfilled. After leaving their

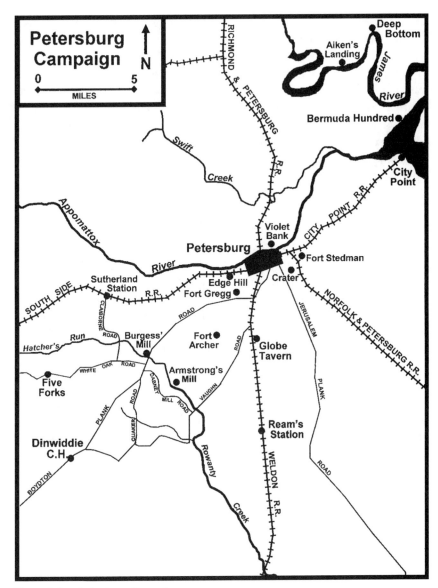

Figure 8.1. Petersburg Campaign.

comrades in the Army of Northern Virginia, Early's command reached Lynchburg on June 17, and although Lee's hope that Early might "demolish Hunter" was not fulfilled, he induced the Federal commander to retreat toward West Virginia. Early was not slow to seize the opportunity this created to push down the Valley and across the Potomac toward the Federal capital.

As Early's intentions became clear, Grant was compelled by the Lincoln administration during the first week of July to weaken his operations against Richmond and Petersburg by sending the Nineteenth Corps, which was then slated to reinforce the Army of the James, and Sixth Corps north to the capital. They arrived just in time to persuade Early, whose command had reached the outskirts of Washington on July 11, to pull back to the Shenandoah Valley. The pursuit of Early's force was badly handled, though, and after winning a victory at the Second Battle of Kernstown on July 24, Early recrossed the Potomac and on July 30 part of his command put the town of Chambersburg, Pennsylvania, to the torch.[7]

These events had many positive benefits for Lee. First, by compelling Grant to detach forces from the operations around Richmond and Petersburg, they significantly hampered his ability to extend his lines westward in order to interdict Petersburg's logistics. They also provided further fuel for critics of the Lincoln administration's conduct of the war and delivered significant blows to Northern faith in the ability of Grant, or any Union commander, to make progress in the war. On July 1, Lee had called Davis's attention to reports in a Northern newspaper of adjustments in the North's policies for raising manpower and increases in the price of gold that indicated growing Northern frustration with the conduct of the war. A little more than a week later, Lee wrote again to Davis to cite reports in a Northern newspaper that indicated Early's operations had "mystified . . . the people in the U.S. . . . teaching them they must keep some of their troops at home and that they cannot denude their frontier with impunity. It seems also to have put them in bad temper as well as bad humour. Gold you will see has gone as high as 271 and closed at 266."[8]

Despite these positive developments, Lee still faced a formidable challenge around Richmond and Petersburg. Even without the Sixth and Nineteenth Corps, the Federals still outnumbered him and, with their operations based on the James, had secure logistics and the freedom to initiate operations at the times and places of their choosing, shifting forces so as to mass them north or south of the great river to gain considerable local superiority at Richmond or Petersburg. This made Lee as eager as ever to take the initiative himself, and in late July he advised Davis that, since Grant had weakened his force to deal with Early's operations, "I have thought much upon the subject of interrupting the enemy's communications on James River." Unless something like this could be done to make Grant less secure about his position in front of Richmond and Pe-

tersburg, Lee complained, "he can attack us at three points, as he may select, &
our success will depend upon our early information and celerity of movement,
as we have not troops sufficient." On the twenty-fourth, Lee sent orders to
Ewell, the officer in charge of the Richmond garrison, advising him that one of
Anderson's divisions had been sent north of the James the previous day with the
intention of seeing if it was possible "to dislodge the enemy, drive them across
the river, and destroy the bridges." Despite Lee's admonition to Ewell that "We
cannot afford to sit down in front of the enemy and allow him to entrench himself whenever he pleases," the Federal positions north of the James were simply
too strong and Grant's line of communications along the James too secure for
Anderson to achieve anything.[9]

As if this were not enough, July was a month of upheaval in the Confederate war effort in Georgia. After defeating Sherman at the Battle of Kenne-
saw Mountain on June 27, Johnston was compelled by a series of skillfully
conceived Federal maneuvers to fall back to the outskirts of Atlanta. Despite
the positive signs regarding Northern morale that Lee called to Davis's attention on July 10, and the fact that Johnston's defensive mind-set placed before his foe the prospect of what was sure to be a frustrating and time-consuming siege that would further strain Northern patience, the Confederate
president was deeply dissatisfied with the situation in Georgia. Davis wanted
a more aggressive military posture, and on July 12 wrote to Lee to advise him
that he was considering a command change in the Army of Tennessee and
asking his opinion of Lt. Gen. John Bell Hood, a former division commander
in the Army of Northern Virginia who was then a corps commander in Johnston's army. Lee wrote back to Davis twice that day that he thought it "a bad
time to release the commander of an army situated as is that of Tennessee.
We may lose Atlanta and the Army too." "Hood," he bluntly added, "is a
bold fighter. I am doubtful as to other qualities necessary." Davis, however,
had had enough of Johnston and, despite Lee's words of caution, replaced
him with Hood on July 17.[10]

Meanwhile, although the loss of the Sixth Corps command did compel a
pause in Grant's efforts to secure the railroads south of Petersburg, it had one
near-fatal consequence for Lee. It undoubtedly made Grant more open than
he would have been to a request for support for a scheme that some of Burnside's men had hatched. This involved digging a tunnel underneath the
ground that separated the two armies, filling it with gunpowder at a point
below a salient in the Confederate defensive works, and then igniting it. If
successful, it was argued, a big enough hole would be created in the Confederate defenses to enable an assault to achieve a penetration large enough
to unravel Lee's entire defensive line and force him to abandon Petersburg.

Despite the extreme skepticism with which the plan was greeted at Army of the Potomac headquarters, Grant approved it, and by the last week in July Burnside's men had completed work on the mine.[11]

To divert Lee's attention from Burnside's mining activities, of which vague reports reached Violet Bank by the third week in July, Grant decided to send Hancock's corps and two divisions of cavalry north of the James at Deep Bottom on the night of July 26–27. Fortunately for Lee, three days earlier he had ordered Anderson to move a division to Chaffin's Bluff in line with his hopes of making a successful attack north of the James. Nonetheless, the Federals enjoyed a considerable manpower advantage when Hancock's force finished crossing the James and began probing toward Richmond on the twenty-seventh. Consequently, Lee was compelled that day to order Anderson to take another division north of the James and assume personal command of the situation there. "Examine the enemy's position," Lee instructed Anderson, "endeavor to ascertain his strength, and if practicable drive him away and destroy his bridges." In line with Lee's instructions, Anderson decided after meeting with Ewell that evening to attack Hancock's right in the morning. The attack on the twenty-eighth, however, failed to achieve any significant results. Neither Lee nor Anderson were discouraged, though, and the former's decision to send yet another division to Anderson's assistance inspired the corps commander to plan another attack for July 29. When Confederate skirmishers went forward that morning, though, they found that except for a small force maintaining the bridgehead at Deep Bottom, the Federals were gone.[12]

Although Lee's dispatch of Anderson's forces to deal with Hancock succeeded in thwarting any possible threat the Federals might have posed to Richmond, it left his forces in front of Petersburg weakened, fulfilling Grant's objective of creating the most favorable conditions possible for Burnside's attack. Once again, though, fortune smiled on Lee, who did not, one officer complained, take the reports of enemy mining at Petersburg that reached him as seriously as he should have. In planning the follow-on assault to the explosion of the mine, Burnside initially assigned the key role to a fresh division of African-American troops. At the last minute, however, Grant and Meade forced Burnside to drop this part of the plan and, as a result, the role the African-American troops were originally to play ended up being assigned to one of the most poorly led divisions in the entire Union army. Consequently, although the mine worked as well as could have possibly been expected on the morning of July 30, ripping a huge hole in the Confederate lines south and east of Petersburg, the Union army failed to exploit it. Due to poor leadership, instead of moving around the crater created by the explosion to exploit the gap in the Confederate line, many of the Federals making the assault plunged into and around the crater and quickly degenerated into a confused mob.[13]

Nonetheless, a huge gap had been created in Lee's lines that had the potential to completely compromise the entire Confederate position at Petersburg. Although the sector of the lines where Burnside attacked was technically under Beauregard's command, Lee did not hesitate in taking action to respond to the crisis. After learning of the explosion of the mine, he ordered reinforcements from Hill's corps to the scene and went there personally to watch the battle. At the Gee House only about five hundred yards from the crater, Lee found Beauregard and together they watched Hill's men drive those Federals who had ventured out of the crater back into it and then turn it into a slaughter pen. By 3:25 p.m., Lee was able to report to Richmond that "we have retaken the salient and driven the enemy back to his lines." In a letter to his wife the next day, Lee only mentioned the fighting in passing, almost as an afterthought. Grant bemoaned in a letter on August 1 that the Battle of the Crater "was the saddest affair I have witnessed in the war. Such an opportunity for carrying fortifications I have never seen and do not expect again." Lee, however, was almost dismissive of the whole operation. "I do not know what [Grant] will attempt next," Lee advised his wife. "He is mining other points along the line. I trust he will succeed no better in his next than his last attempt."[14]

The situation at Petersburg after the Battle of the Crater was hardly cheery, though, with the Federals subjecting the town to an almost constant bombardment that induced Lee to assure a nervous relative on August 12 that although shells occasionally exploded over his headquarters and "pervade all space for miles . . . they have as yet done no harm." Of greater concern to Lee's counterpart at the time, though, was the situation in the Shenandoah Valley. The day after the Crater fiasco, Grant had what must have been a difficult meeting with Lincoln to address the situation in the Valley. Lincoln had acquiesced in Grant's decision to take his army to McClellan's old haunts on the James; however, Halleck had been laying out for just about anyone who would listen the long-standing objections the administration had to the move, and urged Grant to instead keep his army north of Richmond. Early's operations undoubtedly aroused Lincoln's long-standing discomfort with letting the Army of the Potomac operate anywhere that was not between the Confederates and Washington. It also undoubtedly aroused hope in Lincoln, rooted in his belief that operating against Confederate forces in the open and as far north as possible offered the best prospects for decisive victories. Grant managed to assure Lincoln that he understood the problem—and opportunity—the situation in the Valley presented and would compromise the operations on the James in order to address it.[15]

The principal problem was the incompetence with which the Federal response to Early's operations had been managed. Grant had expected Halleck, as senior man in the capital, to handle the matter, but had been badly disappointed by his performance. After encountering resistance to suggestions that William B. Franklin or Meade be sent to take charge of the effort to deal with Early, Grant persuaded the administration to assign the task to Sheridan. During the first week of August, Sheridan assumed command of what would become known as the Army of the Shenandoah with orders to defeat Early and destroy the Valley as a resource for the Confederate war effort. The forces Grant had sent north to Washington from the Petersburg front in July would remain where they were until Sheridan had accomplished these tasks.

To support Early's efforts to deal with Sheridan and continue relieving some of the pressure on Richmond and Petersburg, during the first week of August Lee ordered Anderson to take Maj. Gen. Joseph B. Kershaw's division north to Culpeper Court House. Then, on the eleventh, Lee advised Anderson that he had ordered Hampton's cavalry to join him and urged him to take up a position north of Culpeper and push the cavalry north to operate in the region between the Rappahannock and Washington. If the Federals, in their desire to move across the Blue Ridge to get at Early were to leave their capital uncovered, Lee advised Anderson that the cavalry with him "might cross the Potomac east of the mountains and demonstrate against that city." In any case, Lee directed Anderson that he was expected to act aggressively and make "the presence of our troops be felt beyond the Rappahannock. . . . Any enterprise that can be undertaken to injure the enemy, distract or separate his forces, embarrass his communications on the Potomac or on land is desirable."[16]

As Lee monitored operations in the Valley, thwarted the Crater offensive, and pondered what Grant's next move might be around Richmond and Petersburg during the second half of July, Confederate fortunes in Georgia took a decided turn for the worse. Upon assuming command of the Army of Tennessee, Hood fully fulfilled expectations that he would take a more aggressive approach to dealing with Sherman's advance than had his predecessor. On July 20, 22, and 28, Hood launched attacks against Sherman's army that produced fierce fighting but were bloodily repulsed. Hood was compelled to pull his battered and defeated army back into the defenses of Atlanta and try to figure out how to defend the town, which had taken on great symbolic importance for both sides, against a foe that now clearly had the initiative.[17]

As Sherman endeavored to take advantage of his victories by maneuvering to seize the logistical network that supported Atlanta and Hood's army in August, and as Sheridan and Early cautiously maneuvered against each other in the Lower Shenandoah Valley, Grant was not inactive. Upon learning of Lee's detachment of Anderson's and Hampton's commands north to Culpeper, Grant decided with characteristic alacrity and decisiveness to take the offensive himself. Once again exploiting his numerical superiority and the ability his position astride the James gave him to easily and quickly shift forces laterally to take the initiative, he directed his command to undertake operations both north and south of the James. During the evening of August 13 the first element of Grant's offensive got underway when Hancock's corps again began crossing to the north side of the James at Deep Bottom. Once across, they were to cooperate with a corps from Butler's army and a division of cavalry in an attack on the defenses of Richmond. Grant hoped at the least that Hancock would be strong enough to reach Chaffin's Bluff on the James and secure possession of it.[18]

News that large numbers of Federal troops were crossing to the north side of the James reached Violet Bank early on the fourteenth. Fortunately for Lee, Hancock's crossing fell behind schedule and enabled Maj. Gen. Charles Field, commander of Confederate forces north of the James, to consolidate his command in a strong defensive position on New Market Heights. From this position Field "handsomely repulsed" three attempts to carry the position and brought the Federal advance to a halt. Nonetheless, by the end of the day Lee had deemed it necessary to respond to Field's calls for help by ordering Hampton's command to return to the Richmond front, shifting a division of cavalry and two brigades of infantry over from south of the James, and directing Ewell to push forward forces from the Richmond defenses to Field. "Aid the cavalry all you can," Lee instructed Field, "and drive back enemy." At the same time, though, Lee was not certain of his course and confessed to his wife that he was unable to discern what Grant's intentions were. Consequently, in a message informing Field that reinforcements were heading his way, Lee advised his subordinate that Hancock's activities "may be a feint to draw troops from here. Watch closely and return the troops here at the earliest moment."[19]

Hancock tried to turn Field's position on August 15, but severe heat and humidity decimated his ranks and severely hampered his movements. Consequently, not until the morning of August 16 would an assault actually be

attempted. By then, Lee, who had left Violet Bank that morning, had arrived and was able to personally supervise the battle. The Federals, however, quickly overran a brigade of Georgians near Fussell's Mill early on the
sixteenth, and by mid-morning were threatening the rear of Field's position
on New Market Heights. This created for the Confederate cause what one
man later described as "an hour of fearful apprehension" and compelled Lee
to send a message to Davis recommending that he make sure the Richmond
works were manned. Not content with merely coordinating the response to
the Federal advance, Lee also took a personal hand in directing it. One
man in the Fifth South Carolina later recalled that while moving forward
to join the fight, his colonel caught sight of Lee riding up to them on Traveller and directed the men to dress their lines so they would "show up well
before the General." Removing his hat, Lee told the colonel, "No time for
right dress . . . Charge 'em boys with a hearty shout." The South Carolini-
ans promptly complied with Lee's directive, and their effort contributed to
Field's ability to not only bring the Federal advance to a halt, but recover
his initial positions as well.[20]

  Although there would be no significant fighting north of the James in the
days that followed the engagement of August 16, Lee felt compelled to keep
the forces he had sent to Field's assistance in place to watch Hancock's command and even moved his own headquarters camp to Chaffin's Bluff to
monitor the situation. There Lee learned on August 18 that the second part
of Grant's plan had been put in motion. That day, Warren's Fifth Corps began pushing west toward the Weldon Railroad south of Petersburg with orders to inflict as much damage on the railroad as it could. With Confederate forces south of the Appomattox diminished, Warren had no problem
reaching the railroad, which he did in the vicinity of Globe Tavern at
around nine that morning, and began tearing up the track. Shortly after ten,
Beauregard forwarded to Lee a report from Brig. Gen. James Dearing that
the Federals had driven in his pickets near the Globe Tavern, and at around
noon passed on another message from Dearing stating the Federals were "advancing in force both upon railroad and Vaughn road." Beauregard also advised Lee that he had sent two brigades to Dearing's support. Although too
far away to hope to manage the situation south of the Appomattox in any
case, there is no evidence that Lee disagreed with Beauregard's actions at all.
Indeed, he no doubt hoped that the forces from Hill's corps south of Appomattox, as they had in June, would be able to catch the Federals out of their
strong fortifications and strike a decisive blow that would at the least drive
them away from the Weldon and perhaps even destroy a significant part of
Grant's command.[21]

As hoped, during the afternoon of the eighteenth Maj. Gen. Henry Heth's division was able to catch one of Warren's divisions in the open and with an exposed flank north of Globe Tavern. After routing it, however, Heth encountered other elements of Warren's corps that induced him to break off his attack and pull back to the Petersburg defenses. Warren, who had received orders to maintain his foothold on the railroad, then prudently instructed his men to fortify their position around Globe Tavern, even though he did not have sufficient force to fill the gap between his right and the rest of the Army of the Potomac. When a message arrived after dark from Beauregard reporting that Heth had "driven the enemy about one mile . . . [and] desires re-enforcements to complete his success," Lee responded by ordering a division of cavalry and three brigades from Mahone's division to return to Petersburg from north of the James.[22]

Upon learning of Lee's decision to reinforce him, Beauregard vowed in a message to him early on August 19 to use the forces at his disposal to "endeavor today to dislodge" the Federals from the railroad. True to his word, that afternoon Beauregard attacked Warren's forces, and thanks to the gap between Warren and the rest of the Union army, Mahone's command was able to deliver a devastating blow against Warren's right that netted more than twenty-five hundred prisoners before reinforcements from the Ninth Corps enabled Warren to halt Mahone's attack and maintain his hold on the railroad. Throughout the twentieth, Warren consolidated his position on the railroad by building strong fortifications backed by the powerful Union artillery. Consequently, when the Confederates renewed the attack on August 21, they faced the very sort of tactical situation in which they did not have the means to prevail and were quickly and easily defeated by Union infantry fighting from behind strong fortifications and massed Union artillery. Although able, due to the abandonment the night before by the Federals of their position north of the James, to leave Chaffin's Bluff in order to be closer to the action south of Petersburg, Lee was not able to exert much influence over the fighting on August 21. Conceding defeat, Lee's men had no choice but to pull back to the Petersburg defenses and watch Grant extend his strong line of entrenchments to Globe Tavern.[23]

A disheartened Lee wrote to Davis the next day to report the "enemy availed himself of the withdrawal of troops from Petersburg to the north side of James River, to take a position on the Weldon Railroad" and of the failure of the effort to drive the Federals from that position. The enemy's "late demonstration on the north side of the James," he wrote, "was designed I think in part, to cause the withdrawal of troops from here to favor his movement against the road. . . . As I informed Your Excellency when we first reached Petersburg, I was doubtful of our ability to hold the Weldon road so as to use it. The proximity of the enemy and his superiority of numbers rendered it possible for him to break the road at any time, and even if we could drive him from the position he now holds, we could not prevent him from returning to it. . . . These considerations induced me to abandon the prosecution of the effort to dislodge him." In letters to Richmond on the twenty-third, Lee made clear that his sense of the growing odds against him had received further fuel from the operations of the past week as he appealed for more rigorous efforts to recruit soldiers for his army. "Without some increase of our strength," he warned Secretary of War James Seddon, "I cannot see how we are to escape the natural military consequences of the enemy's numerical superiority."[24]

Then, however, Grant gave Lee an opportunity to both redeem his methods and get a measure of revenge for the setback at the Weldon Railroad. The day after the fighting ended at Globe Tavern, Grant informed Meade, "It is my desire to hold the Weldon road . . . and to thoroughly destroy it as far south as possible." In line with Grant's wishes, Meade ordered a division from Hancock's corps to move south of Warren's position to tear up the track, and by the afternoon of the twenty-third the Federals were at Reams Station. The following evening, Meade ordered more elements from Hancock's to participate in the railroad wrecking expedition, which was to move south along the road toward Rowanty Creek and destroy the track between Globe Tavern and that stream. Hancock promptly complied, and by the morning of August 25 had managed to reach a point only a few miles from the Rowanty.[25]

By then, Lee had found out about the Federal move from Hampton's cavalry and ordered Hill to head south with eight brigades, eagerly hoping that he and Hampton might catch Hancock's command in the open and deliver a decisive blow. Upon learning of Hill's approach, Hancock pulled back to a position at Reams Station where his men took refuge behind some very poorly prepared works that Federals participating in the earlier Wilson-Kautz raid had built. They had not had time to correct the problems with these works or get fully set when the Confederates arrived during the afternoon of the twenty-fifth. In line with Lee's injunction to Hampton to "do all in your power to punish the enemy," Hill and Hampton launched a vicious assault that broke the Union line and forced Hancock to retreat back to Petersburg, with Confederate hopes for a vigorous pursuit frustrated by darkness and rain. "Seven stand of colors, two thousand prisoners, and nine pieces of artillery are in our possession," Lee crowed to Richmond the next day. "The loss of the enemy in killed and wounded is reported to be heavy, ours relatively small."[26]

The Union rout at Reams Station ended the operations along the Weldon on a bright note for Lee and the Confederacy, not the least because it demonstrated that Lee's army and his methods were still capable of winning tactical victories over Grant's forces. Further boosting morale in the Army of Northern Virginia was a bold raid by Hampton's cavalry on September 15–17 into the Federal rear areas that culminated in the overrunning of the defenders of a Union cattle pen at Coggins Point, netted more than three hundred prisoners, and seized nearly twenty-five hundred head of cattle.[27]

Nonetheless, Warren's victory at Globe Tavern demonstrated that there were limits to what Lee's operational and tactical methods could achieve around Petersburg, especially if the Federals conducted their operations with prudent good sense. Moreover, it secured for the Federals a foothold on the Weldon Railroad that Lee did not have the means to overcome and provided the North with a tangible indication that progress was being made around Petersburg. Even worse, Warren's victory was but one in a series of serious military setbacks in August and September 1864 that would do irreversible harm to what faint hopes remained for Confederate victory.

The first setback had actually come a few weeks earlier at Mobile Bay, Alabama, where a Union naval force commanded by Rear Adm. David Farragut won a dramatic victory that secured control of the waters around that important southern port. Then, the same week that Hancock's men were coming to grief at Reams Station, Sherman began a final maneuver designed to complete the effort to secure control of Atlanta's communications. Hood's attempt to check this movement resulted in another defeat, and as a consequence, left him with no alternative but to evacuate Atlanta before it became a death trap for his army. On September 2, Sherman's command took possession of the town. Then, in mid-September Sheridan took the offensive against Early's army in the Shenandoah Valley. On September 19 and 22, Sheridan crushed Early's command in battles at Winchester and Fisher's Hill and then spent a month carrying out Grant's orders to destroy the Valley's resources. To make matters worse, Sheridan's successes enabled Grant to begin making plans to return the forces that had been sent north from Petersburg in response to Early's raid on Washington. Before he could do this, Early launched a surprise attack at Cedar Creek on October 19, but, despite some initial Confederate success, the end result of the battle was a decisive Union victory.[28]

In addition, during the last week of September Grant once again took advantage of the possession of the initiative that superior numbers and the ability operating from the James provided to launch advances against both ends of the Confederate lines around Richmond and Petersburg. Although Grant had been planning such a move for some time, its timing was influenced by a critical decision that Lee made. Detaching Anderson and Kershaw's division to assist Early in the Valley seemed to have paid little in the way of dividends from Lee's perspective in exchange for the costs their absence had entailed. Consequently, in mid-September, Anderson received orders to bring Kershaw's command and a battalion of artillery back across the Blue Ridge to Culpeper Court House. On September 17, however, Lee wrote to Anderson directing him and his staff to return to the Richmond-Petersburg front to "take command of the other divisions of your corps and direct Genl Kershaw to report with his division to Genl Early for the present." Lee sent similar orders to Early, but at some point shortly thereafter it was determined that it was feasible for Kershaw to move to Gordonsville with the rest of Anderson's command. Sheridan then took advantage of Kershaw's absence, promptly reported by Federal intelligence, to defeat Early at Winchester and Fisher's Hill. Lee responded to news of Early's defeats by sending orders to Anderson at Gordonsville to send Kershaw back to Early, but that previous orders that he and his staff return to the Richmond-Petersburg front remained in effect.[29]

Almost as soon as Kershaw began moving back toward the Valley on September 24, Federal intelligence picked up evidence of the move and reported it to Grant. The Union general-in-chief then promptly moved up the start date for his next offensive around Richmond and Petersburg from October 5 to September 29. On the twenty-ninth, two of Butler's corps opened the offensive by crossing to the north side of the James at Aiken's Landing and Deep Bottom and launching powerful assaults against New Market Heights and Fort Harrison, two critical points in Richmond's defenses.[30]

When he learned of Butler's advance at around 6:30 a.m., Lee had only four brigades of cavalry and infantry, operating under Ewell's overall direction, north of the James, and they proved no match for Butler's forces, which by 7:00 a.m. had captured New Market Heights and overrun Fort Harrison. These successes created the very real possibility that the Federals might seize Chaffin's Bluff on the James River, possession of which was vital to defense of the river, and, Butler hoped, maybe even Richmond itself, whose inhabitants could tell, one woman later wrote, "that a most terrific battle was raging. We had never heard peals of artillery in more rapid succession, or more continuously for hours." Upon receiving word of the Federal advance, Lee summoned Field, who along with three of his brigades had been shifted south to Petersburg a few weeks earlier, to his headquarters at Dunn's Hill and directed him to take his forces "at once to Chaffin's Bluff." As more information came in during the morning regarding the situation north of the James, Lee issued orders to Hoke's division, as well as to elements from Hill's corps, Pickett's division, and the cavalry corps, to go to Field's assistance. He also wrote to Richmond requesting that the local defense troops be sent forward, something Ewell had already called for.[31]

At 7:30 a.m., however, this all looked like a case of too little, too late. But then the wounding of the commander of the Federal corps that had seized Fort Harrison and a superb performance by Ewell combined to blunt the momentum of the Federal advance, and by the time Field's men completed their trek to Chaffin's Bluff during the afternoon the situation had already stabilized. By 3:00 p.m. Lee himself was at Chaffin's Bluff and eager to do more than contain the Federal success. Since the early morning, he had been urging Ewell to retake Fort Harrison and not wait for Field to arrive before trying to do so. This was asking too much, for it was all Ewell could do to thwart Federal efforts to exploit their earlier triumphs. Upon his arrival on the scene, Lee himself saw that there simply was not enough Confederate manpower north of the James for an attack to be launched with much prospect of success before nightfall. Consequently, he decided to wait until the next morning, when all of Field's command and Hoke's division were expected to be on the field, before attempting to retake Fort Harrison. Lee then assigned this task to Anderson, who upon his arrival during the morning of the twenty-ninth had assumed command of the situation north of the James from Ewell. Anderson's effort on September 30 to deliver a coordinated attack by all of his forces, however, failed miserably. "It was a very bad charge," one of Hoke's men proclaimed afterward, "as bad a place as I ever was in."[32]

Nonetheless, Lee had managed to contain Butler's offensive. In order to do so, however, he had been forced to reduce the forces south of the Appomattox to a bare four divisions of infantry, with the lines along the Squirrel Level Road just west of Globe Tavern held by a single cavalry brigade. With Lee's departure for Chaffin's Bluff on September 29 and his subsequent preoccupation with the situation north of the James, responsibility for the management of affairs at Petersburg rested squarely on the shoulders of A. P. Hill. (Beauregard had departed from Petersburg just over a week before to see to affairs in South Carolina and would not play a significant role in the war in Virginia again.) Thus, it fell to Hill to deal with the four divisions from the

Union Fifth and Ninth corps—more than twenty thousand troops in all, operating under Warren's overall direction—that Grant and Meade ordered to push westward on September 30 from the Weldon Railroad with an eye on extending their lines to the Boydton Plank Road and, perhaps, the South Side Railroad.[33]

The former road had become especially critical to Lee as, after Warren seized his foothold on the Weldon Railroad, the Confederate commander set up a system whereby supplies coming north on the Weldon from North Carolina would be off-loaded about twenty miles south of Globe Tavern at Stony Creek Depot, then hauled overland to the Boydton Plank Road, which they would follow to Petersburg. If the Federals got possession of the Boydton Plank Road, Lee's ability to hold on at Petersburg would be severely compromised; if they got both the road and the South Side Railroad, Petersburg would be completely untenable. Yet, as the Federal high command anticipated, the threat posed by Butler to Richmond gave Lee no choice but to give Meade's army an opportunity to achieve a truly decisive success south of Petersburg. "If the enemy can be broken . . . follow him up closely," Grant advised Meade. "I can't help believing that the enemy are prepared to leave Petersburg if forced a little."[34]

On the morning of September 30, Warren's forces moved forward to spearhead the Federal advance south of Petersburg. Shortly after noon, Warren made contact near the Peebles Farm with the thinly held Confederate fortifications along the Squirrel Level Road and quickly overwhelmed the defenders of Fort Archer (later to become Union Fort Wheaton), the main strong point and key position in the Confederate line, in what Warren proclaimed to be "splendid style." Just as Butler's men had the morning before at Fort Harrison, Meade's had before them a golden opportunity on the afternoon of September 30 to dramatically hasten the fall of Petersburg. At this point, however, Lee's concept of conducting an active defense in which he would mount counterattacks against enemy advances to catch the Federals in the open and fight them outside fortified positions bore fruit. Rather than continue to push his men forward or move the Ninth Corps forward to sustain the momentum of the advance to the weakly defended Boydton Plank Road, Warren—understandably wary after the heavy losses his command and others had suffered when caught outside of a fortified position during the operations against the Weldon in June and August—ordered a halt to consolidate his position.[35]

Lee was also fortunate at this point that by the afternoon of September 30, whatever offensive inclinations Butler may have possessed when he crossed the James were clearly gone. Consequently, upon learning of the

Federal offensive against the Squirrel Level Road defenses, the Confederate high command felt free to countermand earlier orders to Maj. Gen. Cadmus Wilcox's division to leave Petersburg and join their comrades north of the James. Upon returning to Petersburg and learning of the threat to the Boyd-ton Plank Road, Wilcox led two brigades south to join the force being as-sembled for a counterattack against Warren's force. As the Federal Ninth Corps, now commanded by Maj. Gen. John G. Parke, resumed the advance toward the Boydton Plank Road, Heth ordered his and Wilcox's divisions forward to drive the Federals back while Hampton's cavalry menaced their left flank—roughly the same tactical blueprint that had proven so effective at Reams Station. Disorganized by their advance through wooded terrain

Figure 8.2.   Henry Heth, Confederate, c. 1861–1865. Francis Trevelyan Miller, *The Photographic History of the Civil War*, vol. 10 (New York: The Review of Reviews Co., 1911), 110.

and in an exposed position, the Ninth Corps, just as their comrades had been at the Jerusalem Plank Road, Weldon Railroad, and Reams Station, were in no condition to resist the Confederate counterattack. Parke's command was quickly routed, with Heth and Hampton together claiming nine hundred prisoners, and forced to fall back toward the Squirrel Level Road. There Parke's men were able to rally and, with the assistance of the Fifth Corps, put an end to whatever thoughts Heth might have had of inflicting more damage before nightfall. Heth renewed his attack on October 1, but the Federals, just as they had on August 21 at the Weldon Railroad, held a strong fortified position and were able to easily repulse the Confederate assaults. On October 2, Warren ordered another advance, but it was not strong enough to overcome the reinforced Confederate defenses protecting the Boydton Plank Road.[36]

Thus, the Fifth Petersburg Offensive ended with the Confederate army having again stopped the Federals short of their goals, but by the thinnest of margins and with considerable assistance from their adversaries. The loss of Fort Harrison and extension westward of the Federal lines around Petersburg after the fighting ended also provided clear evidence that Grant's forces were in fact making progress and of Lee's limited ability to prevent them from doing so. All of this was not only important from an operational standpoint, for the Union successes around Petersburg and elsewhere also provided a strong boost to Northern morale prior to the election. At the same time, too much should not be made of this development as a major turning point in shaping the outcome of the war. To be sure, on August 23, Lincoln had drafted a memorandum in which he stated, "it seems exceedingly probable that this Administration will not be re-elected. Then it will be my duty to so co-operate with the President elect, as to save the Union between the election and the inauguration; as he will have secured his election on such ground that he cannot possibly save it afterwards." And the great victories by Farragut, Sherman, and Sheridan, and steady progress Grant was making around Richmond and Petersburg undeniably provided a powerful boost to Northern confidence and morale, which translated into support for the Lincoln administration.[37]

Yet it is also clear in retrospect that the Northern political scene in the late summer and early fall of 1864 should not have provided anyone who hoped for the salvation of the Confederacy much ground for hope. During the last week of August, the Democratic Party convened their national convention in Chicago and nominated George B. McClellan, an unyielding Unionist and War Democrat, for president. Although the platform the Democrats adopted declared the war a "failure" and called for negotiations with the South, it is also fairly clear that the number of individuals within the party who were willing to abandon the effort to restore the Union was too small for them to be considered truly significant. And McClellan made it absolutely clear in his acceptance letter that, as president, he would entertain no resolution of the conflict that did not include restoration of the Union.[38]

No matter how small the possibility that the 1864 election would bring to power a government in the North that would concede independence to the South may have been, it was all that a desperate Lee and the Confederacy had to hang their hopes for victory on, and as long as they had that faint hope, it was enough to inspire them to continue the struggle. On October 7, Lee decided to test the Union position north of the James in hopes that he might find an opportunity to recapture Fort Harrison. That morning, Field's and Hoke's infantry divisions pushed forward from their fortified positions in line with Lee's orders. The operation began well enough. On the Darbytown Road, they encountered a Federal cavalry force and quickly drove it away. However, Field's and Hoke's were unable to locate or create a weak point in Federal defenses on the New Market Road, and their attacks were rather easily repulsed. Content with their defensive success, the Federals made little effort to follow it up and allowed Field and Hoke to pull back to their original positions. Six days later, the forces north of the James once again tangled along the Darbytown Road, but no decisive results were achieved by either side.[39]

In the wake of the cavalcade of successes for Union arms in August, September, and October, Grant might have been forgiven if he had decided to wait until after the election before undertaking another significant operation. However, Grant wanted to keep up the pressure on the Confederates. Consequently, during the last week in October, the Federals once again commenced active operations on both sides of the James. Butler's command would once again test the Confederate defenses north of the river on October 27, with one corps advancing along the Darbytown Road and another pushing north to Fair Oaks and the Williamsburg Road in an attempt to swing around the northern end of the Confederate line. Meanwhile, three corps from Meade's army would again endeavor to extend the Union lines to the Boydton Plank Road and South Side Railroad.[40]

Neither of Butler's corps was able to achieve much against Confederate forces commanded by Longstreet, who had been assigned command of the units north of the James upon returning to the army on the seventeenth. The

Union corps advancing along the Darbytown Road found the Confederate defenses too strong for anything to be accomplished, while the forces sent to Fair Oaks received a sound thrashing at the hands of Field's division. The operations south of the James and Appomattox were no more productive. On October 27 Hancock's corps was able to establish a foothold on the Boydton Plank Road, but the terrain hampered the movements of the other Federal corps participating in the operation and created a gap between them and Hancock's position. Lee and his subordinates were not slow to take advantage. Two divisions from the Third Corps commanded by Heth rushed to the scene and induced Meade to halt Hancock's advance toward the South Side Railroad near Burgess's Mill. Heth then ordered an attack against Hancock's right to take advantage of the gap between his corps and the rest of the Union army. Unlike at Reams Station, however, Hancock's men held their ground and compelled Heth to pull back toward Petersburg. Despite this tactical setback, Heth's efforts enabled Lee to achieve an operational victory. Understandably uneasy about maintaining his position, Hancock decided during the night of October 27–28 to pull back from the Boydton Plank Road to his original lines, thus bringing to an end what one Federal officer despondently proclaimed "a *well*-conducted fizzle." For his part, Lee proclaimed himself "much gratified at the results obtained."[41]

Despite the decidedly frustrating outcome of the Sixth Petersburg Offensive, the political tide in favor of Lincoln and the Republicans created by the earlier victories in Virginia and elsewhere was too strong to be arrested by a minor setback. On November 8, the results of the election were in, with the Republicans winning a resounding victory. With that victory came an indisputable mandate to continue carrying out a policy of applying unrelenting pressure in the effort to crush the Confederacy.

In retrospect, it is clear that the military victories of the late summer and early fall in 1864 had rendered the cause for which Lee was fighting all but hopeless by the second week in November. Sheridan's repeated defeats of Early's command had eliminated for good the tried-and-true method of pushing operations in the Shenandoah Valley to induce Washington to weaken its forces at Richmond and Petersburg. Indeed, with Early's army no longer a serious threat, Grant was able to return the forces that had been sent north from the Richmond-Petersburg front during the summer. And if Lee had only been able to hold off the various Federal offensives north and south of the James during the fall of 1864 by the skin of his teeth, what hope could he possibly have once Grant's forces were reinforced for preventing the fall of Petersburg and Richmond—and with them the fall of the Confederacy?

Yet for those desperate in the late fall of 1864 to find reasons to believe that the cause was not yet lost and there was still a chance for victory, it was possible to find them—albeit not without considerable selectiveness in weighing the facts before them—and, in those, sufficient rationale to justify continuing to do their duty to their nation. First, winter was almost at hand in Virginia, and poor weather could be expected to compel Grant to suspend operations around Petersburg and Richmond for at least a couple of months. Although Grant was clearly too canny to do anything during that time to reduce the long odds Lee could expect to face in the spring, no one familiar with the history of the war in Virginia could completely dismiss the possibility that Washington might do something foolish to cancel out Grant's good sense. And even if Petersburg and Richmond fell, who was to say at the time that this would be necessarily fatal for the cause of Confederate independence? Had not the Continental Army survived the loss of Philadelphia in 1777 and ultimately prevailed? Of course, it is clear in retrospect that the differences between the situation Lee faced in 1865 and the one George Washington faced in 1777 were significant enough to make any Confederate who drew comfort from the former seem rather ludicrous. But Lee and his fellow Confederates were engaged in a desperate cause and had been hanging on against long odds for so long that they could be forgiven if, in their desperation, they clung to what slim reeds were available upon which to hope for victory.

Besides, one could take heart in the fact that, however gloomy things looked in Virginia in November 1864, large segments of the Confederacy were still free of the Yankees. Although Atlanta had been captured, it was not unreasonable to hope that logistical considerations—specifically, his dependency on a single railroad line for supplies and the approach of winter— would compel Sherman to pause for a considerable amount of time to consolidate his hold over what he had gained during the spring and summer. Moreover, there was the fact that, despite the beating his forces had taken around Atlanta, Hood still had a respectable army in Georgia and the possibility that, freed from its fixed position in Atlanta, it might be able to maneuver in such a way as to severely complicate for months Sherman's efforts to consolidate his position and prepare for a renewal of offensive operations. And in the weeks that followed the fall of Atlanta, Hood did make an attempt to loosen Sherman's grip on Atlanta by operating against his communications that induced the Federal commander to dispatch troops northward in response. If Sherman could continue to be stymied in Georgia, the Confederacy would gain a not inconsiderable period of time to draw sustenance from areas still untouched by Yankee occupation and, the diehard

Confederate might hope, perhaps this would allow a continuation of the contest for some time.[42]

Of course, these proved to be very thin reeds upon which to rest hopes for Confederate independence. The prospects for a collapse of Northern will before Southern luck and resources ran out—which had probably never existed anyway—were completely eliminated as a consequences of Lincoln's reelection and the boost Northern confidence in ultimate victory received from the victories achieved by Union arms in August, September, and October. In addition, Grant had so skillfully managed the war effort and his dealings with his superiors that any hopes that Washington would do something during the winter of 1864–1865 to impede the execution of his soundly conceived and ultimately irresistible plans for rendering Richmond and Petersburg untenable for Lee's army in the spring of 1865 were likewise in vain. Moreover, by the first week in November 1864, Sherman had already stopped responding to Hood's activities and was actively preparing to unleash on yet-untouched segments of the South an operation that would render hopeful assumptions about the Confederate situation outside Virginia completely invalid.

This operation would see the implementation of the method of army-sized raids that Grant and Sherman had conceived in 1863. In part to overcome the operational problems that could give partisans of the Confederacy cause for hope that the Federals could be contained in Georgia, Sherman broke off the effort to counter Hood's operations against his railroad communications and proposed another course of action. He would lead his army east from Atlanta toward the Atlantic Coast. While the territory in his path would not be formally occupied, with all the headaches that consolidating one's hold on enemy territory entailed, its war resources would be used to the benefit of the Union army. Whatever might be left over would be destroyed. Crippling the South's ability to continue the war through the physical destruction of its resources, however, was but one of Sherman's objectives. Equally important, Sherman believed, would be the effect of such a campaign on the South's will to fight. "If we can march a well appointed Army right through his territory," Sherman argued on November 7, "it is a demonstration to the world, foreign and domestic, that we have a power which Davis cannot resist. . . . there are thousands of people abroad and in the South who will reason thus—'If the North can march an Army right through the South, it is proof positive that the North can prevail in this contest,' leaving only open the question of its willingness to use that power." Grant needed little convincing to accept Sherman's proposal and persuaded Lincoln to approve it. On November 15, Sherman's command left Atlanta. "The Confederacy is a mere shell," Grant remarked a few days later, "a hollow shell, and Sherman will prove it to you."[43]

Sherman did just that. By mid-December, his army had completed a relatively bloodless march and reached the coast. On the twenty-first, Sherman took possession of Savannah and then sent a jaunty message to Washington offering the city as "a Christmas gift . . . with 150 guns & plenty of ammunition & also about 25,000 bales of cotton." For those unfortunates who resided in the area between Atlanta and Savannah in late 1864, Sherman's March to the Sea was no laughing matter. The Federals had thoroughly wrecked the region, and the trail of destruction they left behind them dealt a crushing blow to Confederate hopes and assumptions regarding the viability of their nation and the Richmond government's ability to defend it. And as if this were not enough, even with Sherman's forces marching through Georgia, in mid-December a Federal army commanded by Maj. Gen. George H. Thomas still had the ability to defeat Hood's army at the Battle of Nashville. Hood had hoped that by leading his army north into Tennessee he could reverse the tide of the war in the West by winning battlefield victories over the Federals in that state. But this, like so many Confederate hopes in 1864, proved a forlorn one that was destined to be crushed under the weight of superior numbers and firepower soundly applied.[44]

Meanwhile, in early December Lee too found himself confronted with a Federal operation south of the James similar in its objective to Sherman's— albeit far smaller in terms of the number of forces participating and the extent of damage the Federals sought to inflict. On the seventh, a scout informed Lee, whose headquarters were now located just west of Petersburg on an estate known as Edge Hill, that a large body of Federal forces had been seen moving south down the Jerusalem Plank Road. The following day Lee learned that this force consisted of the Fifth Corps and two divisions from the Second Corps, along with some cavalry, under the overall command of Warren. He responded by ordering Hill and Hampton to pursue them and prevent them from invading North Carolina. This, however, was not Warren's objective. Rather, it was simply to destroy as much of the railroad as they could south of the Stony Creek Depot, and at around sunset on the eighth, three Federal infantry divisions had reached the railroad. They spent that evening and much of the following morning wrecking the railroad, while their cavalry kept Hampton's cavalry at bay.[45]

Meanwhile, back in Petersburg, Lee sent a message to Longstreet asking him to see if the situation may have been altered to the point that it might be possible to make a successful attack north of the James. Longstreet pushed his command forward to New Market Heights on December 11, but was unable to find a weak spot in the Federal lines north of the James and decided to return to his own fortifications. By then Warren's force was already back in Petersburg. After reaching the Meherrin River on the ninth, Warren decided, after finding a fortified Confederate position on the south side and seeing the bad weather that had accompanied his march so far was about to take a turn for the worse, that he had achieved all that he could and ordered his men to return to Petersburg. When Hill and Hampton attempted to launch a counterstrike against Warren's flank and rear on the morning of the tenth, they found their quarry had prudently left the scene. Hampton attempted a pursuit, but it accomplished little, while Warren gloated on December 14 that his men had thoroughly destroyed about seventeen miles of track.[46]

Although Lee could claim a measure of success in turning the Federals back at the Meherrin, he lamented to one of his sons afterward that "we did them little harm." And in the weeks that followed, Lee's correspondence contained little of cheer as it chronicled the experience of an army in crisis that was serving a dying nation. "A tale of disaster which has filled the land with gloom," one official in the War Department proclaimed on Christmas Day as he reflected on recent events. "Ten days ago the last meat ration was issued and not a pound remained in Richmond." "The men are getting very discouraged, and to tell the truth, they have cause to be," one of Lee's soldiers candidly advised his family in mid-January. "If the men are not fed, they will not stay." Supplies of meat, corn, and other vital supplies were a constant source of concern, as was the thinness of the force with which Lee had to hold a system of fortifications that extended from north of the James all the way to Hatcher's Run south and west of Petersburg. Further exacerbating the problem was an alarming increase in desertions from the Army of Northern Virginia, which Lee attributed in late January 1865 to "the insufficiency of food and non-payment of troops." When Richmond authorized Lee, as a consequence of problems maintaining one of the railroads that connected his army, to impress supplies from the local population, the general complained that such a move would be impossible due to the fact that "there is nothing within reach of this army is to be impressed; the country is swept clear. Our only reliance is upon the railroads."[47]

Making matters worse, the prospects for maintaining possession of these roads dramatically diminished over the course of the fall and winter of 1864–1865. To be sure, Lee's strength in manpower received a welcome boost in November and December with the return of Kershaw's division and the Second Corps (now commanded by Maj. Gen. John B. Gordon) to the Richmond-Petersburg front. Yet this paled in comparison to the reinforcements the Federal armies north and south of the James received during this time as the forces Grant had sent to the Valley returned to the Richmond and Petersburg fronts. And, of course, there was the constant stream of gloomy news from the south and west: Sherman's march; the loss of Savannah; Hood's defeat at Nashville; and a successful joint Federal assault on Fort Fisher on January 15, 1865, which effectively sealed off the last major Confederate port of Wilmington, North Carolina.[48]

In the wake of these disasters came appeals to Richmond that troops be sent from Lee's forces in Virginia to the Carolinas. Lee greeted these with sympathy and even acquiesced in a decision to send forces from his army south to the Carolinas. However, he noted there was no way he could meet all of the demands elsewhere for manpower from his army without crippling his ability to fend off Grant. On January 19, Lee responded to a request for troops to assist in the defense of South Carolina by agreeing that it was important to avoid the loss of Charleston, defeat Sherman's army, and by doing so boost "the spirits of the people." Yet he added, "I do not think that this would be accomplished by so weakening this army as to enable the enemy to disperse it, and achieve what he has been struggling to obtain the whole campaign. It seems to me that it would only aggravate our disasters by adding the loss of Richmond." Instead, he argued Sherman could be effectively checked if the people of South Carolina and Georgia themselves turned "out in all their strength, aided by the troops now in that department."[49] The weeks that followed would prove Lee's hopes that Confederate forces in the Carolinas could handle Sherman's army without help from the Army of Northern Virginia were badly misplaced.

Throughout the second half of 1864, Lee faced an almost impossible situation, and it is rather difficult to see how he could have accomplished much more than he did. As he had predicted in June—and indeed had believed from the time he assumed command two years earlier—once the main Federal army in Virginia was on the James, the fall of Richmond, and with it the Confederacy, was but a "mere question of time." The best Lee could hope for was to buy sufficient time for the Federals to commit blunders, either in his immediate front or elsewhere, which would relieve the Confederacy of its near-indefensible operational situation and/or elevate Northern frustration to the level where it would lead to a political revolution. And Lee, by his timely dispatch of Early's force to the Valley, by conducting an active defense around Richmond and Petersburg that instilled caution in his adversaries, and by taking advantage of the not insignificant assistance he received from the Federals, managed to buy a truly impressive amount of time. Yet in retrospect it is fairly clear that the prospect of a government coming to power in the North that would grant Confederate independence was never good, even in 1864, and with Grant firmly in control of the Union war effort to a degree that none of his predecessors had enjoyed, the Federals could not be induced to commit an error that would deny them the opportunity to exploit the overwhelming operational advantage operating from the James provided. Moreover, if Grant's various offensives north and south of the James had not achieved immediate decisive results, they did have the cumulative effect of pushing Lee's army and with it the fate of the Confederacy to the edge of complete and total defeat. In 1865, the Federals would finish the job.

Notes

1. Meade to his wife, June 1, 1864, in *The Life and Letters of George Gordon Meade, Major-General United States Army*, 2 vols., edited by George Gordon Meade Jr. (New York: Charles Scribner's Sons, 1913), vol. 2: 200; Lee to Davis, June 19, 1864, in *Wartime Papers*, eds. Dowdey and Manarin, 794. Compared to the other campaigns in Lee's Civil War career, the operations around Petersburg in 1864 and 1865 have not received much attention from historians, although Noah Andre Trudeau provides a fine short account of Lee's efforts in his "A Mere Question of Time," 539–46. The best full accounts of the campaign can be found in Humphreys, *Virginia Campaign*, 226–372; and Noah Andre Trudeau, *The Last Citadel: Petersburg, Virginia June 1864–April 1865* (Boston: Little and Brown, 1991). Excellent studies of particular phases of the campaign covered in this chapter have, however, been published. See John Horn, *The Destruction of the Weldon Railroad: Deep Bottom, Globe Tavern, and Reams Station, August 14–25, 1864*, 2nd ed. (Lynchburg, VA: H.E. Howard, 1991); Michael Cavanaugh and William Marvel, *The Battle of the Crater: "The Horrid Pit," June 25–August 6, 1864* (Lynchburg, VA: H.E. Howard, 1989); and, especially, Richard J. Sommers, *Richmond Redeemed: The Siege of Petersburg* (Garden City, NY: Doubleday, 1981).

2. Lee to [Hill?], June ———, 1864, OR, vol. 40, pt. 2: 703.

3. Alexander, *Fighting for the Confederacy*, 438–39.

4. Albert Castel, *Decision in the West: The Atlanta Campaign of 1864* (Lawrence: University Press of Kansas, 1992), 125–276; Richard M. McMurry, *Atlanta 1864: Last Chance for the Confederacy* (Lincoln: University of Nebraska Press, 2000), 55–103.

5. Meade to Grant, June 20, 1864, OR, vol. 40, pt. 2: 233; Birney to Williams, June 26, 1864, OR, ibid., 325–27; Wilson to Forsyth, February 18, 1865, ibid., pt. 1: 620–24; William Mahone, "The Occasion of 22nd June 1864 . . . at Johnson's Farm," Mahone Family Papers, LV; Lee to Seddon, June 22, 1864, in *Wartime Papers*, eds. Dowdey and Manarin, 802.

6. Field, "Campaign of 1864 and 1865," 549–50; Venable, "Campaign from the Wilderness to Petersburg," 539–40; Lee to Seddon, June 24, 1864, OR, vol. 40, pt. 1: 750; Beauregard, "General instructions for a proposed attack on the enemy to-morrow morning," June 23, 1864, ibid., 804–05.

7. Lee to Davis, June 21, 1864, in *Lee's Dispatches*, eds. Freeman and McWhiney, 254; Hattaway and Jones, *How the North Won*, 585–87, 600–03.

8. Lee to Davis, July 1, 10, 1864, in *Lee's Dispatches*, eds. Freeman and McWhiney, 265–67, 279–80.

9. Alexander, *Fighting for the Confederacy*, 417, 436–37; Lee to Davis, July 23, 1864, in *Wartime Papers*, eds. Dowdey and Manarin, 823; Lee to Ewell, July 24, 1864, ibid., 824–25.

10. Castel, *Decision in the West*, 309–61; McMurry, *Atlanta 1864*, 107–20, 131–40; Lee to Davis, July 12, 1864, in *Wartime Papers*, eds. Dowdey and Manarin, 821–22.

11. Grant, *Memoirs*, 523–24; Humphreys, *Virginia Campaign*, 250.

12. Taylor to Bettie, July 22, 1864, in *Lee's Adjutant*, eds. Tower and Belmont, 175; Anderson to Taylor, 1865, OR *Supplement*, vol. 7: 252–53; Lee to Anderson, July 27, 1864, in *Wartime Papers*, eds. Dowdey and Manarin, 826; Hancock to Williams, November 11, 1864, OR, vol. 40, pt. 1: 308–11.

13. Alexander, *Fighting for the Confederacy*, 449.

14. Ibid., 464; Lee to Seddon, July 30, 1864, in *Wartime Papers*, eds. Dowdey and Manarin, 827; Lee to his wife, July 31, 1864, ibid., 828; Grant to Halleck, August 1, 1864, OR, vol. 40, pt. 1: 17.

15. Lee to Carter Lee, August 12, 1864, Lee Papers, WL. The Federals' problems dealing with Early's force and resolution of them have been extensively documented; a very good and brief recent look at this matter can be found in Joseph T. Glatthaar, "U.S. Grant and the Union High Command during the 1864 Valley Campaign," in *The Shenandoah Valley Campaign of 1864*, edited by Gary W. Gallagher (Chapel Hill: University of North Carolina Press, 2006), 42–49.

16. Anderson to Taylor, 1865, OR *Supplement*, vol. 7: 253; Lee to Anderson, August 11, 1864, in *Wartime Papers*, eds. Dowdey and Manarin, 832.

17. Castel, *Decision in the West*, 366–436; McMurry, *Atlanta 1864*, 141–57.

18. Grant, *Memoirs*, 531; Grant to Hancock, August 13, 1864, OR, vol. 42, pt. 2: 148.

19. Field, "Campaign of 1864 and 1865," 551–52; Lee to Hampton, August 14, 1864, in *Wartime Papers*, eds. Dowdey and Manarin, 835; Lee to Field, August 14, 15, 1864, ibid., 835, 836, 837; Lee to his wife, August 14, 1864, ibid., 837.

20. Taylor to Bettie, August 15, 1864, in *Lee's Adjutant*, eds. Tower and Belmont, 181; "Newspaper account of demonstrations at Richmond and Deep Bottom, Virginia, August 13–20, 1864," OR *Supplement*, vol. 7: 455; John D. McConnell, "Recollections of the Civil War," Winthrop College Archives and Special Collections, copy in bound vol. 113, FSNMP; Lee to Davis, August 16, 1864, in *Wartime Papers*, eds. Dowdey and Manarin, 838; Lee to Seddon, August 16, 1864, ibid.

21. Taylor to Wilcox, August 18, 1864, in *Wartime Papers*, eds. Dowdey and Manarin, 839; Beauregard to Lee, August 18, 1864, OR, vol. 42, pt. 2: 1186.

22. Beauregard to Lee, August 18, 1864, ibid., 1187; "Report of Major-General Henry Heth, C.S. Army, on the Battle of Reams' Station, Virginia, August 26, 1864," OR *Supplement*, vol. 7: 473–74; Horn, *Destruction of the Weldon Railroad*, 67.

23. Beauregard to Lee, August 19, 1864, OR, vol. 42, pt. 2: 1190; Hill to Beauregard, August 19, 1864, ibid., 940; Warren to Williams, August 25, 1864, ibid., 429–32; Alexander, *Fighting for the Confederacy*, 473.

24. Lee to Davis, September 22, 1864, in *Wartime Papers*, eds. Dowdey and Manarin, 842; Lee to Seddon, September 23, 1864, ibid., 844; Lee to Seddon, September 22, 23, 1864, OR, vol. 42, pt. 2: 1194–95, 1199.

25. Grant to Meade, August 22, 1864, ibid., 391; Hancock to Williams, September 12, 1864, ibid., pt. 1: 222–23.

26. Hampton to Taylor, August 29, 1864, ibid., pt. 1: 942–44; Lee to Hampton, August 24, 1864, in *Wartime Papers*, eds. Dowdey and Manarin, 844; Lee to Seddon, August 26, 1864, ibid., 845.

27. Hampton to Taylor, September 27, 1864, ibid., vol. 46, pt. 1: 944–47; Lee to Seddon, September 17, 1864, in *Wartime Papers*, eds. Dowdey and Manarin, 853.

28. Castel, *Decision in the West*, 485–529; McMurry, *Atlanta 1864*, 169–76; Hattaway and Jones, *How the North Won*, 617–25.

29. Anderson to Taylor, 1865, OR Supplement, vol. 7: 256–58; Lee to Early, September 17, 1864, OR, vol. 42, pt. 2: 1257–58; "Diary of the First Corps, Army of Northern Virginia . . . August 1–October 18," ibid., pt. 1: 875; Lee to Anderson, September 17, 23, 1864, in *Wartime Papers*, eds. Dowdey and Manarin, 852–53.

30. Sommers, *Richmond Redeemed*, 4–5, 21, 29–31, 38–40.

31. Taylor to Gregg, September 29, 1864, OR, vol. 42, pt. 2: 1302; Lee to Bragg, September 29, 1864, OR, vol. 42, pt. 2: 1302; Ewell to Bragg, September 29, 1864, ibid., 1303; Sallie B. Putnam, *Richmond During the War: Four Years of Personal Observation* (New York: G.W. Carleton and Co., 1867), 330; Field, "Campaign of 1864 and 1865," 555; Sommers, *Richmond Redeemed*, 28, 50–51, 110.

32. Lee to Ewell, September 29, 1864, OR, vol. 42, pt. 2: 1303, 1304; Field, "Campaign of 1864 and 1865," 556–58; Anderson to Taylor, 1865, OR Supplement, vol. 7: 258–59; Entry for September 30, 1864, Washington L. Dunn Diary, Georgia Department of Archives and History, copy at Petersburg National Battlefield Park, Petersburg, VA.

33. Sommers, *Richmond Redeemed*, 210–18; Meade to Bowers, November 1, 1864, OR, vol. 42, pt. 1: 31.

34. Grant to Meade, September 30, 1864, ibid., pt. 2: 1119.

35. Warren to Humphreys, September 30, 1864, ibid., 1131; Sommers, *Richmond Redeemed*, 240–41, 245–59.

36. Heth to Palmer, [n.d.], OR Supplement, vol. 7: 476–77; Lee to Seddon, October 1, 1864, OR, vol. 42, pt. 1: 852; Hampton to Taylor, November 21, 1864, ibid., 947–48.

37. Abraham Lincoln, "Memorandum Concerning . . . Probable Failure of Reelection," August 23, 1864, *Works of Lincoln*, vol. 7: 514.

38. William W. Freehling, *The Reintegration of American History: Slavery and the Civil War* (New York: Oxford University Press, 1994), 226–28; McClellan to the Democratic Nomination Committee, September 8, 1864, in *The Civil War Papers of*

George B. McClellan: Selected Correspondence, 1860–1865, edited by Stephen W. Sears (New York: Ticknor and Fields, 1989), 595–96.

39. Anderson to Taylor, 1865, OR Supplement, vol. 7: 259–60; Lee to Seddon, October 7, 13, 1864, in *Wartime Papers*, eds. Dowdey and Manarin, 861–62, 863.

40. Butler to Terry, October 26, 1864, OR, vol. 42, pt. 3: 366–68; Orders, Headquarters, Army of the Potomac, October 25, 1864, ibid., 340–42.

41. Special Orders No. 248, Headquarters, Department of Northern Virginia, October 17, 1864, Lee Headquarters Papers, series 7; Longstreet to Taylor, [n.d.], OR, vol. 42, pt. 1: 871–72; Meade to Bowers, October 28, 1864, ibid., pt. 3: 404–06; Heth to Palmer, February 1, 1865, OR Supplement, vol. 7: 480–83; Lyman, *Meade's Headquarters*, 251; Lee to Hill, October 31, 1864, Lee Headquarters Papers, VHS, series 7.

42. Hattaway and Jones, *How the North Won*, 629–33; Anne J. Bailey, *The Chessboard of War: Sherman and Hood in the Autumn Campaign of 1864* (Lincoln: University of Nebraska, 2000), 19–20, 26–36, 41–44.

43. Hattaway and Jones, *How the North Won*, 634, 637–39, 641–43; Bailey, *Chessboard of War*, 49–51; Sherman to Grant, November 7, 1864, in *Sherman's Civil War*, eds. Simpson and Berlin, 751; Simpson, *Ulysses S. Grant*, 391.

44. Sherman to Lincoln, December 22, 1864, in *Sherman's Civil War*, eds. Simpson and Berlin, 772; Bailey, *Chessboard of War*, 44–51, 53–108, 112–30, 151–63; Hattaway and Jones, *How the North Won*, 639–40, 643–54.

45. Lee to Seddon, December 7, 8, 1864, in *Wartime Papers*, eds. Dowdey and Manarin, 874; Warren to Williams, December 14, 1864, OR, vol. 42, pt. 1: 443–44.

46. Longstreet to Lee, December 9, 10, 11, 1864, ibid., pt. 3: 1260–61, 1264; Warren to Williams, December 14, 1864, ibid., pt. 1: 444–46; Hampton to Taylor, January 21, 1865, ibid., 950–51; Lee to Seddon, December 10, 1864, in *Wartime Papers*, eds. Dowdey and Manarin, 875.

47. Kean, *Inside the Confederate Government*, 184; Battle to his sister, January 18, 1865, Battle Letters, FSNMP; Lee to G.W.C. Lee, December 13, 1864, in *Wartime Papers*, eds., Dowdey and Manarin, 876; Lee to Davis, December 14, 1864, ibid., 877; Lee to Seddon, December 26, 1864, January 11, 27, 1865, ibid., 879, 881, 879, 886; Seddon to Lee, January 11, 1865, OR, vol. 46, pt. 2: 1034–35.

48. John B. Gordon, *Reminiscences of the Civil War* (New York: Charles Scribner's Sons, 1903), 374; Lee to Davis, December 19, 1864, in *Wartime Papers*, eds. Dowdey and Manarin, 878.

49. Lee to Davis, January 10, 15, 1865, in *Lee's Dispatches*, eds. Freeman and McWhiney, 315, 316–17; Lee to Miles, January 19, 1865, in *Wartime Papers*, eds. Dowdey and Manarin, 885–86.

CHAPTER NINE

To Appomattox

Although Ulysses Grant and his armies had made the fall of Richmond and Petersburg but a matter of time by then, there was much that remained to be decided by the force of arms in January 1865. There was no telling just how much time and what measures it would take to bring about the final defeat of Lee's army after the loss of its logistics base and the Confederacy's political capital and industrial heart—much less convince Lee and his legions to once again submit to the authority of the Lincoln government. If powerless to stop the Federal armies on the James in an operational sense, there was still room in the strategic realm for Lee to shape events. And there were strong incentives for continued resistance, for the higher the cost the South could impose on the North for ending the rebellion, the stronger its hand would be when the time came to submit to the verdict of Mars.[1]

For Lee, the question of how to strengthen the South's military hand was a matter of grave concern throughout the winter of 1864–1865. Although the near exhaustion of just about every war resource provoked consternation, what appeared to be a rapidly shrinking pool of available and willing manpower by January 1865 led many members of the Confederate high command to accept the idea of turning to the people whose oppression was the central, defining institution in the economic, political, and cultural life of the antebellum and wartime South. Of course, African-Americans had been serving the Confederate war effort in critical ways since 1861, not the least of which in helping construct fortifications. It was their use in this capacity that had inspired the first step in the North's turning the war for the Union into one that had the destruction of slavery as one of its goals—the declaration that slaves laboring in support of the Confederate military could be legitimately seized and liberated as "contraband of war." In December 1864, the U.S. Congress had taken a major step in the process of destroying slavery by passing the Thirteenth Amendment to the Constitution of the United States, which abolished slavery forever in the nation.

In the South, the idea of turning to the slaves to meet the Confederacy's need for manpower had first been seriously raised in January 1864. That month a division commander in the Army of Tennessee, Maj. Gen. Patrick Cleburne, suggested to an assemblage of generals that the Confederacy offer freedom to slaves who volunteered to serve in the army. When Cleburne's proposal was forwarded to Richmond, the Davis administration immediately proclaimed it unacceptable and mandated that it receive no further discussion. But as the South's military situation became more and more desperate, the logic of doing something along the lines Cleburne proposed became so compelling that Davis himself raised the issue openly in his November 1864 annual message to the Confederate Congress.[2]

A few months before this, Lee had advised the president that he believed in order to place as many men as possible on the firing line, it should be the government's policy to relieve "all able bodied white men employed as teamsters, cooks, mechanics, and laborers, and supplying their places with negroes." Lee eventually adopted this policy on his own, but by January had come to accept that more must be done. During the second week of that month, a letter arrived at the Army of Northern Virginia headquarters from Virginia senator Andrew Hunter asking its commander's opinion as to whether "by a wisely devised plan and judicious selection Negro soldiers can be made effective and reliable." Lee replied on January 11 that he would prefer not to disturb the existing relationship between the races in the Confederacy and to rely on "our white population to preserve" a favorable balance "between our forces and those of the enemy." Unfortunately, he declared, the Union policies of emancipation and employing African-American troops promised to end slavery "in a manner most pernicious to the welfare of our people." "We must decide," he wrote, "whether slavery shall be extinguished by our enemies and the slaves be used against us, or use them ourselves at the risk of the effects which may be produced upon our social institutions. My own opinion is that we should employ them without delay." This required, he added, "giving immediate freedom to all who enlist, and freedom at the end of the war to the families. . . . with a well-digested plan of gradual and general emancipation. . . . We should not expect slaves to fight for prospective freedom when they can secure it at once by going to the enemy."[3]

As if the challenge of coping with Grant's forces in Virginia alone were not enough, on February 1 Lee learned the Senate had just confirmed his appointment as general-in-chief of all the Confederate armies. Lee assumed his new position with little enthusiasm. Only two weeks earlier he had protested an offer from Davis to expand his command to encompass the South Atlantic states on the grounds that he did not think he had the ability to direct the armies there and effectively command the Army of Northern Virginia. "If I had the ability I would not have the time," he protested. "I do not think I could accomplish any good." Nonetheless, there was no other man Davis could appoint general-in-chief when Congress created the position, although it failed to provide, Lee complained, "instructions as to my duties."[4]

Hopes that some negotiated settlement to bring an end to the fighting might be reached were kindled that same week with the passage through the lines on February 3 of three officials from the Confederate government for a meeting at Hampton Roads with Lincoln and his secretary of state. The conference, however, only made it clear that there was little chance of the war ending with anything but the complete destruction of the Confederacy. Lincoln told his guests in no uncertain terms that there could be no resolution of the conflict without the restoration of the Union and the death of slavery. Despite the dire situation their military commanders faced, the Confederate commissioners informed Lincoln that these terms were unacceptable. Thus, the Hampton Roads Conference ended having vindicated the low expectations informed men on both sides had that it might bring an end to the conflict.[5]

Although Lee needed no reminder of just how difficult a situation he faced in February 1865, two days after the Hampton Roads Conference, Grant decided to provide one. On February 2, Lee received a message from Davis that he had a report that the Federals intended to undertake an operation north of the James if the unseasonably good weather continued. During this time, Longstreet was also advising Lee that he believed that with the fall of Fort Fisher, Grant would probably not deem the cutting of Petersburg's southern communications as critical as he had before and would instead make his next major offensive north of the James. Although Davis's and Longstreet's concerns were seemingly confirmed on February 4 when reports arrived of a buildup of Union forces near Fort Harrison, this was not where Grant planned to deliver his next blow. Instead, he had decided to make an attempt to "destroy or capture as much as possible of the enemy's wagon train" moving along the Boydton Plank Road. To this end, he and Meade sent a division of cavalry to seize Dinwiddie Court House on February 5, directed Warren's corps to push west across Hatcher's Run to support the cavalry, and ordered Maj. Gen. Andrew A. Humphreys' Second Corps to move to Armstrong's Mill on Hatcher's Run to support Warren.[6]

Reports that the Federals were pushing across Hatcher's Run reached Lee at around noon on the fifth, and he promptly dispatched elements from Gordon's and Hill's corps to the scene. They were unable to prevent the Federal cavalry from reaching Dinwiddie Court House and found Humphreys' command already entrenched north of Hatcher's Run near Armstrong Mill. Lee's subordinates then launched an attack against Humphreys' position that, although repulsed, induced Meade to pull Warren's command back across Hatcher's Run, while the Federal cavalry, which had already pulled back from Dinwiddie Court House, covered this movement. The following morning, Warren and Gordon each pushed forward a division along the Dabney's Steam Saw Mill Road, and when they made contact a sharp engagement ensued that ended with the Federals pulling back. Feeling "it was not a bad fight and in no way discouraged," Warren sent out another division-size reconnaissance the following day. Although the Federals managed to drive the Confederate pickets out of their advanced position, bad weather and a determination that he could achieve no decisive results led Warren to fall back behind Hatcher's Run at the end of the day, which effectively brought the whole operation to an end.[7]

Although his thin lines had been stretched even further, after Hatcher's Run Lee expressed greater concern about the condition of the troops that had participated in the fighting. "Some of the men," he wrote Richmond on the eighth, "had been without meat for three days, and all were suffering from reduced rations and scant clothing, exposed to battle, cold, hail, and sleet." He then reported that his chief commissary officer had "not a pound of meat at his disposal." If nothing were done about these problems, he added, "I apprehend dire results. . . . Taking these facts in connection with the paucity of our numbers, you must not be surprised if calamity befalls us." The following day, after issuing orders announcing his assumption of the post of general-in-chief, Lee asked Davis for permission to offer amnesty to all deserters and absentees who returned to their command within thirty days and announce that any who did not comply by then "would receive the full sentence of the courts upon their conviction, without suspension, remission, or delay, from which there need be no appeal for clemency." Davis wrote back the following day approving Lee's proposal, and the general promptly issued general orders announcing the new policy. The general's appeal for greater exertions to improve the conditions under which his men were serving would not and, as a consequence of the irreversibly broken Confederate economy and transportation network, could not receive such a satisfactory resolution.[8]

In his orders promulgating the new policy toward desertion, Lee proclaimed on February 11 that for the soldiers of the Confederacy, "The choice between war and abject submission is before them. . . . Taking new resolution from the fate which our enemies intend for us, let every man devote his energies to the common defense. Our resources, wisely and vigorously employed, are ample, and with a brave army, sustained by a determined and united people, success with God's assistance cannot be doubtful." But even as he drafted this document, Lee must have known that his sentiments regarding the South's "ample resources" and determination to employ them were more a product of wishful thinking than cold logical analysis. And if he needed any further evidence that this was the case, to the south Confederate military authorities were impotently contending with Sherman's legions, which were advancing north from Savannah with the intention of doing to the Carolinas what they had done to Georgia.[9]

Responsibility for dealing with Sherman's army rested with Beauregard, the overall commander of Confederate forces in the Carolinas, who was unable to prevent the Federals from seizing possession of the South Carolina state capital on February 17. Even before then, Lee had been receiving messages urging him to put the forces in the Carolinas under the overall command of Gen. Joseph E. Johnston. Although Lee had received "unfavorable" accounts of the situation in the Carolinas, where in addition to Sherman's army there was also a Federal force commanded by Maj. Gen. John M. Schofield threatening to push inland from the coast, he was not quite ready on February 19 to concede that the situation was beyond repair. "I do not see," he wrote Richmond that day, "that Sherman can make the march [from Columbia to North Carolina to link up with Schofield] anticipated by Genl Beauregard if our troops can do anything. They can at least destroy or remove all provisions in this route." This, the removal of every provision from the Carolinas to allow the accumulation of supplies in Virginia, and concentration of the dispersed forces, he argued, might make possible a successful stand at the Roanoke River. At the same time, he advised Richmond that he thought "it prudent that preparations be made" for the evacuation of Wilmington, Richmond, and Petersburg, "in anticipation of what may be necessary . . . to abandon all our cities."[10]

As he monitored events to the south, Lee continued pursuing the idea of giving freedom to slaves in order to get them to enlist in the army. On February 11 Secretary of State Judah Benjamin wrote to Lee complaining about problems the government was having getting public opinion to come around on the issue and asking if it might be possible for him to "get from the army an expression of its desire to be re-enforced by such negroes as for the boon of freedom will volunteer to go to the front." If this were secured, Benjamin predicted, "the measure will pass without further delay, and we may yet be able to give you such a force as will enable you to assume the offensive." By the sixteenth, orders were making their way to division commanders in the Army of Northern Virginia asking them to discreetly glean from their men their opinions on providing freedom to slaves who volunteered for the army. Two days later, Lee received a message from Gordon that the men in the Second Corps were "decidedly in favor of the voluntary enlistment of the negroes as soldiers. . . . The opposition to it is now confined to a very few, and I am satisfied will soon cease to exist." While one recent historian has found considerable evidence that Gordon greatly exaggerated the degree of unanimity that existed within the Army of Northern Virginia on the matter, his report did reflect a larger shift in opinion both in and out of the army. Finally, on March 13, the Confederate Congress passed legislation authorizing the recruitment of African-American soldiers, and by the end of the month Lee's headquarters was actively corresponding with Ewell on improving implementation of the new policy. Even before then, in a message to new Secretary of War John C. Breckinridge on March 14, Lee had expressed concern that the measure would have to be implemented so carefully that it was unlikely to produce much benefit anytime soon.[11]

While the debate over whether to enlist African-American troops was coming to a resolution, Lee demonstrated he was by no means averse to seeking other measures that might produce something other than the total conquest and subjugation of the South. During the last week of February, Longstreet and the new commander of the Union Army of the James, Maj. Gen. Edward O. C. Ord, had a meeting in which they conceived the idea of arranging a cease-fire to allow for the organization of a convention to negotiate an end to the conflict. After discussing the matter with Davis, Longstreet, and Breckinridge, Lee decided to encourage his subordinate's efforts and, after a second meeting with Ord, on February 28 Longstreet suggested Lee write directly to Grant on the matter. Lee did so on March 2 and proposed he and Grant meet at 11:00 a.m. on March 6, "with the hope that upon an interchange of views it may be found practicable to submit the subjects of controversy between the belligerents to a convention." Lee, however, advised Richmond he was not optimistic that anything would come of this effort, as he did not think Grant would consent to anything "unless coupled with the condition of our return to the Union." And indeed after forwarding Lee's message to Washington, Grant received a message from Secretary of War Edwin Stanton stating that Lincoln would authorize "no conference with General Lee, unless it be for the capitulation of General Lee's army or on some minor and purely military matter." "You are not," Stanton added, "to decide, discuss, or confer upon any political question. Such questions the President holds in his own hands, and will submit them to no military conferences or conventions." Thus, on March 4, Grant informed Lee there could be no conference along the lines he had proposed.[12]

While Longstreet and Ord were hatching their scheme for a convention, Lee was dealing with Richmond's response to his suggestion that it might prove necessary to abandon the capital. When asked by Breckinridge where the army might go after leaving Richmond, Lee replied on February 21 that he would "endeavor to unite the corps of this army about Burkeville (junction of South Side and [Richmond and] Danville Railroads)." The following day, Lee responded to a message from Breckinridge advocating the sending of troops from western Virginia and the Shenandoah Valley to the Carolinas. Lee agreed that something must be done to defeat Sherman but was unsure of the wisdom of taking troops from elsewhere to reinforce Beauregard. Not only did he doubt there would be sufficient time for forces in western Virginia and the Shenandoah Valley to reach Beauregard, but asked Breckinridge, "What then will become of those sections of the country?" Lee also made clear that he was mentally prepared for the fact that the struggle for Richmond and Petersburg would soon be at an end. "Grant, I think, is now preparing to draw out by his left," he advised Breckinridge, "with the intent of enveloping me. He may wait till his other columns approach nearer, or he may be preparing to anticipate my withdrawal. . . . I am endeavoring to collect supplies convenient to Burkeville. Every thing of value should be removed from Richmond."[13]

That same day, at Lee's request, the Davis administration directed General Johnston to make contact with Lee who, on February 22, sent Johnston a message instructing him, "Assume command of the Army of Tennessee and all troops in Department of South Carolina, Georgia, and Florida. . . . Concentrate all available forces and drive back Sherman." Knowing Davis's relationship with Johnston was extremely bitter, Lee immediately made a point of writing to the president to express gratitude for agreeing to Johnston's restoration to command and tell him he hoped this would produce "favourable results . . . and that Sherman may still be driven back." Lee also

Figure 9.1.   General Joseph E. Johnston, Confederate, c. 1861–1865.
National Archives

made a point of ensuring the president was fully aware of the thinking at headquarters regarding the future. "I will do all in my power to strengthen [Johnston]," Lee wrote, "and should he be forced across the Roanoke, unite with him in a blow against Sherman before the latter can join Genl. Grant. This will necessitate the abandonment of our position on James River for which contingency every preparation should be made."[14]

Johnston, however, immediately recognized that he did not have the means to defeat Sherman's and Schofield's forces and that the only purpose for continued resistance would be to secure the best terms possible from the North. Whether Lee possessed such a realistic view of matters in March 1865 is unclear, but it is hard to believe that he held out much hope for victory. Indeed, on March 9, he advised Breckinridge that the forces around Richmond and Petersburg were so exhausted logistically that it seemed "almost impossible to maintain our present position." He also pointed out that Johnston's force was clearly "inferior to that of the enemy, and its condition gives no prospect of a marked success"—and that this was the case for armies throughout the Confederacy. Straining to find grounds for optimism, Lee also remarked that the military situation, though "not favorable, it is not worse than the superior numbers and resources of the enemy justified us in expecting from the beginning. Indeed, the legitimate military consequences of that superiority have been postponed longer than we had reason to anticipate." At the same time, Lee refused to accept any responsibility for determining whether this meant the cause of Southern independence remained worth fighting for. The fate of the Confederacy, he argued, ultimately rested not on her armies and their commanders, but on "the disposition and feelings of the people." Responsibility for determining whether they were equal to the challenges the Confederacy faced, in his mind, lay not with the military leadership, but the people's representatives.[15]

The first three weeks of March certainly brought no grounds for optimism. The month opened with bad news from the Shenandoah Valley, where Sheridan attacked and effectively destroyed what was left of Early's command at Waynesboro on March 2. Further south, Schofield's forces advanced into the interior of North Carolina and, after fighting off a series of attacks at Kinston on March 8–10, continued their push westward to a rendezvous with Sherman. Meanwhile, after crossing into North Carolina, Sherman's command steadily advanced northward, with his cavalry winning an engagement at Monroe's Crossroads on March 10 and his right wing overcoming stiff resistance at Averasborough on March 15–16. Three days later, Johnston, after concentrating his forces at Bentonville, made a determined attempt to destroy one wing of Sherman's command. Sherman's forces were simply too strong and its commanders too cautious, though, for the Confederates to achieve a decisive success. Nonetheless, Johnston was able during the night of March 21–22 to extricate his army from the field. This at least preserved its existence, while Johnston maneuvered it after Bentonville in such a way as to deny the Federals the ability to inflict more damage, acting very much in line with Lee's belief that as long as the Confederate armies could "be maintained, we may recover from our reverses, but if lost we have no resource."[16]

While Johnston licked his wounds after Bentonville, Lee braced for a renewal of Federal operations against Richmond and Petersburg. After learning of Early's defeat, it was not difficult to divine that Sheridan's next step would be to unite with the forces operating along the James. On the nineteenth, his cavalry reached the Pamunkey and five days later crossed the James and Appomattox to rejoin the Army of the Potomac. That same day, March 24, Grant issued orders for what would be the final offensive against Petersburg. On the night of the twenty-seventh, he directed, three divisions from Ord's army would cross to the south side of the James and Appomattox and take up a position where they would support two corps from the Army of the Potomac that were to cross Hatcher's Run on March 29 and advance toward the Boydton Plank Road and Dinwiddie Court House. By doing so, these corps would in turn support a push by Sheridan's cavalry for the South Side and Danville Railroads. Successful execution of this plan would not only give the Federals possession of Petersburg's last supply lines, but also put Grant's forces in positions from which they would be able to block any attempt by Lee to link up with Johnston. This was something Grant desperately hoped to prevent.[17]

The same day Grant issued orders for the final push against Petersburg, Lee decided to make one more attempt to loosen the vise in which Grant had him. As Grant extended his lines south of the Appomattox, the possibility had always existed that he might weaken his position east of Petersburg enough that an attack against his lines there might be able to achieve success. Now with Grant clearly preparing another major push south and west of the city, Lee decided the time had come to test whether his adversary had in fact done so. Consequently, he directed Gordon to launch an assault with his corps and elements from Longstreet's and Hill's against a point in the Federal line south and east of Petersburg. At best, Lee hoped Gordon might, after breaking through the Federal lines, swing south and force an abandonment of the entire Federal position south of Petersburg by threatening to cut the bulk of the Army of the Potomac off from its supply base at City Point. Lee, of course, was too much of a realist to expect to achieve such great results from Gordon's attack, but it was the only course of action available to him at the time that held out any possibility (however slim) of accomplishing something positive and of real significance. Moreover, Lee could hope that a successful attack on the Federal lines east of Petersburg might at least induce his enemy to, he later wrote, "curtail his lines, that upon the approach of Genl Sherman, I might be able to hold our position with a portion of the troops, and with a select body unite with Genl Johnston and give him battle. If successful, I would then be able to return." Besides, he believed with some justification that, even if the attack were "unsuccessful I should be in no worse condition, as I should be compelled to withdraw from James River if I quietly awaited his approach."[18]

Gordon's morning assault on March 25 initially achieved some success, seizing possession of Fort Stedman and briefly opening a significant gap in the Union line. The Federals, however, quickly regrouped and by the end of the day had regained their original lines. Indeed, the Federals won the fight for Fort Stedman so easily that at no time did it arouse any anxiety in Grant or even the much less phlegmatic Lincoln, who was visiting the general at his headquarters. After meetings with Lincoln and Sherman, who after joining his forces with Schofield's at Goldsboro on March 23 had come up to City Point, in which all three agreed on the need to deliver vigorous blows to bring about the surrender of the remaining Confederate armies followed by generous terms to discourage further resistance, Grant issued orders for the final Petersburg offensive. "I now feel like ending the matter," he wrote Sheridan on March 29.[19]

That day, Sheridan led three divisions of cavalry through a heavy rain to Dinwiddie Court House, while Meade pushed Warren's and Humphreys' corps forward across Hatcher's Run. When news arrived that the Federal offensive had begun, Lee responded as he always had—by seeking an opportunity for a successful counterattack that would catch the Federals in the open, put them back on their heels, and disrupt their plans. Thus, he directed Lt. Gen. Richard H. Anderson, now commanding what was designated the Fourth Corps but one of whose two divisions had been detached for service in North Carolina, to push his command forward from the Confederate defensive lines near the intersection of the Boydton Plank Road and White Oak Road. Anderson promptly complied and, at around three that afternoon, his men ran into the lead brigade from Warren's corps as it was advancing north along the Quaker Road toward its intersection with the Boydton Plank Road. This produced a brief, but sharp engagement near the Lewis Farm that did little to disrupt the Federal offensive or prevent Warren's men from establishing a foothold shortly after dark parallel to and across the Boydton Plank Road, while Anderson was compelled to pull back to his original lines. As this was going on, Maj. Gen. George Pickett's division from Longstreet's command marched south and west from Petersburg to take up a position where they would extend the Confederate right flank.[20]

As Pickett's men completed their march during the night of March 29–30, Grant decided that, instead of letting Sheridan continue moving south and west to attack the railroads, the cavalry commander would instead endeavor to envelop the western end of Lee's defensive line. To facilitate Sheridan's efforts, Warren's infantry was directed to continue its push against Confederate positions along the Boydton Plank Road at Hatcher's Run. Heavy rains throughout the thirtieth, however, badly impeded the Federal offensive.

They also gave Lee the ability to shift Pickett's five brigades to Five Forks, a critical road junction west of the Boydton Plank Road, to assist cavalry there commanded by Maj. Gen. Fitzhugh Lee, who on the morning of the thirtieth managed to turn back a reconnaissance by Sheridan's cavalry from Dinwiddie Court House. "Skirmishing was frequent along the lines today," Lee reported as March 30 came to a close, "but no serious attack."[21]

The following day would be quite different. That morning, the Federal offensive resumed in earnest, with Sheridan's cavalry driving north from Dinwiddie Court House toward Five Forks and Warren's infantry advancing toward the Confederate position along the Boydton Plank and White Oak Roads. Once again, Lee and his subordinates refused to wait passively in their fortifications for the Federals. Instead, Fitz Lee's cavalry and Pickett's infantry pushed south from Five Forks to confront Sheridan, while General Lee personally ordered Anderson's command to once again sally forward from its trenches in an attempt to catch Warren's advancing forces while they were in the open. Anderson's advance initially achieved some success, with his men delivering a crushing attack on the front and left flank of Warren's lead division, which by two in the afternoon had driven the Federals back more than a mile. Warren, however, was able to rally his forces and break the momentum of the Confederate attack. He then brought up more of his command, pushed Anderson's men back to the White Oak Road, and managed to secure a position on the road west of the Claiborne and Boydton Plank Roads by nightfall. Meanwhile, to the south and west, Fitz Lee and Pickett were able to blunt an attempt by Sheridan's cavalry to push north toward Five Forks and drive the Federals almost all the way back to Dinwiddie Court House.[22]

Nonetheless, when night fell on March 31 the Federals were in a much more favorable position than they had been when the day started. Warren had not only secured a Federal foothold on the White Oak Road but also put his infantry in a position from which it could assist Sheridan the following day. Recognizing this, Grant and Meade ordered Warren to move west to Sheridan's support on April 1, while instructing Humphreys to take over the fight with the Confederates posted at Hatcher's Run and the Boydton Plank–White Oak Road intersection. Learning of the threat posed by Warren's command as a result of the events of March 31, Pickett ordered his infantry and Fitz Lee's cavalry to pull back and take up a position north of Five Forks behind Hatcher's Run. Then, however, he received a message from army headquarters to "hold Five Forks at all hazards" and instead began fortifying a position around the road junction. Robert E. Lee, however, was under no illusions about the prospects for success on April 1. The Federal movements of the past few days, he informed Davis that morning, had secured for them "an advantageous point on our right and rear" from which they could "I fear . . . readily cut both the South Side and the Danville Railroads. . . . This in my opinion obliged us to prepare for the necessity of evacuating our position on James River at once, and also to consider the best means of accomplishing it."[23]

Lee's assessment of the situation was proven correct that afternoon as Warren's and Sheridan's commands overwhelmed Pickett's defenses around Five Forks. This placed the South Side Railroad in Grant's reach and made it possible to talk of the fall of Petersburg in terms of hours, not days or weeks. Lee responded by directing Longstreet to send Field's division to Petersburg and come himself. Longstreet personally reached Edge Hill early on the second. Then, shortly after Lee informed Longstreet his command would be sent to the assistance of the forces at Hatcher's Run, more bad news arrived. Earlier that morning, they learned, the Union Sixth Corps had broken through a section of the Confederate line held by elements from Heth's and Wilcox's divisions of Hill's corps. As the Federals, Wilcox later wrote, "turned both to the right and left, sweeping everything before them," Hill attempted to rally his command but was killed by some stray Union soldiers. The news was almost immediately brought back to Lee. "He is now at rest," Lee remarked, "and we who are left are the ones to suffer." He did not have much time to mourn, though, for the defeat at Five Forks and the Federal breakthrough meant that Lee could, as he advised Breckinridge, "see no prospect of doing more than holding our position here till night. . . . I advise that all preparation be made for leaving Richmond tonight. . . . If I can I shall withdraw tonight north of the Appomattox."[24]

Once this had been accomplished, and the forces north of the James and at Bermuda Hundred had evacuated their lines, Lee hoped to reconcentrate his command somewhere along the Richmond and Danville Railroad and then follow it to North Carolina to link up with Johnston. By three in the afternoon, Lee had finished developing his plan for the retreat from Richmond and Petersburg and notified Davis of his decision and the reasons behind it. To fill the void left by Hill's death, Lee had earlier dispatched a message to Henry Heth directing him to take command of the Third Corps. Unfortunately, by the time Lee's message reached Heth elements from two Union corps were interposed between him and Edge Hill, and between Lee and the forces south and west of the breakthrough, which had themselves been compelled to abandon their positions around Hatcher's Run during the morning. Under Heth's direction, some of these forces managed to establish a defensive position covering the South Side Railroad at Sutherland Station. Yet because Heth was unable to reach army headquarters to accept his new assignment, Lee changed his mind and decided to place both the First and Third Corps under Longstreet's command.[25]

According to Lee's plan for the retreat, during the night of April 2–3, Longstreet's two corps would cross to the north side of the Appomattox using a pontoon bridge while Gordon's did the same using two bridges slightly downstream from Longstreet. The three corps would then recross the Appomattox at Bevill's Bridge and proceed to Amelia Court House on the Richmond and Danville Railroad. There they would rendezvous with the forces that had been driven from the lines at Hatcher's Run and Five Forks, as well as those commanded by Mahone and Ewell that had been holding the lines at Bermuda Hundred and north of the James.[26]

The retreat from Petersburg and Richmond, Lee instructed his subordinates, would begin at eight that evening and was to be completed by three the following morning. Lee also made a point of sending a message to Davis informing him that he had given orders for the retreat and that he would send an officer "to Your Excellency to explain the routes to you by which the troops will be moved to Amelia Court House, and furnish you with a guide and any assistance that you may require." Lee also responded to an earlier message from Davis in which the president, after reading the general's earlier message to Breckinridge about his intention to retreat from Richmond and

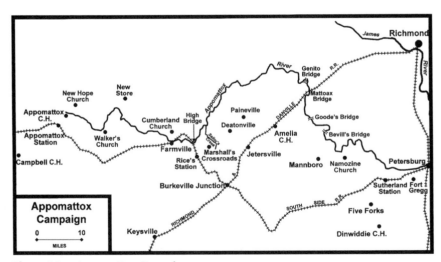

Figure 9.2.   Appomattox Campaign.

Petersburg, complained that many valuables would be lost due to a lack of time and available transportation. The abandonment of Richmond and Petersburg that night, Lee once again explained, was "absolutely necessary. . . . The enemy is so strong that they will cross above us and close us in between the James and Appomattox Rivers if we remain."[27]

What prospects existed for the success of Lee's plan rested first on whether he could prevent the complete collapse of his defenses around Petersburg before night fell on April 2. In addition to the successes that had been achieved south and west of Petersburg during the morning of the second, the Federals had also managed to penetrate Confederate defenses south and east of the town along the Jerusalem Plank Road. Gordon's men were able to contain this breakthrough and make their escape back to and across the Appomattox that evening without too much difficulty. Despite Lee's hopes that Heth might be able to do the same, the story was different to the west. During the afternoon, elements from the Union Second Corps managed to crush the Confederate position at Sutherland Station and sever the South Side Railroad. More seriously, after pushing through the hole in the Confederate lines along the Boydton Plank Road created by the Sixth Corps, the Union Twenty-fourth Corps turned north and east and began pushing toward the lightly held western defenses of Petersburg. While Lee anxiously awaited the arrival of Field's division, the Federals reached the two key strong points that stood between them and the last Confederate defensive line west of Petersburg. The vastly outnumbered defenders of Forts Gregg and Whitworth, however, put up a truly heroic fight and by doing so bought enough time for Field's men to reach the line of defense Longstreet and Lee had put together in the western section of the old Dimmock Line. Fortunately for Lee, this line proved strong enough to prevent the exhausted Federals from following up their capture of the two forts with an assault on Petersburg itself from the west on April 2.[28]

Nonetheless, in line with Lee's orders, the evacuation of Petersburg and Richmond began that night, and by dawn on April 3, the cities' defenders were gone. As his men occupied Richmond and Petersburg that morning, Grant sent orders to Sheridan to push his cavalry and the Fifth Corps west to the Danville Railroad to block the route Grant anticipated Lee would try to use to reach Johnston. To support Sheridan's forces, Grant ordered Meade to take two corps from the Army of the Potomac and follow them to the Danville Railroad. A few miles south of Sheridan and Meade, Ord and the elements from his army that had participated in the fighting of April 2 and two divisions from Parke's Ninth Corps would follow the South Side Railroad until they reached its junction with the Danville line at Burkeville Junction.[29]

As Grant put together his pursuit plan, Lee's various commands were moving toward Amelia Court House. As he rode west accompanying Longstreet and his command, Lee learned to his consternation that Bevill's Bridge, which he had intended to use to get Longstreet's and Gordon's commands across the Appomattox, was unusable due to the fact that its approaches were under water. This compelled him to order those commands further up the river to Goode's Bridge, which Longstreet reached at around nightfall and then used to push two divisions across to establish a bridgehead. Meanwhile, the Confederates south of the Appomattox also moved steadily toward Amelia Court House, with their rear guard fighting sharp engagements with Sheridan's cavalry at Namozine Church and Mannboro during the afternoon. Nonetheless, by heroic marching on largely empty stomachs, Lee and his legions managed to secure a respectable head start in their race with Grant's forces. After the army had concentrated at Amelia Court House—where it was expected the Richmond government had dispatched supplies in response to orders from Lee's headquarters—and gathered rations, Lee could then lead it south toward Burkeville, Danville, and then to North Carolina before the Federals could prevent him from doing so.[30]

Unfortunately, when Lee reached Amelia Court House on the morning of April 4, he learned something had gone seriously awry. Richmond had indeed dispatched large quantities of supplies to the small village, but Lee found "not a pound of subsistence for man or horse." Orders to send Richmond's reserve subsistence stores along the Richmond and Danville Railroad had reached the responsible officer too late for him to secure available space on the trains leaving the capital before other government officials had claimed them. Consequently, Lee was compelled to dispatch foraging parties to the surrounding countryside around Amelia Court House with messages to the local population offering vouchers in payment for their goods and appealing to their "generosity and charity to supply as far as one is able the wants of the brave soldiers who have battled for your liberty for four years. We require meat, beef, cattle, sheep, hogs, flour, meal, corn, and provender in any quantity that can be spared."[31]

The pause at Amelia Court House also provided time to deal with a problem that had come to Lee's attention during the afternoon of April 3. For some reason, that afternoon the pontoon bridges Lee had ordered laid over the Appomattox at Genito Bridge for Ewell's command had not appeared. Consequently, Lee instructed Ewell to see if he could make it across at that point or some other point in the vicinity, but expecting he would not, directed him to make his way to the rest of the army's crossing at Goode's Bridge. Ewell eventually managed to find another convenient crossing at

Mattoax Bridge, which carried the Richmond and Danville Railroad over the Appomattox, but news of this did not reach Lee until after night fell on April 4. Lee also spent the fourth issuing orders designed to lighten his army's logistical tail. He instructed artillery chief Brig. Gen. William Pendleton to go among the various commands and reduce the number of guns to only what would be required in the field and have the rest forwarded to "Danville, or to some point south of it." The chief quartermaster was ordered to do the same with the army's wagons and teams.[32]

As Lee's men straggled into Amelia Court House on April 4, President Davis made it clear that even though the capital had been lost, he did not consider the fall of the Confederacy at all inevitable. In a proclamation that day "to the people of the Confederate States of America," Davis conceded that the loss of Richmond was a serious blow to the country, but argued it would be a mistake if the people of the Confederacy were to at all become disheartened or relax their efforts. The loss of Richmond, he stated, was "not without compensation." The enemy, he predicted, would draw confidence from their victory and anticipate that it "would be the signal for our submission to their rule, and relieve them from the burden of war," but would soon learn the loss of Richmond in fact only marked the beginning of "a new phase" in the conflict. No longer shackled to the defense of "cities and particular points," fresh strategic and operational options had become open to the armies of the Confederacy that would enable them to burst Federal hopes for a swift end to the war. Now Lee and other Southern commanders were, Davis proclaimed, "Free to move from point to point and strike in detail the detachments and garrisons of the enemy, operating on the interior of our own country, where supplies are more accessible, and where the foe will be far removed from his own base and cut off from all succor in case of reverse, nothing is now needed to render our triumph certain but the exhibition of our own unquenchable resolve." He then assured the people of Virginia and any other state that might find itself under the Yankee heel that "again and again will we return, until the baffled and exhausted enemy shall abandon in despair his endless and impossible task of making slaves of a people resolved to be free."[33]

Yet, even as Davis's proclamation was being prepared, military operations outside Virginia were crushing his hopes that there would be some place where the Confederacy's political and military institutions might be able to once again operate advantageously against the Federals and that the southern population's will and ability to continue the war could be sustained. After the victory at Nashville, Union military authorities west of the Appalachians conceived a plan for again using the raiding method that had proven so effective in Georgia. They organized a force of cavalry and mounted infantry under the command of Maj. Gen. James H. Wilson and gave it the mission of conducting a massive raid into the interior of Alabama to destroy the war resources in that region and further impress upon the Southern people the impotence of the Confederate government. Meanwhile, an operation was put together under the direction of Maj. Gen. Edward R.S. Canby for an attack against the land defenses of Mobile. On March 22 Wilson's command began its push south. After tearing up northern Alabama for nine days, they encountered a Confederate force commanded by Lt. Gen. Nathan Bedford Forrest at Montevallo and routed it. On April 2, they once again thrashed Forrest's forces at Selma and then went to work wrecking that town's munitions-producing facilities, while further to the south, Canby's command was conducting siege operations against the fortifications guarding Mobile. By April 9, Canby's forces had seized enough of these to render the city defenseless. The following day, Wilson's command left Selma and began advancing toward Montgomery, Alabama, the first capital of the Confederacy, whose virtually defenseless posture vividly symbolized the emptiness of the strategy and hopes for Southern independence contained in Davis's proclamation.[34]

Of course, between Alabama and Lee's hard-pressed forces in Virginia, there was the Confederate army in North Carolina. On April 9, Johnston had known about the evacuation of Richmond and Petersburg for about four days, and had his army concentrated around Smithfield so it could oppose advances by Sherman against the North Carolina state capital, Raleigh, or directly north toward Virginia. For their part, Sherman's forces were at Goldsboro, while their commander prepared a push north toward Burkeville to interpose his command between Lee and Johnston. The fall of Richmond led Sherman to drop that plan and make Raleigh his next objective. Meanwhile, Johnston understood his next move was to link up with Lee, but a lack of solid information regarding the movements of the Army of Northern Virginia made it difficult to discern how this was to be done. When reports that Sherman's advance had begun arrived on the morning of April 10, Johnston ordered his three corps to move to Raleigh in order to cover the state capital and preserve a position on the railroad that ran from Raleigh to Greensboro, where it connected with the Richmond and Danville Railroad.[35]

Yet for Lee's hopes of reaching North Carolina, the pause at Amelia Court House proved "fatal," as the general later advised Davis. As Lee's foraging parties engaged in a fruitless search of the countryside for food and the general waited for word from Ewell, the Federals were pushing to Jetersville. At about five in the afternoon, Sheridan personally reached Jetersville, with the Fifth Corps marching hard behind his cavalry. As the infantry arrived, Sheridan ordered it to begin entrenching astride the railroad and nervously kept a look out toward Amelia Court House. "It seems to me," he later wrote, "that this was the only chance the Army of Northern Virginia had to save itself, which might have been done had General Lee promptly attacked and driven back the comparatively small force opposed to him and pursued his march to Burkeville Junction." In truth, much of Lee's army had not even reached Amelia Court House yet and even had Lee managed to break through Sheridan's position, it is difficult to see how he could have accomplished much. Grant already had Ord's command moving to Burkeville, and Lee would have had to make his march along the railroad with Meade's three corps and Sheridan's cavalry operating against his eastern flank and rear.[36]

To Sheridan's relief, Lee decided to remain at Amelia Court House throughout the fifth to give those parts of the army that still had yet to reach the village time to do so. He also issued orders the night before to a member of his staff to put the army's wagon train and reserve artillery in motion during the morning of the fifth to the north and west. During the afternoon, however, a brigade of Union cavalry suddenly appeared at Paineville and pounced on a section of the Confederate wagon trains. When Lee learned of this, he sent some cavalry to the scene that chased the Federals back to Jetersville; however, more than six hundred prisoners, more than a dozen pieces of artillery, and two hundred wagons had been lost.[37]

More importantly, during the afternoon of April 5, two more Union corps reached Jetersville, as Lee ordered Longstreet to probe south from Amelia Court House along the railroad. At around one in the afternoon, Longstreet began his advance and as his lead elements made contact with Sheridan's cavalry, Lee and Longstreet rode forward to see for themselves what would be necessary to clear the route to Danville. Given the urgency of the situation, it is hardly surprising that one officer later wrote, "I never saw Gen. Lee seem so anxious to bring on a battle in my life as he seemed this afternoon." However, after being advised that enough Federal infantry had reached Jetersville to eliminate any hopes for a successful attack, Lee decided to abandon his effort to push south along the railroad. Instead, when the army left Amelia Court House that night, it would move north and west to Paineville, and from there via Deatonville to Rice's Station on the South Side Railroad and then follow the railroad to Farmville. Once at

Farmville, he hoped to resupply his army and then push south to reach the Danville Railroad near Keysville.[38]

Lee could not have been under any illusion that such a move would be easy. However, fortune initially smiled on him, for after arriving at Jetersville and assuming overall command of the Federal force there on the fifth, Meade decided he would advance toward Amelia Court House the next morning, following the tracks of the railroad. He did so over the objections of Sheridan, who correctly believed that Lee would march west on the sixth and argue that Meade's plan would give him a clear route to do so. Sheridan was so convinced that this was the case that he persuaded Grant to come personally to Jetersville to hear his argument. Although he agreed with Sheridan's assessment of the situation, after reaching Meade's headquarters around midnight, Grant told that officer that his plan to advance the three corps of infantry toward Amelia Court House was approved, but also persuaded him to modify it to have Sheridan's cavalry swing out further to the left. For his part, Ord, who had reached Burkeville Junction that afternoon, received instructions to push forward from there along the tracks of the South Side Railroad to the Appomattox at High Bridge.[39]

As Grant mediated the dispute between Meade and Sheridan, Lee's men were already on the move. With cavalry screening their advance, the First and Third corps, still under the combined command of Longstreet, led the march from Amelia Court House, followed by Mahone's division, and then Anderson's two divisions. Next in line was Ewell's command, then the army's wagon train, and, finally, Gordon's corps. Longstreet managed to reach Rice's Station early on the morning of April 6 and shortly after his arrival learned that he had just missed a raiding force Ord had sent forward from Burkeville Junction to burn High Bridge. After sending a cavalry force commanded by Brig. Gen. Thomas Rosser in pursuit of the Federal raiders, Longstreet, aware that a substantial body of enemy troops was moving in his direction from Burkeville Junction, began establishing a fortified position covering the roads between that place and Rice's Station.[40]

As Longstreet's command reached Rice's Station, Meade's infantry was advancing toward Amelia Court House, but soon after starting their advance evidence arrived that Lee was on the move, and Meade began reorienting his movements in response. While Federal infantry pushed north and west toward Amelia Springs to nip at the heels of Lee's army, Sheridan's cavalry moved west a bit further south with an eye on cutting off the Confederate retreat. As the Confederates fought off their pursuers throughout the late morning and early afternoon, a significant gap opened in the Confederate line of march between Mahone's and Anderson's commands. Then, after crossing Sailor's Creek and pushing about a mile to Marshall's Crossroads, Anderson learned Federal cavalry had managed to interpose themselves between his command and Mahone's. Consequently, it was decided that the wagon train and Gordon's corps would have to take a different route to Farmville, one that crossed Sailor's Creek about a mile upstream from the direct road to Rice's Station. The last of Lee's forces to use the latter road to cross the creek, Ewell's, then took up a position on the heights overlooking the stream, while the wagon train and Gordon's command turned off onto the new route across Sailor's Creek.[41]

Shortly thereafter, the Union Sixth Corps appeared on the ridge on the opposite side of the creek from Ewell and at about six that evening, began advancing across the creek to attack Ewell. Meanwhile, at Marshall's Crossroads, Anderson's men found themselves battling Sheridan's cavalry. By the time the day was over both Ewell's and Anderson's positions had been overwhelmed and eight Confederate generals were prisoners, which one Union general subsequently crowed "were counted by thousands." Gordon's men were not even able to make it across the creek before they found themselves under attack by a superior Union force. Fortunately, although the Federals were able to overlap both of his flanks, it was late in the day when they attacked and this enabled much of Gordon's command to escape from the field. Nonetheless, it too had lost heavily on April 6.[42]

As had been the case ever since he left Petersburg, Lee spent most of April 6 with Longstreet, whose efforts that day were focused on dealing with the raiders Ord had dispatched to High Bridge and the advance of Ord's command toward Rice's Station from Burkeville. The former was handled rather easily by Rosser's cavalry, which captured nearly the entire Union raiding force, while later in the day Longstreet was able to drive back a heavy skirmish line Ord advanced toward Rice's Station. By then, news that the rest of his command was in trouble had prompted Lee to ride back toward Sailor's Creek and direct Mahone's division and some units from Heth's to do the same. By the time they reached the heights overlooking Sailor's Creek, however, there was nothing they could do but provide a point for refugees from Anderson's and Ewell's commands to gather around. As Lee looked over the wreckage from the battle, Mahone later recalled, he "straightened himself in his saddle, and, looking more of the soldier if possible than ever, exclaimed as if talking to himself, 'My God! Has the army dissolved?'" Shortly thereafter Lee grabbed a battle flag and began personally rallying the remnants of Anderson's and Ewell's commands around Mahone's men. When Anderson himself arrived, an angry Lee sternly directed him to take command of his stragglers and lead them to the rear, "signaling the emphasis," Mahone later wrote, "by a violent sling of his left hand."[43]

Once the situation was stabilized at Sailor's Creek, Lee instructed Mahone to take his troops and the refugees from Ewell's and Anderson's commands across the Appomattox at High Bridge during the night of April 6–7. Gordon's command would do the same. The bridge would then be destroyed as the two commands followed the railroad to Farmville, where the rest of the army was to move to from Rice's Station during the night. At Farmville the army would gather eighty thousand rations that were waiting for them there before crossing to the north side of the Appomattox. Then, with all the bridges in the area destroyed, Lee could feed his men and put some distance between them and the Federals. A few hours after returning to his headquarters near Rice's Station during the early evening, a courier from President Davis arrived and was told by Lee, "I shall have to be governed by each day's developments." Lee then bluntly remarked, "A few more Sailor's Creeks and it will all be over." For their part, the Union high command was scenting victory. That night, Sheridan wrote to Grant, "If the thing is pressed I think that Lee will surrender." "Let the *thing*," Lincoln directed Grant upon seeing Sheridan's message, "be pressed."[44]

After a tough night march, Longstreet's men reached Farmville early on April 7 and were issued rations before crossing to the north side of the Appomattox. There Lee called for Longstreet's artillery chief, Col. E. Porter Alexander, and gave him the responsibility of destroying the two bridges over the Appomattox at Farmville. Before Alexander left to take care of this, Lee showed him a map and indicated the next objective point for the army was Appomattox Court House, as supplies for the army were then being collected at the nearby station on the South Side Railroad. When Alexander noted that the shortest road from Farmville to that point was actually south of the Appomattox, Lee responded by questioning whether the map was in fact accurate. Then, however, Alexander located a local resident who confirmed that the map was correct. Of course, it was too late at that point to do anything other than pursue the course Lee had already chosen. "Well," he resignedly told Alexander, "there is time enough to think about that. Go now and attend to these matters here."[45]

Meanwhile, the reconcentration of the army proceeded through the morning as Gordon managed to reach Farmville after following the railroad from High Bridge. Unfortunately, Lee learned shortly thereafter, the job of destroying High Bridge and the lower wagon bridge that ran along it had been botched. This enabled Humphreys' Union corps to use it to cross the

Appomattox and then nip at Gordon's heels as he marched to Farmville and at Mahone's as his command took the road leading from the bridge to Cumberland Church. As Lee and his subordinates established a position on the high ground upon which the church rested, with Mahone's division on the left, Gordon's corps in the center, and Longstreet's command on the right, Federal cavalry occupied Farmville. However, until a pontoon bridge could be laid across the Appomattox, the Federals declined to cross to the north side of the river in strength. Consequently, when Humphreys attacked Mahone during the afternoon, Lee was able to send part of Longstreet's command to his assistance without worrying about his southern flank.

Despite the repulse of Humphreys' attack, Lee had no illusions about his prospects if he remained at Cumberland Church and ordered yet another night march. As Lee was conferring with Longstreet near the church and preparing the army for its departure, a message arrived from Grant. "The results of the last week must convince you," it read, "of the hopelessness of further resistance on the part of the Army of Northern Virginia. I feel that it is so, and regard it as my duty to shift from myself the responsibility of any further effusion of blood, by asking of you the surrender of that portion of the C.S. Army known as the Army of Northern Virginia." After showing the message to Longstreet, and receiving a blunt, "*Not yet*," Lee wrote back to Grant that he did not share his view "of the hopelessness of further resistance on the part of the Army of Northern Virginia," but, sharing his desire to avoid "useless" bloodshed, asked what terms of surrender Grant was prepared to offer. That same evening William N. Pendleton informed Lee that an impromptu council of high ranking officers had asked him to tell the commanding officer they believed the time had come to end the war and open negotiations with Grant for the surrender of the Army of Northern Virginia. "I trust it has not come to that," Lee replied. "We have yet too many bold men to think of laying down our arms."[46]

As his response to Grant's message made its way through the lines, Lee's forces left Cumberland Church and began pushing west toward Appomattox Court House. By a good night's march Lee hoped he might get enough of a head start to enable him to reach Appomattox Station, feed his army, push south from there to Campbell Court House, and thence to Danville and North Carolina. When the Federals discovered the Confederates had left early the next morning, they immediately pushed west in pursuit. While two corps followed Lee's march north of the Appomattox, the rest of Grant's command, with Sheridan's hard-driving cavalry in front, would move toward Appomattox Station south of the river.[47]

Lee's response to Grant's first message reached Union headquarters during the morning of April 8. Although displeased with Lee's message, Grant immediately drafted a reply. "Peace being my great desire," he wrote, "there is but one condition I would insist upon, namely: that the men and officers surrendered shall be disqualified for taking up arms again against the Government of the United States until properly exchanged. I will meet you, or will designate officers to meet any officers you may name for the same purpose, at any point agreeable to you, for the purpose of arranging definitely the terms upon which the surrender of the Army of Northern Virginia will be received."[48]

Meanwhile, Lee's army continued its desperate march, reaching Appomattox Court House during the morning and afternoon of April 8. They were too late. Shortly before dusk, Sheridan's cavalry reached Appomattox Station and seized the loaded supply trains that had been sent there from Lynchburg for the Army of Northern Virginia. Shortly after learning there were Federals at Appomattox Station, Lee called a council of war at his headquarters just north of Appomattox Court House. There he laid out the situation to Longstreet, Gordon, and Fitz Lee, presented to them his correspondence with Grant on the matter of surrendering the army, and decided on an attempt the next morning by the cavalry and Gordon's infantry to break through the Federal force in their front and clear the way to Campbell Court House. "In case nothing but cavalry were discovered," Fitz Lee later wrote, "we were to clear it from our route and open a way for our remaining troops; but in case they were supported by heavy bodies of infantry the commanding general should be at once notified, in order that a flag of truce should be sent to accede to the only alternative left us."[49]

It is unclear, however, whether the correspondence with Grant that Lee showed his subordinates included his response to Grant's second note. In that note, Lee stated, "I do not think the emergency has arisen to call for the surrender of this army. . . . I cannot, therefore, meet you with a view as to surrender the Army of Northern Virginia; but as far as your proposal may affect the C.S. forces under my command, & tend to the restoration of peace, I should be pleased to meet you at 10 a.m. tomorrow, on the old stage road to Richmond, between the picket lines." As Lee awaited Grant's response early on the morning of April 9, the effort to break out from Appomattox Court House began. By 8:00 a.m., however, it was clear that a strong force of Union infantry blocked the road to Campbell Court House and could not be driven from it, while four miles to the north and east, the lead elements of Meade's two corps were advancing on Longstreet's command near New Hope Church.[50]

When Lee learned from Gordon that infantry was in his front and that there was no prospect for a successful breakout, he was on a ridge about two miles from Appomattox Court House. Spotting Colonel Alexander nearby, he called the artillerist over and, Alexander later recalled, remarked: "Well here we are at Appomattox, and there seems to be a considerable force in front of us. Now, what shall we have to do today?" Alexander replied that he thought the army should "be ordered to scatter in the woods and bushes. . . . If there is any hope for the Confederacy it is in delay. For if the Army of Northern Va. surrenders every other army will surrender as fast as the news reaches it." By not rendering their military manpower "absolutely helpless and the mercy of the enemy" by surrendering, Alexander thought it would at least ensure the war would not end on terms as dishonorable as those "Unconditional Surrender" Grant would surely demand. After hearing Alexander out, Lee rejected his suggestion. While he agreed that the surrender of the Army of Northern Virginia would effectively be the end of the Confederacy, Lee argued that the consequences of Alexander's proposed course of action would be much worse. First, he did not think that enough men were left for them to accomplish much as bushwhackers in any case. More importantly, though, he stated that if he took Alexander's proposed course, "the men would have no rations and they would be under no discipline. . . . They would have to plunder and rob to procure subsistence. The country would be full of lawless bands . . . and a state of society would ensue from which it would take the country years to recover." Besides, from their correspondence, Lee told Alexander that did not think Grant would demand terms as harsh as he feared should Lee take "the only proper and dignified course . . . to surrender myself and take the consequences."[51]

After talking to Alexander, Lee summoned Longstreet to discuss the situation. "He was dressed," Longstreet later wrote of his commander that day, "in a suit of new uniform, sword and sash, a handsomely embroidered belt, boots, and a pair of gold spurs. At first approach his compact figure appeared as a man in the flush vigor of forty summers, but as I drew near, the handsome apparel and brave bearing failed to conceal his profound depression." Longstreet's counsel did nothing to lift this, nor did Mahone's. Instead, they confirmed their chief's sense that, as he had told a member of his staff shortly before that, "there is nothing left me but to go and see Grant." Thus, Lee gathered some members of his staff and led them north along the Richmond-Lynchburg Stage Road with the intention of having the meeting with Grant he had proposed the previous evening.[52]

Grant, however, had only a few hours earlier drafted a message to Lee stating that "the meeting proposed for ten a.m. today could lead to no good." He had, Grant reminded Lee, no authority to negotiate with him on anything other than the surrender of his army, and stated, "The terms upon which peace can be had are well understood. By the South laying down their arms. They will hasten that most desirable event, save thousands of human lives, and hundreds of millions of property not yet destroyed." This note reached Lee after he and his party had passed through his rear guard and encountered Federal pickets near New Hope Church. Lee then had a message drafted for Grant stating he had received the Federal commander's note and "now request an interview in accordance with the offer contained in your letter of yesterday . . . with reference to the surrender of this army." When this reached Meade, he agreed to grant Lee's request for a one-hour suspension of hostilities and suggested that Lee send a duplicate message to Grant requesting an interview elsewhere through the lines to expedite its reaching the Union general-in-chief.[53]

After doing so, Lee rode back toward Appomattox Court House and dismounted just before reaching the Appomattox River. There beside the stage road he took a seat under the shade of an apple tree to await Grant's reply, which was delivered to him by Lt. Col. Orville Babcock of Grant's staff around one o'clock. "I am at this writing," wrote Grant, "about four miles west of Walker's Church [which placed him about six miles from Appomattox Court House] and will push forward to the front for the purpose of meeting you." Upon receiving this, Lee proceeded to Appomattox Court House with two members of his staff, Babcock, and another Federal orderly. There they encountered resident Wilmer McLean, who offered the use of his home for the meeting between Grant and Lee.[54]

About an hour after Lee settled into the parlor of the McLean House, Grant arrived. After shaking hands, the two men sat down with Grant trying in vain to discern what the Confederate commander's feelings were at that moment. After briefly conversing, Grant later wrote, "about old army times," Lee suggested Grant put down in writing the terms he intended to offer for the surrender of the Army of Northern Virginia. After Grant drafted them, he passed them over to Lee. Lee found that Grant asked only that the men in his army, once given parole not "take up arms against the Government of the United States until properly exchanged," return home, where they were "not to be disturbed so long as they observe their paroles and the laws in force." All arms and other property belonging to the army were to be turned over, but officers could keep their sidearms and private horses and baggage. Lee declared the terms acceptable and even managed to persuade Grant to also allow his officers to keep their mounts as well. Lee then directed the staff officer accompanying him to

Figure 9.3. General Robert E. Lee's Return to His Lines after the Surrender. Robert Underwood Johnson and Clarence Clough Buel, eds., *Battles and Leaders of the Civil War*, vol. 4 (New York: The Century Magazine, 1884–1888), 747.

put in writing his acceptance of Grant's terms. Before departing, Lee also secured an offer of twenty-five thousand rations from Grant to feed his men.[55]

It was around three in the afternoon when both men signed the documents laying out the terms of surrender, after which Lee walked out the door of the McLean House and called for his warhorse. One Union officer later recalled watching Lee as he "stood on the lowest step, and gazed sadly in the direction of the valley beyond, where his army lay—now an army of prisoners. He thrice smote the palm of his left hand slowly with his right fist in an absent sort of way . . . and appeared unaware of everything about him." After he snapped out of his "reverie" and mounted Traveller, Lee looked to the porch of the McLean House and saw Grant step down from it and lead his men in raising their hats in salute. Lee returned the salute and then began riding toward his own camps. As Lee's party approached, some of Longstreet's artillerists decided to salute his return with uncovered heads and silence. But then a mob of infantrymen rushed forward and began cheering the general with such enthusiasm that the artillerists abandoned their plan and joined in. As their cheers echoed through the hills and valleys around Appomattox Court House, Lee told them, one officer later recalled, "that he had done his best for them and advised them to go home and become as good citizens as they had been soldiers that he had done all that he could for them."[56]

Notes

1. In preparing the account of events provided in this chapter, I relied heavily on the accounts of the latter stages of the Petersburg Campaign contained in the works by Trudeau and Humphreys previously cited, as well as A. Wilson Greene, *Breaking the Backbone of the Rebellion: The Final Battles of the Petersburg Campaign* (Mason City, IA: Savas Publishing, 2000); Chris Calkins, *The Appomattox Campaign, March 29–April 9, 1865* (1997; New York: Da Capo Press, 2001); and William Marvel, *Lee's Last Retreat: The Flight to Appomattox* (Chapel Hill: University of North Carolina Press, 2002). Also of value were Trudeau, "A Mere Question of Time," 546–54; and Mark Grimsley's wonderfully insightful "Learning to Say 'Enough': Southern Generals and the Final Weeks of the Confederacy," in *The Collapse of the Confederacy*, edited by Mark Grimsley and Brooks D. Simpson (Lincoln: University of Nebraska Press, 2001), 40–79.

2. Herman Hattaway and Richard E. Beringer, *Jefferson Davis, Confederate President* (Lawrence: University Press of Kansas, 2002), 329–32.

3. Lee to Davis, September 2, 1864, in *Wartime Papers*, eds. Dowdey and Manarin, 847–48; Hunter to Lee, January 7, 1864, OR, series 4, vol. 3: 1007–09; Lee to Hunter, January 11, 1864, ibid., 1012–13.

4. Lee to Davis, January 19, 1865, in *Wartime Papers*, eds. Dowdey and Manarin, 884; Lee to Cooper, February 4, 1865, ibid., 888.

5. Donald, *Lincoln*, 557–60.

6. Davis to Lee, February 2, 1865, OR, vol. 46, pt. 2: 1192; Longstreet to Lee, February 1, 4, 1865, ibid., 1189, 1203; Grant to Meade, February 4, 1865, ibid., 367; Circular, Hdqrs. Army of the Potomac, February 4, 1865, ibid., 370.

7. Lee to Cooper, February 5, 1865, ibid., 1204; Humphreys to Webb, February 13, 1865, ibid., pt. 1: 192–93; Gregg to Ruggles, February 13, 1865, ibid., 366; Gordon to Taylor, February 9, 1865, ibid., 390; Lee to Cooper, February 6, 1865, ibid., pt. 2: 1206; Warren to Ruggles, February 15, 1865, ibid., pt. 1: 254–56.

8. Lee to Seddon, February 8, 1865, in *Wartime Papers*, eds. Dowdey and Manarin, 890; General Orders No. 1, Hdqrs. Confederate Army, February 9, 1865, ibid., 891; Davis to Lee, February 10, 1865, OR, vol. 46, pt. 2: 1228.

9. General Orders No. 2, Hdqrs. Armies of the Confd. States, February 11, 1865, ibid., 1229–30.

10. Longstreet to Lee, February 2, 1865, OR, vol. 42, pt. 2: 1192; Lee to Alexander H. Stevens et al., February 13, 1865, in *Wartime Papers*, eds. Dowdey and Manarin, 894; Lee to Breckinridge, February 19, 1865, ibid., 904–05; Lee to Davis, February 19, 1865, ibid., 905–06.

11. Benjamin to Lee, February 11, 1865, OR, vol. 46, pt. 2: 1229; Latrobe to Kershaw, February 16, 1865, ibid., 1236; Gordon to Taylor, February 18, 1865, ibid., vol. 51, pt. 2: 1063; Bruce Levine, *Confederate Emancipation: Southern Plans to Free and Arm Slaves During the Civil War* (New York: Oxford University Press, 2006), 113–17; Marshall to Ewell, March, 27, 30, 1865, Campbell Brown Collection, LV; Lee to Breckinridge, March 14, 1865, Lee Headquarters Papers, VHS, series 8.

12. Jeffry D. Wert, *General James Longstreet: The Confederacy's Most Controversial Soldier* (New York: Simon & Schuster, 1993), 397–98; Lee to Grant, March 2, 1864, in *Wartime Papers*, eds. Dowdey and Manarin, 911; Lee to Davis, March 2, 1865, ibid.; Stanton to Grant, March 3, 1865, OR, vol. 46, pt. 2: 802; Grant to Lee, March 4, 1865, ibid., 825.

13. Breckinridge to Lee, February 20, 21, 1865, ibid., 1242, 1245; Lee to Breckinridge, February 21, 22, 1865, ibid., 1244, 1247.

14. Johnston, *Narrative*, 370; Lee to Johnston, February 22, 1865, OR, vol. 47, pt. 2: 1247; Lee to Davis, February 23, 1865, in *Wartime Papers*, eds. Dowdey and Manarin, 909–10.

15. Johnston, *Narrative*, 372; Breckinridge to Lee, March 8, 1865, OR, vol. 46, pt. 2: 1292; Lee to Breckinridge, March 9, 1865, in *Wartime Papers*, eds. Dowdey and Manarin, 912–13.

16. Mark L. Bradley, *This Astounding Close: The Road to Bennett Place* (Chapel Hill: University of North Carolina Press, 2000), 12–25; Lee to Davis, March 14, 1865, in *Wartime Papers*, eds. Dowdey and Manarin, 915.

17. Longstreet to Lee, March 5, 1865, OR, vol. 46, pt. 2: 1281–82; Lee to Breckinridge, March 7, 1865, ibid., 1285; Grant to Stanton, July 22, 1865, OR, vol. 46, pt. 1: 50–52.

18. Gordon, *Reminiscences*, 403; Lee to Davis, March 26, 1865, in *Wartime Papers*, eds. Dowdey and Manarin, 917.

19. Lee to Breckinridge, March 25, 1865, in *Wartime Papers*, eds. Dowdey and Manarin, 916; Grant to Sheridan, March 29, 1864, OR, vol. 46, pt. 3: 266.

20. Grant to Stanton, July 22, 1865, ibid., pt. 1: 53; Sheridan to Rawlins, May 16, 1865, OR, vol. 46, pt. 1: 1101–2; Lee to Breckinridge, March 29, 1865, in *Wartime Papers*, eds. Dowdey and Manarin, 920; R. H. Anderson, "Narrative of Services Oct '64–April '65," June 15, 1866, OR Supplement, vol. 7: 817–18, 820; Pickett to Taylor, May 1, 1865, ibid., 779.

21. Grant to Stanton, July 22, 1865, OR, vol. 46, pt. 1: 53; F. Lee to R.E. Lee, April 22, 1865, ibid., 1298–99; Pickett to Taylor, May 1, 1865, OR Supplement, vol. 7: 779–80; Lee to Breckinridge, March 30, 1865, in *Wartime Papers*, eds. Dowdey and Manarin, 921.

22. Johnson to Dabney, April 10, 1865, OR, vol. 46, pt. 1: 1287–88; F. Lee to R.E. Lee, April 22, 1865, ibid., 1299; Pickett to Taylor, May 1, 1865, OR Supplement, vol. 7: 780–81; Lee to Breckinridge, March 31, April 1, 1865, in *Wartime Papers*, eds. Dowdey and Manarin, 922, 923.

23. F. Lee to R.E. Lee, April 22, 1865, OR, vol. 46, pt. 1: 1299; Freeman, R.E. Lee, vol. 4: 36; Lee to Davis, April 1, 1865, in Wartime Papers, eds. Dowdey and Manarin, 922.

24. Longstreet to Taylor, April 11, 1865, OR Supplement, vol. 7: 775; Cadmus M. Wilcox, "Petersburg Campaign Report," Lee Headquarters Papers, VHS, series 5; Freeman, R.E. Lee, vol. 4: 46; Lee to Breckinridge, April 2, 1865, in Wartime Papers, eds. Dowdey and Manarin, 924–25.

25. Lee to Davis, April 2, 1865, ibid., 927–28; Heth to Palmer, April 11, 1865, OR Supplement, vol. 7: 811.

26. T. M. R. Talcott, "From Petersburg to Appomattox," SHSP, vol. 32: 67; Hdqrs. Army of Northern Virginia, April 2, 1865, OR, vol. 46, pt. 3: 1379; Taylor to Ewell, April 2, 1865, ibid., 1380.

27. Davis to Lee, April 2, 1865, ibid., 1378; Lee to Davis, April 2, 1865, in Wartime Papers, eds. Dowdey and Manarin, 925–26, 928.

28. Gordon to Taylor, April 11, 1865, OR Supplement, vol. 7: 796; Longstreet to Taylor, April 11, 1865, ibid., 775–76; Lee to Heth, April 2, 1865, Lee Papers, WL.

29. Grant, Memoirs, 610.

30. Talcott, "From Petersburg to Appomattox," 68; Longstreet to Taylor, April 11, 1865, OR Supplement, vol. 7: 776; Anderson, "Narrative of Services," ibid., 821; Lee to Ewell, April 3, 1865, in Wartime Papers, eds. Dowdey and Manarin, 929.

31. St. John to Lee, June 20, 1865, Lee Headquarters Papers, VHS, series 10; Freeman, R.E. Lee, vol. 4: 67.

32. Lee to Ewell, April 3, 4, 1865, in Wartime Papers, eds. Dowdey and Manarin, 929, 929–30; Special Orders No. ——, Hdqrs. Army of Northern Virginia, April 4, 1865, OR, vol. 46, pt. 3: 1384.

33. Davis to the People of the Confederate States of America, April 4, 1865, ibid., 1382–83.

34. Wilson to Whipple, May 3, 1865, OR, vol. 49, pt. 1: 350–51; Canby to Chief of Staff, Headquarters of the Army, June 1, 1865, ibid., 92–98.

35. Johnston, Narrative, 395–96; Sherman to Halleck, April 4, 1865, OR, vol. 47, pt. 1: 30.

36. Lee to Davis, April 12, 1865, in Wartime Papers, eds. Dowdey and Manarin, 936; Sheridan to Rawlins, May 16, 1865, OR, vol. 46, pt. 1: 1106.

37. Taylor, Special Orders No. ——, April 4, 1865, ibid., pt. 3: 1384; F. Lee to R.E. Lee, April 22, 1865, ibid., pt. 1: 1301; Davies to Weir, April 14, 1865, ibid., 1145.

38. Alexander, Fighting for the Confederacy, 521; Lee to Davis, April 12, 1865, in Wartime Papers, eds. Dowdey and Manarin, 936.

39. Grant, Memoirs, 617–18, 621.

40. Lee to Davis, April 12, 1865, in Wartime Papers, eds. Dowdey and Manarin, 936; Longstreet to Taylor, April 11, 1865, OR Supplement, vol. 7: 776; Ord to Rawlins, OR, vol. 46, pt. 1: 1161.

41. Humphreys, Virginia Campaign, 378–80; Anderson, "Narrative of Services," OR Supplement, vol. 7: 821; Gordon to Taylor, April 11, 1865, ibid., 797; Ewell to Lee, December 20, 1865, OR, vol. 46, pt. 1: 1294.

42. Ewell to Lee, December 20, 1865, ibid., 1294–95; Wright to Ruggles, April 29, 1865, ibid., 906; Gordon to Taylor, April 11, 1865, OR Supplement, vol. 7: 798.

43. Longstreet, Manassas to Appomattox, 612, 614–15; Alexander, Fighting for the Confederacy, 524; William Mahone, "On the Road to Appomattox," edited by William C. Davis, Civil War Times Illustrated 9 (January 1971): 9–10.

44. Calkins, Appomattox Campaign, 116; Sheridan to Grant, April 6, 1865, OR, vol. 46, pt. 3: 610; Lincoln to Grant, April 7, 1865, Works of Lincoln, vol. 8: 392.

45. Longstreet, Manassas to Appomattox, 615–16; Alexander, Fighting for the Confederacy, 525.

46. Grant to Lee, April 7, 1865, OR, vol. 46, pt. 3: 619; Longstreet, Manassas to Appomattox, 619 (italics in original); Lee to Grant, April 7, 1865, in Wartime Papers, eds. Dowdey and Manarin, 931–32; A. L. Long, Memoirs of Robert E. Lee: His Military and Personal History (New York: J.M. Stoddart and Company, 1886), 416–17.

47. Lee to Davis, April 12, 1865, in Wartime Papers, eds. Dowdey and Manarin, 937; Grant to Stanton, July 22, 1865, OR, vol. 46, pt. 1: 56.

48. Grant, Memoirs, 623; Grant to Lee, April 8, 1865, OR, vol. 46, pt. 3: 641.

49. Sheridan to Grant, April 8, 1865, ibid., 653; F. Lee to R.E. Lee, April 22, 1865, ibid., pt. 1: 1303; Gordon, Reminiscences, 434–36.

50. Lee to Grant, April 8, 1865, in Wartime Papers, eds. Dowdey and Manarin, 997; Lee to Davis, April 12, 1865, ibid., 937.

51. Alexander, Fighting for the Confederacy, 531–33.

52. Longstreet, Manassas to Appomattox, 626–27; Mahone, "On the Road to Appomattox," 45; Long, Memoirs, 421; Marshall, Lee's Aide-de-Camp, 262.

53. Grant to Lee, April 9, 1865, OR, vol. 46, pt. 3: 664; Lee to Grant, April 9, 1865, ibid.; Marshall, Lee's Aide-de-Camp, 262–64.

54. Alexander, Fighting for the Confederacy, 537–38; Lee to Grant, April 9, 1865, OR, vol. 46, pt. 3: 665; Grant to Lee, April 9, 1865, ibid., 665; Marshall, Lee's Aide-de-Camp, 267–69.

55. Grant, Memoirs, 629–33; Grant to Lee, April 9, 1865, OR, vol. 46, pt. 3: 665; Marshall, Lee's Aide-de-Camp, 269–73.

56. Porter, Campaigning With Grant, 485–86; Alexander, Fighting for the Confederacy, 539–40.

CHAPTER TEN

The Fall of the Confederacy

After Lee's surrender, whatever resolve remained in the South to follow President Davis's calls for continued resistance crumbled fairly quickly. In Alabama, Wilson's command claimed possession of Montgomery on April 12, encountering few willing to put up much of a fight for the birthplace of the Confederacy. The only significant conventional force capable of continuing resistance along the lines proposed in Davis's April 4 proclamation remained Johnston's. Johnston, however, could see no good that could come from prolonging the war after he received reports on April 11 of Lee's surrender. Shortly thereafter, he met with Davis, Beauregard, and Breckinridge in Greensboro, North Carolina, and told them, he later wrote, "it would be the greatest of human crimes for us to attempt to continue the war" and that "the effect of our keeping the field would be, not to harm the enemy, but to complete the devastation of our country and ruin of its people." Davis told his generals that he still did not think the cause was lost, but agreed to let Johnston send a message to Sherman asking him to contact Grant to see if a general "suspension of active operations" could be arranged "to permit the civil authorities to enter into the needful arrangements to terminate the existing war."[1]

On April 18, Johnston met with Sherman and not only got liberal terms for the surrender of his army, but persuaded Sherman to enter into an agreement covering far broader matters. All Confederate armies still in the field, they agreed, would disband, return to their state capitals, and deposit their arms and other public property there. Furthermore, the existing state governments would be recognized and the political rights of the people of the

Southern states would be guaranteed, as would their "rights of person and property," by the Federal government. Once the disbanding of the Confederate
armies had been completed, a general amnesty would be granted to their officers and men. Sherman agreed to these points to ensure as much as possible the
disbanded rebel armies would not become guerrilla bands and to give the states
the ability to repress any impulse that might exist to engage in guerrilla warfare. His actions, however, produced a firestorm when the terms he negotiated
reached Washington, where nerves were especially frazzled as a result of Lincoln's death at the hands of an assassin on April 15. Consequently, Sherman
was forced to inform Johnston on the twenty-fourth that their agreement had
been disapproved by Washington and unless they worked out a new one in
which Johnston surrendered on the same terms Grant had given Lee "purely
and simply" within two days, he would once again resume operations. When
Davis learned of this development, he directed Johnston to take advantage of
the open route of retreat south he still possessed and continue the war. Johnston, however, refused to do anything other than release some cavalry to serve
as an escort for Davis and surrendered his army to Sherman on April 26 on the
same terms Lee had accepted at Appomattox.[2]

As the effort to bring the war in North Carolina to an end played out,
Robert E. Lee returned to Richmond on a rainy April 15. There, on April 20,
he took up his pen to explain to President Davis the factors that had compelled
his surrender and advise him on his future course of action. After describing
the disintegration of his army's "moral condition" over the course of the winter of 1864–1865 and how this was manifest in its poor performance during the
operations of late March and early April, Lee told Davis that he did not think
Virginia had either the physical or moral resources necessary to ever again raise
and support an army for the Confederacy. He also wrote that, "as far as I know
the condition of affairs, the country east of the Mississippi is morally and physically unable to maintain the contest." He noted the South could turn to partisan warfare to protract the conflict, but also made clear he had no interest
whatsoever in seeing this course pursued. It would, he argued, only cause "individual suffering and the devastation of the country," and there was "no
prospect by that means of achieving a separate independence." Although he
told Davis that decisions regarding the South's future course ultimately rested
with him, Lee also made it clear that he no longer had the will to support continuing the struggle for Confederate independence. "To save useless effusion of
blood," he concluded, "I would recommend measures be taken for suspension
of hostilities and the restoration of peace."[3]

The Union army effectively delivered the final blow to anyone who still
harbored hopes that the cause of Southern independence was worth fighting

Figure 10.1.   General Robert E. Lee in Richmond, Virginia, April 1865.
National Archives

for less than three weeks after Lee conceded he did not. On May 10, elements from Wilson's command captured Jefferson Davis near Irwinville, Georgia, foiling his hopes of reaching the Mississippi River and continuing the strug-gle. By the end of the month, the last significant Confederate command had surrendered to the Federals. The Confederacy had fallen.

How had it happened? How could Robert E. Lee, who less than two years earlier at Chancellorsville had achieved such a magnificent military success that the scene inspired one man to proclaim him nearly elevated to the level of a god, end up surrendering his army in April 1865 and giving up on the cause for which he had fought so hard and sent so many young men to their deaths? What had he and his country gotten wrong? How had they fallen so far short of victory? To Lee, the answer to these questions was clear one day after he surrendered his army. "After four years of arduous service, marked by unsurpassed courage and fortitude," Lee told his men on April 10, "the Army of Northern Virginia has been compelled to yield to overwhelming numbers and resources."[4]

Lee's contention that the North's superiority in manpower and material resources was decisive to the fall of the Confederacy undeniably had much truth to it. Without its great superiority in "numbers and resources," it is indeed difficult to see how the North could have prevailed in its effort to destroy the Confederacy by persuading the people residing in the South to once again consent to be governed by Washington—and killing enough of those who could never be persuaded to do so.

Yet the Civil War was far too complex for monocausal explanations of its outbreak, course, or outcome to be sufficient. Moreover, history abounds with examples of people fighting wars in which they faced great disadvantages in numbers and resources, and prevailing. In the late eighteenth century, the American revolutionaries took on Great Britain, the world's mightiest nation, and won. A few decades later Napoleon repeatedly humbled coalitions of nations whose combined wealth in manpower and resources far outnumbered his own to make France the greatest military power in Europe—and then was in turn humbled by the militarily and materially inferior Spanish. Barely a year after Lee surrendered at Appomattox, Prussia surprised Europe by winning a spectacular victory in a war against the more populous Austrian Empire. And a little more than a hundred years later, Israel managed to win a spectacular victory over a far wealthier and more populous Arab coalition in the Six Day War of 1967, while during that same period the Vietnamese communists waged what would be a successful war of liberation (at least in their eyes) against a government backed by the great wealth and military power of the United States.

So, while possession of superior resources was unquestionably essential to Union victory, to focus exclusively on this factor in the defeat of the Confederacy would produce at best an incomplete understanding of this event. Clearly, another factor in the failure of the Confederacy to emulate the American revolutionary, Spanish insurgent, Prussian, Israeli, and Vietnamese communist successes in defeating materially superior foes was the way the political and military leadership of the South organized and applied the resources they had at their disposal.

In the wars waged by the American revolutionaries, Spanish insurgents, and Vietnamese communists mentioned above, victory came because a more powerful nation was unable to overcome a combination of an effective conventional military force operating in conjunction with guerrilla or irregular forces, aid from outside nations, and access to areas where they could find sanctuary from the military power of their foes possessed by the victorious insurgents.[5] In waging their own war of national liberation, the Confederacy's political and military leaders did, of course, raise and maintain armies that were capable of conducting conventional operations. They did not, however, fully take advantage of the potential their large body of manpower and access to weapons provided for an effective guerrilla force whose efforts, if properly directed, encouraged, and coordinated, could have complemented and enhanced the effectiveness of the Confederacy's conventional forces. Nor did they secure the sort of assistance from foreign governments the American revolutionaries, Spanish insurgents, and Vietnamese communists received or take advantage of areas of safe haven from Northern military power that possession of a large country with many features inhospitable to an invading army provided.

While the ability to secure foreign assistance was never something the Southern political and military leadership had much control over, their failure to develop an effective guerrilla force and incorporate it into their strategy or take advantage of potential areas of sanctuary was the consequence of fundamental strategic choices.[6] Yet the freedom the Confederate military and political leadership possessed strategically was severely constricted by several factors. The most important of these was the nature of the society they were defending, and the purpose for which the South had left the Union and the government of the Confederate States of America had been organized to fulfill. The rationale for an independent Confederacy that made it worth fighting for, according to the men who created it and directed its defense, was a belief that the South's distinctive political, economic, and social life, and the institution upon which it rested, slavery, were mortally threatened within the Union by Yankee contamination. Only by breaking away from the old Union and forming their own independent government to defend slavery and the civilization that rested upon it, they argued, could the people of the South be certain they and their society would be secure.

Having sufficiently convinced the people of the South of the validity of this idea to win their consent for secession and the establishment of an independent Confederacy, the new nation's political and military leaders could only retain legitimacy in the eyes of their people if they were able to fulfill their promise of physically defending the South and its people from the threat to their civilization posed by the North. If the leaders of the Confederacy would not or could not prevent Northern armies from physically violating the territorial integrity of the South and exercising power directly against its people—which could only be done through conventional military means—their ability to maintain the consent of the people for the government they had created and their will to fight on its behalf would be fatally compromised.

Moreover, the people of the South believed the superior society they created a separate government to defend fostered qualities in its people that made them superior martially to the Yankees. Consequently, they would not have placed much confidence in a government that shrank from confronting the Yankees wherever and whenever they threatened the territorial integrity of the South. Thus, the Confederate government was compelled to make an effort to defend as much of its territory as possible and could not follow the example of Washington and the American Revolutionaries, to whom the loss of significant sections of their country was deemed an acceptable (if unpleasant) price to pay if it made it possible for their government and armies to find and take advantage of places that offered sanctuary from superior British military power. Also compelling in convincing the South's military and political leadership that they had to contest every possible inch of Confederate soil through conventional military means was the fact that fate had located the South's most valuable provinces in terms of manpower, agricultural resources, and industrial production—the loss of which would be fatal to the Confederacy's ability to successfully resist Union military power—close to the frontier. Thus a strategy of abandoning parts of the Confederacy to find sanctuary for their armies or to lure the Federals into the South so they would be vulnerable to guerrilla operations was practically unsuitable as well.

As has been amply documented by recent historians, pro-Confederate Southerners did not hesitate to engage in guerrilla warfare when the conditions were right, and where they did so were quite effective, presenting serious problems to the North's political and military leadership. Yet the idea of making unconventional operations a central feature of Confederate strategy received a decidedly cool reception from the nation's military leaders—and for compelling reasons.[7] First, the conservative and hierarchical social, economic, and political system the South seceded from the Union to preserve could not be reconciled easily with the chaotic and informal nature of guerrilla warfare. In addition, to most effectively employ guerrilla warfare, Northern armies would have to actually be in occupation of significant sections of the South, something the Confederacy's leadership could not accept for moral, economic, or political reasons.

Whether the enthusiasm expressed in many quarters of the Confederacy for following the lead of practitioners of guerrilla tactics from the Revolution like Francis Marion and Thomas Sumter could have ever become powerful enough to convince the South's political and military leaders to drop their resistance to making guerrilla operations a central component of Confederate strategy is impossible to tell with absolute certainty. Ironically, perhaps the most serious blows to prospects for this happening were inflicted by the Confederacy's 1861 victories at Big Bethel, Wilson's Creek, and, above all, First Manassas. On the surface, these events certainly provided compelling evidence to support the argument that the South could prevail in a conventional war with the North, and there was no need to accept the social, economic, and political costs that making guerrilla war a central component of Confederate strategy entailed. And to any doubters who might have emerged as a consequence of the North's wave of success in early 1862, Lee's victories that summer probably delivered the final blow to the effort of advocates of unconventional warfare to fundamentally reshape Confederate strategy. And so the people of the Confederacy staked the fate of their nation on the ability of their armies to win a conventional war against a foe possessing overwhelming advantages in the means to fight such a war.

Was Southern victory in such a war possible? The examples cited above of Napoleon, Prussia, and Israel demonstrate that it is possible for a nation to defeat an enemy possessing superior numbers and resources in a conventional war. Generally, this has been done through successful pursuit of a "strategy of annihilation," in which a nation focuses its efforts on crushing the armed forces of their enemies on the battlefield. By achieving decisive successes in the field, these nations render their enemy's military ineffective and make continued resistance appear unfeasible to their political leadership. The problem for the Confederacy, however, was that the North's major armies would prove to be too powerful physically—due to their sheer size and firepower— and their commanders too able for the Confederacy to hope to achieve the truly decisive battlefield success necessary for a strategy of annihilation to succeed. Likewise, a "strategy of attrition," in which Union armed forces would be destroyed gradually over time, rather than in a single engagement or campaign, was unfeasible for the materially inferior Confederacy.

That left Confederate strategists by default to pursue a "strategy of exhaustion." A strategy of exhaustion seeks to destroy an enemy nation's will or the resources that enable it to wage war over time. Destroying the North's ability to wage war was, of course, beyond the capabilities of the materially inferior South. That left only the former—the North's will—as a suitable and viable target for Confederate military strategists.

Of course, all wars are ultimately contests of will. One side tries to impose its will on an enemy through physical force, to compel the enemy to agree to a particular set of policy demands that it would otherwise find unacceptable. The challenge for the strategist is to determine what is the most important factor supporting the enemy's will to fight, and organize and manage his own resources in a way that makes achieving his policy goals feasible and acceptable. Strategies of annihilation and attrition are adopted on the assumption that the enemy's military is the decisive point, and the elimination of its effectiveness—whether quickly or over time—is the key to persuading the enemy to cease resistance. As Lee saw it, in the conventional war of exhaustion he was forced to fight, the key factor sustaining the North's will to prosecute the war and crush the Confederacy was the populace's faith that the South could be defeated and that preservation of the Union was worth the costs necessary to do this. Only if the North came to the conclusion that preservation of the Union could be not be achieved at an acceptable cost, Lee correctly believed, could the militarily inferior Confederacy win a war of exhaustion with the North.

This was the key to the ability of the Israelis, Prussians, and Napoleon to defeat their materially superior enemies. They were able to achieve victories through strategies of annihilation due to the fact that while their enemies may have still possessed the resources to continue fighting, they lacked the will to do so because the terms offered by the military victors made the costs of continuing the war less compelling than the benefits for ending it. After defeating the Austrians in 1805 and Russians in 1807 on the battlefield, for example, Napoleon was able to persuade his foes to end resistance by offering their governments terms that their leaders were willing to accept. The Prussians did the same in 1866, making the benefits of continuing the war for the Austrians far less compelling than the costs. While the victory of 1967 did not bring a formal peace treaty, the Arab states did accept an armistice and end the fighting because Israeli victories on the battlefield made the costs for doing so less severe than those a continuation of the fighting would impose.

Here, however, was the insurmountable obstacle to Confederate victory. If Lee was correct in his belief that the only way the Confederacy could prevail in the conventional war of exhaustion its society compelled it to fight was if the North's determination to preserve the Union could not be maintained, he was wrong to hope that the South could make it happen. The ultimate problem for the Confederacy was that the terms it demanded for ending the war were never acceptable to the North. Though this could only be recognized fully in retrospect, for all the great success its armies achieved tactically and operationally, at no point did the South ever come close to push-ing the North to the point where it was willing to consent to the destruction of the Union and accept the existence of an independent Confederacy.

The elections in the North Lee hoped might provide the opportunity for a "political revolution" that would bring to power officials willing to concede Confederate independence were never, for all the noise and exaggerated rhetoric that accompanied them, referendums on the end of preserving the Union. Northern politicians understood that, to the vast majority of the vot-ing public, the idea of recognizing the independence of the Confederacy was completely unacceptable. While there certainly were some in the North will-ing to see the Union sundered, their numbers never were so great, nor their message so popular, that there was ever a threat of leaders who held this view gaining power. Indeed, they could not even take control of the Democratic Party, as evidenced by the fact that when the time came for the party to put up a challenger to Lincoln in 1864, they chose a staunch Unionist—even though they made their selection at a time when discontent with the progress of the war was at perhaps its highest level. Since both parties agreed that the Union needed to preserved, what elections in the North were over was the question of whether the leaders and policies put forward by the Re-publicans were the best means for achieving the end of restoring the Union. Thus, Republican victories did not so much bolster or reflect the determi-nation of the Northern populace that to let the Confederacy survive was unacceptable—that was never at any time in question—but confidence that the Lincoln administration and its policies were the most effective means for achieving that end.

Of course, Republican politicians recognized the overwhelming sentiment of the Northern public was for making whatever effort was necessary to pre-serve the Union, as evidenced by the great effort they expended to foster in the minds of the electorate a perception (which many Republicans no doubt sincerely believed to be correct) that opposition to their party and its poli-cies was synonymous with disunionism. That this was the case, of course, is only clear in retrospect—although in much scholarship on the war there is still a tendency to conflate opposition to the Republicans and support for Southern independence. And if historians working with the benefit of hind-sight can still be confused on this point, certainly actors at the time such as Lee can be forgiven for hoping that the existence of dissatisfaction with the Republican Party meant that there was a chance that a large enough segment of the Northern populace could be convinced to bring to power leaders who would concede Confederate independence. Thus, the outcome of the Civil War was determined by this combination of the Southern people's decision to pit the fate of their nation on winning a conventional war of exhaustion and the superiority of Northern resources and unshakable resolve to preserve the Union that made such an effort an exercise in futility.

Yet victory for the North did not by any means come easily. Undoubtedly, one of the most important reasons for this—perhaps the preeminent one—was the generalship of Robert E. Lee, for without his consistently inspired, driving leadership and brilliance at the operational and tactical levels of war it is difficult to see how the war in Virginia could have lasted as long as it did. From the time he assumed direction of the Army of Northern Virginia, his keen understanding of the virtues and drawbacks of the society he served and those of his opponent enabled him to formulate and rigorously execute the only operational vision that could have saved Richmond from an early capture in 1862, shape the course of the war in a way that enabled the Confederacy to hold out as long as it did, and inspire Southern belief in the possibility of victory. To be sure, like all great commanders, he had more than his share of luck on the battlefield, but it was luck that he did much to manufacture. It was a keen understanding of Lee's generalship that fostered a degree of caution in the commanders he faced that, although on the whole proper, led them to miss significant tactical opportunities at various points in the war. More importantly, he so intimidated the North's political leadership that it—with much less justification—became preoccupied with avoiding defeat in the East and ensuring Washington was completely secure. Instead of pursuing victory by doing all it could to capture Richmond, the Northern government resigned itself to a long drawn-out war and imposed its operationally defensive mentality on the high command of its most important army.

As suggested in these last few sentences, a complete explanation for why it took the North so long to win the war in Virginia cannot be found by only, or even primarily, looking at the Southern side of the field. Whatever his merits as a general, it is difficult to dispute the wisdom demonstrated by George Pickett when he proclaimed, in response to debates over why the Army of Northern Virginia was defeated at Gettysburg, "I believe the Union Army had something to do with it."[8] The Union army and its leaders did indeed have "something to do with it," and not just at Gettysburg.

Contrary to popular stereotype, the generals Lee faced in the course of the war were capable commanders who demonstrated the ability to make—and more often than not did make—sound decisions in maneuvering their armies and managing them on the battlefield. To be sure, they did not exhibit the ruthless aggressiveness, tactical boldness, or operational daring that Lee did. This was not, however, a consequence of deficiencies in intellect, courage, or the other qualities required of effective commanders. Rather it was because circumstances did not require them to march and fight the way Lee did and, indeed, sober analysis of the matter suggests it would have been foolish and counterproductive for them to do so. Lee's generalship was distinguished by the aforementioned qualities because otherwise there was no way the Confederacy could have hoped to survive as long as it did. Inferior resources meant that the Army of Northern Virginia would almost always face a quantitative disadvantage, which could only be countered by taking advantage of the greater speed and maneuverability its smaller numbers and lighter logistical tail gave it by being aggressive and taking risks in an attempt to compel the Federals to engage in a war of maneuver.

The situation was very different on the other side of the field. With its superiority in resources, a cautious and methodical approach to operations made eminent sense for the Army of the Potomac. The surest way for the Union to defeat Lee was to eschew a war of movement in which speed, the ability to react quickly to circumstances, and aggressiveness to the point of recklessness—something Lee's smaller and more desperate army would always possess in greater degree—would determine the outcome of operations, and instead carefully and methodically manage its own forces to deny the Confederates opportunities for tactical success and then gradually wear them down over time.

A clear understanding of these facts and an approach to operations emphasizing caution and methodically directed movements that properly flowed from that recognition enabled McClellan to reach the gates of Richmond and shackle the Confederate army to the defense of its capital, and then turn back Lee's invasion of Maryland. When exercising good caution during the opening phases of the Second Manassas Campaign, John Pope effectively thwarted attempts by Lee to catch him at a disadvantage. Unfortunately, Pope then attempted to translate the public derision of the McClellan paradigm of operations that had secured him his position as commander of the Army of Virginia into aggressive tactics that provided Lee the opportunity to drive him from the field at Second Manassas. During his tenure in command of the Army of the Potomac, Ambrose Burnside faced so many troubles—due to circumstances Washington had more to do with than he did—that it is difficult to see how even the ablest commander could have succeeded.

For his part, Hooker demonstrated considerable operational skill at Chancellorsville, luring Lee into an engagement in which the Union army was able to fight concentrated in a strong defensive position in which nearly all the advantages would be on its side. That more was not achieved (and it can be argued that the campaign ended with more damage having been done to Lee's cause than Hooker's), was a consequence of gross mismanagement by a corps commander that left the army vulnerable to Jackson's flanking march and the fact that Hooker suffered a serious head injury at a critical point in the battle. Hooker subsequently demonstrated good judgment and skill in the opening phases of the Gettysburg Campaign, effectively maneuvering his command in line with a well-conceived plan that held great promise for achieving a decisive victory over Lee's army. Although he adopted a different plan from Hooker's upon taking command, Meade also managed his army effectively as it moved north toward its collision with Lee at Gettysburg. And even though that battle commenced under circumstances different from what Meade intended in his plan—and indeed a case can be made that Lee might have come away from the campaign much worse off than he did had Meade's subordinates not precipitated a fight at Gettysburg and induced Meade to toss aside his original plan—he recovered smartly and through prudent and cautious management of his army compelled Lee to fight a battle he could not win. Meade's generalship in the months that followed was likewise commendable, as he avoided any serious mistakes and managed to achieve a respectable number of operational and tactical successes of his own.

While it would ultimately fall to Grant to lead the North to victory in Virginia, his efforts were facilitated by those commanders who had gone before him. If McClellan, Pope, Burnside, Hooker, and Meade had not decisively defeated Lee's army, they had conducted their campaigns in a way that ensured that the Confederacy never achieved sufficient success to shatter Northern faith in the ultimate triumph of the Union. And even when they suffered tactical and operational setbacks, these officers were able enough to contain the damage and ensure that good and bad fortune on the battlefield would be balanced sufficiently so that the North's advantages in resources could ultimately be decisive. In the process they also did Grant the great favor of exhausting Lee's army so badly that it was no longer the sharp instrument in 1864 that it was in 1862 and 1863.

For all their merits, however, the efforts of the men who commanded the Army of the Potomac were consistently undermined by incessant meddling by Washington. To be sure, the troubles in the relationship between Washington and the Army of the Potomac were not all one-way, but as the superior in these relationships, ultimate responsibility for the problems that existed rested squarely with the Lincoln administration. And there were many. The constant intrusion of Lincoln administration officials and Congress into the army's internal affairs—although fully in line with their constitutional responsibilities—played a critical role in the absence of the level of harmony and mutual trust in the high command of the Army of the Potomac that Lee enjoyed with his principal subordinates. From the time Lincoln imposed corps commanders on the Army of the Potomac that he knew McClellan did not enjoy a fully cooperative relationship with in early 1862, the army's high command would be racked with internal turmoil that precluded any commander from being able to develop plans with full confidence that they would be executed in good faith. Consequently, throughout the war, a lack of mutual confidence among the members of the Army of the Potomac's high command would hamper its effectiveness and facilitate Lee's ability to achieve battlefield success.

The fact that these problems endured despite changes at the head of the eastern armies that brought a considerable range of personalities, political perspectives, and military temperaments to the position—from the politically and militarily conservative McClellan to the militarily aggressive and politically radical Pope to modest and middle-of-the road Burnside to the politically pragmatic and militarily aggressive Hooker and back to the politically and militarily conservative Meade—suggests the problem was not individual personalities, but systemic. And there were two things that did not change through all of these changes: that Union commanders had to contend with an enemy army commanded by Robert E. Lee and that they had to operate under the close supervision of Washington. It is certainly suggestive that Union armies tended to more successful the further they were from Lee and Washington.

Perhaps the most important contribution the Lincoln administration made to Lee's efforts was its denying the Army of the Potomac high command the ability to conduct operations where its army would be most effective—on the James River. Of all the decisions that shaped the war in the East, three were most critical to the ability of Lee and the Confederacy to stave off defeat in Virginia for as long as they did: the withholding of forces from McClellan's army during the Peninsula Campaign in 1862, its withdrawal from the banks of the James River after the Seven Days' Battles, and the imposition in the months that followed of the "headquarters doctrine" that mandated the Army of the Potomac would have to conduct its operations on a line that kept it at all times between Richmond and Washington. Both times the Army of the Potomac operated on the James, in 1862 and 1864, Lee found himself in an operational nightmare: pinned to the defenses of Richmond, unable to successfully attack the Federals or force them into a campaign of maneuver, and almost at the complete mercy of the enemy. Yet, thanks to the aforementioned decisions by the Lincoln administration, instead of being compelled to fight campaigns of seigecraft and position against a foe based on the James that he was almost guaranteed to lose for much of the war, Lee was able to conduct a war largely of maneuver in central and northern Virginia, and by doing so extended the war in Virginia and the life of the Confederacy beyond what a sound operational approach on the part of the Union high command would have allowed. None of these decisions were made at the Army of the Potomac headquarters; indeed, they were all made over the known opposition of many of the officers who dominated that army's high command.

Of Grant's many virtues as a commander, his most important may well have been his great ability—thanks to the prestige of his office and his consummate skill in handling his political superiors—to neutralize the influence of Washington on how the campaign in Virginia would be conducted in 1864–1865. Thus, Grant was able to make getting the Army of the Potomac to the James—where Lee's army and Richmond could be targeted in the methodical campaign of trenches, material, and firepower at which the Union army was most effective—the objective of his campaign. By breaking away from the "headquarters doctrine," he forced Lee back into the near-hopeless operational and tactical situation the great Confederate commander had endeavored to avoid ever since McClellan's campaign had vividly demonstrated its danger to the fate of the Confederacy in 1862.

Yet, even in 1864, fortune smiled on Lee. Even Grant had to bend to the will of the administration and begin his main campaign in Virginia north of Richmond. In combination with the failure of the operation under Butler along the James to fully realize its potential, this condemned Grant and the Army of the Potomac to a bloodletting so horrific that it inspired hope in the Confederacy that Union will might be broken, and continues to unnecessarily stain Grant's reputation as a general. Nonetheless, he ultimately got the Army of the Potomac where it could once again be most effective and Lee would be rendered operationally impotent. By succeeding in his objective of getting the Army of the Potomac to the James, Grant made the fall of the Confederacy's indispensable capital and defeat of its most important army, as Lee predicted, a mere matter of time.

To be sure, when Richmond fell and Lee surrendered his army a week later, there were still thousands of men of military age and beyond who could have continued the fight. But with the South's major industrial centers either occupied by the Yankees or wrecked by Yankee raiders, the tools of war would not be available to sustain a conventional contest. There was the option of abandoning the conventional war and turning to guerrilla warfare, but a willingness to pursue this course of action and accept its costs on behalf of the Confederacy just was not there. In April 1865, the will of Robert E. Lee and the people of the South to continue the desperate fight for southern independence was gone. The Yankees had crushed it.

Notes

1. Wilson to Whipple, May 3, 1865, OR, vol. 49, pt. 1: 352; Johnston, *Narrative*, 396–98; Johnston to Sherman, April 14, 1865, OR, vol. 47, pt. 3: 206–7.

2. Sherman and Johnston, "Memorandum," April 18, 1865, ibid., 243–44; Sherman to Grant or Halleck, April 18, 1865, ibid., 243; Grant to Stanton, April 24, 1865, ibid., 293; Sherman to Johnston, April 24, 1865, ibid., 293–94; Johnston to Breckinridge, April 25, 1865, ibid., 836; Sherman and Johnston, "Terms of a Military Convention," April 26, 1865, ibid., 313.

3. Lee to Davis, April 20, 1865, in *Wartime Papers*, eds. Dowdey and Manarin, 938–39.

4. General Orders No. 9, Hdqrs. Army of Northern Virginia, April 10, 1865, in *Wartime Papers of R.E. Lee*, eds. Dowdey and Manarin, 934.

5. One historian has recently coined the term "fortified compound warfare" to describe a strategy in which a combatant possesses and uses in combination conventional forces, irregular forces, sanctuary, and external assistance. Thomas M. Huber, "Compound Warfare: A Conceptual Framework," in *Compound Warfare: That Fatal Knot*, edited by Thomas M. Huber (Fort Leavenworth, KS: U.S. Army Command and General Staff College Press, 2002), 3–5.

6. Ethan S. Rafuse, "Why the Confederate Insurgency Failed: Another Take on the Essential Question," *North and South* 7 (November 2004): 29–34.

7. Daniel E. Sutherland, "Guerrilla Warfare, Democracy, and the Fate of the Confederacy," *Journal of Southern History* 68 (May 2002): 259–82.

8. Reardon, "Pickett's Charge," 84.

Bibliographic Essay

Given the massive volume of literature on Lee and the parameters of the series of which this book is a part, it was somewhat difficult to determine how to fully and accurately acknowledge all of the sources that have shaped this study. In an attempt to do so, the method used by David Herbert Donald in his 1995 biography of Lincoln has largely been adopted. This essay lists major biographies or general secondary works, with studies consulted for information on specific campaigns generally listed in a single note at the beginning of each chapter's section of notes.

The place for any student of Lee to begin is the best modern biography of the general, Emory M. Thomas's *Robert E. Lee: A Biography* (New York: W. W. Norton, 1995), which provides many useful and compelling insights into Lee's personality. Further information and intriguing analysis of Lee the man is provided in Elizabeth Brown Pryor's massive and revealingly titled *Reading the Man: A Portrait of Robert E. Lee through His Private Letters* (New York: Viking, 2007). The same year Thomas's biography appeared, an excellent anthology of writings on Lee's military career was published under the editorship of Gary W. Gallagher, *Lee the Soldier* (Lincoln: University of Nebraska Press, 1995). The fullest treatments of Lee's life and military career remain Douglas Southall Freeman's *R.E. Lee: A Biography*, 4 vols. (New York: Scribner's, 1934–1935), and *Lee's Lieutenants: A Study in Command*, 3 vols. (New York: Scribner's, 1942–1944). Readers looking for a good survey of Lee's entire military career will find much of value in Brian Holden Reid, *Robert E. Lee: Icon for a Nation* (Amherst, NY: Prometheus Books, 2007).

Critical analyses of Lee and his generalship form a distinct subgenre in Civil War studies. The best work along these lines is Thomas L. Connelly, *The Marble Man: Robert E. Lee and His Image in American Society* (New York: Alfred A. Knopf, 1977); and his essay "Robert E. Lee and the Western Confederacy: A Criticism of Lee's Strategic Ability," which originally appeared in *Civil War History* in June 1969. As Albert Castel pointed out in a pugnacious response to Connelly's essay that appeared in the March 1970 *Civil War History* (both essays are republished in Gallagher's *Lee the Soldier*), some of Connelly's objections to Lee's generalship were previously presented in J. F. C. Fuller's *Grant and Lee: A Study in Personality and Generalship* (1932; Bloomington: Indiana University Press, 1957), whose then-revisionist take on Grant remains compelling and persuasive, while his criticisms of Lee are less so. Other studies critical of Lee include Alan T. Nolan, *Lee Considered: General Robert E. Lee and Civil War History* (Chapel Hill: University of North Carolina Press, 1990); Bevin Alexander, *Robert E. Lee's Civil War* (Holbrook, MA: Adams Media, 1998); Edward H. Bonekemper, *How Robert E. Lee Lost the Civil War* (Fredericksburg, VA: Sergeant Kirkland's Press, 1998); and John D. McKenzie, *Uncertain Glory: Lee's Generalship Re-examined* (New York: Hippocrene Books, 1997).

Efforts, in Castel's words, "to do a job on Bobby Lee" have been more than effectively answered in recent scholarship. Among the most important studies in this regard have been Joseph L. Harsh's *Confederate Tide Rising: Robert E. Lee and the Making of Southern Strategy, 1861–1862* (Kent, OH: The Kent State University Press, 1998); and *Taken at the Flood: Robert E. Lee and Confederate Strategy in the Maryland Campaign of 1862* (Kent, OH: Kent State University Press, 1999). Two collections of superb essays by Gary W. Gallagher are also essential: *Lee and His Generals in War and Memory* (Baton Rouge: Louisiana State University Press, 1998) and *Lee and His Army in Confederate History* (Chapel Hill: University of North Carolina Press, 2001). An excellent collection of essays that offer mixed assessments of Lee's generalship has been compiled by Peter S. Carmichael in *Audacity Personified: The Generalship of Robert E. Lee* (Baton Rouge: Louisiana State University, 2005). Carmichael also contributed one of the essays to the June 2000 issue of *North & South* magazine, which focused on Lee's generalship, and included Joseph L. Harsh's wonderfully compelling and insightful "'As Stupid a Fellow As I Am': On the Real Military Genius of Robert E. Lee."

Readers will also benefit from a thorough grounding in the military history of the Civil War. In addition to being the best work of its kind, Herman Hattaway and Archer Jones's *How the North Won: A Military History of the Civil War* (Urbana: University of Illinois Press, 1983) is one of the true landmark studies in the field and essential reading for any student of the Civil War. Russell F. Weigley places Lee's generalship and the military conduct of the Civil War in the context of the evolution of the United States's approach to warfare in *The American Way of War: A History of United States Strategy and Policy* (New York: Macmillan, 1973); and his essay "American Strategy from Its Beginnings through the First World War," in Peter Peret et al., eds. *Makers of Modern Strategy: From Machiavelli to the Nuclear Age* (Princeton, NJ: Princeton University Press, 1986).

Outstanding general histories of the Confederacy include Frank E. Vandiver, *Their Tattered Flags: The Epic of the Confederacy* (New York: Harper's Magazine Press, 1970); Emory M. Thomas, *The Confederate Nation: 1861–1865* (New York: Harper and Row, 1979); and William C. Davis, *The Lost Cause: A History of the Confederate States of America* (New York: Free Press, 2002). Further analysis of the Confederate war effort can be found in Gabor Boritt, ed., *Why the Confederacy Lost* (New York: Oxford University Press, 1992); and Robert G. Tanner, *Retreat to Victory? Confederate Strategy Reconsidered* (Wilmington, DE: Scholarly Resources, 2001). A controversial explanation of the Confederacy's failure can be found in Richard E. Beringer, Herman Hattaway, Archer Jones, and William N. Still, *Why the South Lost the Civil War* (Athens: University of Georgia Press, 1986). Rebuttals to some of the ideas advanced by Beringer and his coauthors are offered in Gary W. Gallagher's *The Confederate War: How Popular Will, Nationalism, and Military Strategy Could Not Stave Off Defeat* (Cambridge, MA: Harvard University Press, 1997).

Jefferson Davis's life and presidency career are thoroughly chronicled in William J. Cooper Jr., *Jefferson Davis: American* (New York: Alfred A. Knopf, 2000), while a recent study that focuses on Davis's presidency is Herman Hattaway and Richard E. Beringer, *Jefferson Davis: Confederate President* (Lawrence: University Press of Kansas, 2002). A fine account of Davis's management of the war in the East and his relationship with Lee, whose central theme is clearly indicated in its title, is Steven E. Woodworth's *Davis and Lee at War* (Lawrence: University Press of Kansas, 1995).

Many of those who served Lee during the last two years of the war at a significant level of command wrote memoirs, and nearly all have been the subject of recent studies. For the sake of brevity, officers who wrote memoirs will be indicated by an asterisk by their name. Readers interested in the life and career of the Confederate officer who stood second only to Lee in importance during the final stages of the war will find much of value in Craig L. Symonds' *Joseph E. Johnston*: A Civil War Biography* (New York: W.W. Norton, 1992). William Garrett Piston's compelling *Lee's Tarnished*

Lieutenant: James Longstreet* and His Place in Southern History (Athens: University of Georgia, 1987) did much to rehabilitate Longstreet's military reputation and explains the factors that made such an effort necessary, although Jeffry D. Wert's *General James Longstreet, the Confederacy's Most Controversial Commander: A Biography* (New York: Simon & Schuster, 1993), is the best full biography. Another corps commander who supposedly let Lee down is the subject of Donald C. Pfanz's outstanding *Richard S. Ewell: A Soldier's Life* (Chapel Hill: University of North Carolina Press, 1998). Stonewall Jackson's great biographer James I. Robertson is also the author of *General A.P. Hill: The Story of a Confederate Warrior* (New York: Random House, 1987). Stuart's life is best chronicled in Emory M. Thomas, *Bold Dragoon: The Life of J.E.B. Stuart* (New York: Harper & Row, 1986), while his successor's is examined in Robert K. Ackerman, *Wade Hampton III* (Columbia: University of South Carolina Press, 2007). Two officers who, like Hampton, emerged as stalwarts in the Army of Northern Virginia high command during the second half of the war are the subject of Charles C. Osborne, *Jubal: The Life and Times of General Jubal A. Early*, CSA* (Chapel Hill, NC: Algonquin Books, 1992); and Ralph Lowell Eckert, *John Brown Gordon*: Soldier, Southerner, American* (Baton Rouge: Louisiana State University Press, 1989). Men who cut conspicuous figures in command of divisions in the Army of Northern Virginia are the subject of Lesley J. Gordon's *General George E. Pickett in Life and Legend* (Chapel Hill: University of North Carolina Press, 1998); and Nelson Blake, *William Mahone of Virginia: Soldier and Political Insurgent* (Richmond, VA: Garrett and Massie, 1935).

Many important and necessary insights are to be gleaned from scholarship on Lee's foes. The best one-volume study of Lincoln is Donald's *Lincoln* (New York: Simon & Schuster, 1995), while Phillip Shaw Paludan's *The Presidency of Abraham Lincoln* (Lawrence: University Press of Kansas, 1995) contains many valuable insights. T. Harry Williams's *Lincoln and His Generals* (New York: Alfred A. Knopf, 1952) is still the best study of Lincoln's management of military affairs, although it is in fundamental disagreement with much of the analysis contained in this study. Joseph Hooker needs a modern biographer, although Walter Hebert's *Fighting Joe Hooker* (Indianapolis: Bobbs-Merrill, 1944) is a very good study. Freeman Cleaves's *Meade of Gettysburg* (Norman: University of Oklahoma Press, 1960) is the fullest account of the life of its subject, although readers will also find value in Richard Sauers's *Meade* (Potomac, MD: Brassey's, 2003) and my *George Gordon Meade and the War in the East* (Abilene, TX: McWhiney Foundation Press, 2003). Anyone interested in Ulysses S. Grant should begin by consulting *The Personal Memoirs of U.S.*

Grant, 2 vols. (New York: Charles L. Webster, 1885). The best study of Grant's life and military career to 1865 is Brooks D. Simpson, *Ulysses S. Grant: Triumph over Adversity, 1822–1865* (New York: Houghton Mifflin, 2001). A survey of recent scholarship on Grant is provided in my essay "Still a Mystery? General Grant and the Historians, 1981–2006," which appeared in the July 2007 issue of *The Journal of Military History*.

Index

About the Author

Ethan S. Rafuse is associate professor of military history at the U.S. Army Command and General Staff College in Fort Leavenworth, Kansas. His publications include *A Single Grand Victory: The First Campaign and Battle of Manassas*, *McClellan's War: The Failure of Moderation in the Struggle for the Union*, and over one hundred essays, articles, and reviews in a variety of academic and popular history journals, including *Civil War Times Illustrated*, *Civil War History*, *North & South*, and *The Journal of Military History*.